ASIAN AMERICAN
VOICES

ASIAN AMERICAN VOICES

Deborah Gillan Straub, *Editor*

DETROIT • NEW YORK • TORONTO • LONDON

AN IMPRINT OF GALE

ASIAN AMERICAN VOICES

Deborah Gillan Straub, *Editor*

Staff

Sonia Benson, *U•X•L Senior Editor*
Carol DeKane Nagel, *U•X•L Managing Editor*
Thomas L. Romig, *U•X•L Publisher*

Margaret Chamberlain, *Permissions Associate*

Shanna Heilveil, *Production Associate*
Evi Seoud, *Assistant Production Manager*
Mary Beth Trimper, *Production Director*

Michelle DiMercurio, *Art Director*
Cynthia Baldwin, *Product Design Manager*

 This book is printed on acid-free paper that meets the minimum requirements of American National Standard for Information Sciences—Permanence Paper for Printed Library Materials, ANSI Z39.48-1984.

Library of Congress Cataloging-in-Publication Data
Asian American Voices/Deborah Gillan Straub.
      p. cm.
   Includes bibliographical references and indexes.
      ISBN 0-8103-9676-9 (alk. paper)
      1. Asian Americans–Biography. 2. Asian Americans–History. 3. Speeches, addresses, etc., American–Asian
      American authors.
      E184.06A842 1997
  973'.0495–dc21

                                                    97-6449
                                                  CIP

Printed in the United States of America
10 9 8 7 6 5 4 3 2 1

Contents

Daniel K. Inouye

Speech Topics at a Glance

Liliuokalani

For a more detailed listing of information covered in this volume, consult subject index.

Multiculturalism

Science and Technology

Social Unrest

Vietnam War

Women's Issues

World War II

Reader's Guide

Patsy Takemoto Mink

In the mid-1800s only several hundred Chinese were counted in the U.S. census and the first Japanese had just arrived. Although people of Asian ancestry had lived in the United States for centuries, it was not until the first half of the twentieth century that the number of Chinese, Japanese, Asian Indian, and Korean immigrants rose significantly. Their numbers grew despite widespread anti-Asian sentiments that led to restricted immigration and barred the newcomers from citizenship, public schools, labor unions, social arenas, and even from owning land. For the early pioneers from Asia, the United States often offered a cold—sometimes even a brutal—welcome.

Today Asian Americans are the fastest-growing minority in the nation. Racial and national restrictions have been lifted from U.S. immigration policies and basic civil rights have been recognized. Traditions from the diverse cultures of Asia are being celebrated by many Americans of Asian and non-Asian ancestry. While anti-immigrant hostilities directed at Asian Americans as well as ignorance and discrimination still exist,

Asian Americans involved in politics, the arts, and social issues have made their voices heard. If few Asian American speeches went on record before World War II, they have abounded since then.

Asian American Voices collects in a single source complete and excerpted speeches delivered by fifteen Asian American activists, political figures, educators, and other prominent men and women who have helped shape the history and culture of the United States since the late nineteenth century. *Voices* selections include such historical documents as Hawaiian Queen Liliuokalani's statement to the court during her trial for treason against the American-run Republic of Hawaii that had recently overthrown her monarchy. Also included is Syngman Rhee's 1948 speech upon taking over the presidency of a newly independent South Korea after World War II. The most prominently addressed issue in *Voices* is the internment of more than 120,000 people of Japanese ancestry in the United States during World War II. The speeches of Robert T. Matsui, Spark M. Matsunaga, Norman Y. Mineta, and Clifford I. Uyeda relate the anguish caused by this act and argue passionately for constructive measures to ensure that nothing of the kind will ever happen again. In another speech, Daniel K. Inouye recalls very different World War II experiences in the all-Japanese American 442nd Regimental Combat Team, the most decorated unit in military history. Also among the many topics featured in this volume, playwright David Henry Hwang discusses "authenticity" in writing about being Asian American, writer Bette Bao Lord calls for U.S. involvement in the international human rights movements, and Helen Zia urges Asian American journalists to help fight the stereotyping of Asian Americans in the media.

It is not possible in this first edition of *Asian American Voices* to include all of the many prominent Asian American speakers who have contributed to American culture and history. *Voices* does, however, provide a compelling array of perspectives on recent U.S. history, from the annexation of Hawaii to World War II, and from the Vietnam War and student protest to the 1992 riots in Los Angeles. The speeches were chosen for their accessibility to students and for the first-hand—and often quite dramatic—insight they provide into the issues, events, and movements of Asian American history.

The entries in *Asian American Voices* are arranged alphabetically by speaker. Each begins with introductory material, providing a brief biography of the speaker and the historical context of the speech that follows. Informative sidebars expand on topics mentioned within the entries. A "Sources" section directs the student to further readings on the speechmaker and his or her speeches.

Asian American Voices also contains more than eighty photographs, a cumulative subject index, and a timeline. Words and phrases are defined as they appear throughout the book.

Related Reference Sources

Asian American Almanac explores the culture and history of the diverse groups of Americans who descend from Asian and Pacific Island countries: Asian Indian, Cambodian, Chinese, Filipino, Native Hawaiian, Hmong, Indonesian, Korean, Japanese, Laotian, Pacific Island, Pakistani, Thai, and Vietnamese Americans. The *Almanac* is organized into subject chapters on topics including family, health, religion, employment, civil rights and activism, education, law, demographics, literature and theater, and sports. More than eighty black-and-white photographs and maps, a glossary, and a subject index are included in the volume.

Asian American Biography profiles more than 130 Americans who trace their ancestry to Asia and the Pacific Islands. The individuals featured are notable for their achievements in fields ranging from civil rights to sports, politics to academia, entertainment to science, religion to the military. Early leaders in Asian America as well as contemporary figures are among those included. A black-and-white portrait accompanies most entries, and a list of sources for further reading or research is provided at the end of each entry. The volumes are arranged alphabetically and conclude with an index listing all individuals by field of endeavor.

Asian American Chronology explores significant social, political, economic, cultural, and professional milestones in Asian American history. Arranged chronologically by date, the volume spans from prehistory to modern times and contains more than sixty illustrations, extensive cross references, and a cumulative subject index.

Acknowledgments

The editor wishes to thank the following people who served as advisors on this project: Wil A. Linkugel, Professor of Communication Studies, University of Kansas, Lawrence, Kansas; Suzanne Lo, Branch Manager, Asian Branch, Oakland Public Library, Oakland, California; and Hilda K. Weisburg, Media Specialist, Sayreville War Memorial High School, Parlin, New Jersey.

Your Suggestions Are Welcome

The editor welcomes your comments and suggestions for future editions of *Asian American Voices*. Please write: The Editor, *Asian American Voices*, U•X•L, 835 Penobscot Building, Detroit, Michigan 48226-4094; call toll-free: 1-800-877-4253; or fax: (313) 961-6347.

Introduction

Asian Pacific Americans and Oral Public Discourse

Asian Pacific Americans are a diverse group. They include East Asians (Chinese, Japanese, Koreans), Southeast Asians (Filipinos, Vietnamese, Cambodians, Laotians, Thais, Indonesians, Malaysians), South Asians (Indians, Pakistanis, Bangladeshis, Sri Lankans), and Pacific Islanders (Hawaiians, Samoans, Guamanians). Besides their diverse origins and cultures, Asian Pacific Americans have a varied past in America. Hawaiians settled their island home possibly as early as the third century B.C. and were forcibly annexed by the United States in 1898. Filipino communities formed in North America as early as the 1760s. Chinese and Asian Indians were on the East Coast by the 1790s, and Chinese settled in Hawaii and California before 1850. However, the majority of Asian Americans have been in the United States only since 1965, when immigration laws that discriminated against them (as well as against Latinos) were lifted. That ethnic diversity gives an in-

David Henry Hwang

dication of how difficult it is to write about an "Asian Pacific American tradition" in oral public discourse.

In the face of those historical and cultural differences, a striking commonality [common feature or characteristic] about Asian Pacific American public discourse is its apparent absence. We find very little evidence of Asian Pacific American speechmaking. I suppose that we in America generally think about public speaking as an arena where leaders—mainly politicians and social and labor reformers—address audiences to move masses of people into action. Most Americans couldn't name an Asian Pacific American social movement or an Asian Pacific American leader. Part of this difficulty is due to the historical fact that Asians were legally barred from participating fully in American life from the time of their arrival to the 1950s.

What were some of those barriers? For one, most Asians weren't even permitted to become naturalized citizens until 1952. In addition, they were restricted in their work and housing opportunities, they were prohibited from joining labor unions, and their children were forced to attend segregated schools. Hawaiians lost most of their land and were encouraged to abandon their language and culture. Asian Pacific Americans thus were generally excluded from the life of the mainstream, from politics to labor to the social and cultural arenas.

But Asian Pacific Americans *did* participate in the American pageant, and within their own communities Asian Pacific American leaders galvanized [energized] social movements that involved large numbers of people. For instance, after having been removed from her throne by force of arms in 1898, Liliuokalani, the last Hawaiian queen, argued the cause of Hawaiian independence. "Oh, honest Americans, as Christians hear me for my downtrodden people!" she pleaded. "Their form of government is as dear to them as yours is precious to you. Quite as warmly as you love your country, so they love theirs."

Beginning in 1901, the Reverend Wu P'an-chao (also known as Ng Poon Chew), a Christian minister and newspaper publisher in San Francisco, California, made several national tours during which he addressed English and Chinese-speaking audiences about the need for immigration reform and the Chinese contribution to American society. Another distinguished speaker of Chinese ancestry was Jinqin Xue, who had studied at the University of California, Berkeley, in 1902 as a sixteen-year-old. She went on to become a leading feminist in China, and when she revisited California, she appeared before hundreds of San Francisco Chinatown residents to discuss ending China's patriarchal [headed by a father or by a male authoritarian figure] system and advancing women's liberation.

Between 1908 and 1910, Taraknath Das, a self-described "itinerant [wandering] preacher," devoted himself to "explaining the economic, educational, and political conditions to the masses of the people." He spoke to audiences in Canada and the United States urging India's independence from British colonialism and calling for an end to discriminatory laws against Asian Indians in North America.

Waka Yamada, a woman of Japanese ancestry who had been tricked into marriage and forced into prostitution around the turn of the century, escaped the brothels [buildings where prostitutes work] of Seattle, Washington, and San Francisco to become a leading writer, social critic, and feminist in Japan. She returned to America in 1937 on a lecture tour of West Coast Japanese American communities, riveting listeners with her insights on politics, peace, and women's liberation.

By and large, however, precious little survives of what these pioneering leaders actually said and what the reactions of their listeners were. Hawaiians in particular comprise a largely silent people because Americans have too easily ignored their articulate and persistent voices. An oral culture before contact with Europeans and Americans, Hawaiians told stories of their past in chants and dances of the hula. Those were deemed "uncivilized" by Christian missionaries who tried to forbid and change the meanings of those traditions, but they survived and have seen a revitalization in the resurgence of Hawaiian culture and language since the 1960s.

Furthermore, we know of few instances in which Asian Americans addressed large numbers of Americans outside of their communities. Only since World War II and the African American civil rights movement of the 1960s have Asian

Americans become a part of American politics in any significant way.

Asian Pacific America has therefore not been devoid of [lacking, without] leaders or social movements—they have simply not been recognized or widely mentioned. Asian Pacific Americans organized and participated in labor unions, initiated civil rights suits that resulted in landmark Supreme Court decisions, engaged in feminist struggles against patriarchy, and formed societies for the liberation of colonized Asia. Ministers preached sermons, labor leaders mobilized masses of workers, and feminists and civil rights leaders testified in courts and lectured to audiences from Hawaii to New York.

Within their own communities, Asian Pacific Americans took part in lively and vigorous public discourse. Among those who did so were people such as American-educated Syngman Rhee, the first president of the Republic of Korea, and D. S. Saund, who gave public lectures on Indian independence while a student at the University of California, Berkeley, during the 1920s and who in 1956 became the first Asian American elected to the U.S. Congress. They in turn paved the way for contemporary civil rights, feminist, and political leaders such as Clifford I. Uyeda, Helen Zia, S. I. Hayakawa, Norman Y. Mineta, and Robert T. Matsui. Meanwhile, Asian Pacific Americans such as Hiram L. Fong, Spark M. Matsunaga, Daniel K. Inouye, Patsy Takemoto Mink, and Daniel K. Akaka have played key roles in transforming the political landscape of Hawaii in the last half of the twentieth century.

Asian Pacific American voices have resonated throughout America's past and present, if we will only listen.

Dr. Gary Y. Okihiro
Director of Asian American Studies Program and Professor of History
Cornell University
Ithaca, New York

Suggested Readings

Espiritu, Yen Le, *Filipino American Lives,* Temple University Press, 1995.

Lee, Mary Paik, *Quiet Odyssey: A Pioneer Korean Woman in America,* University of Washington Press, 1990.

Liliuokalani, *Hawaii's Story by Hawaii's Queen,* Charles E. Tuttle, 1964.

Saund, D. S., *Congressman from India,* E.P. Dutton, 1960.

Yamazaki, Tomoko, *The Story of Yamada Waka: From Prostitute to Feminist Pioneer,* Kodansha International, 1985.

Yung, Judy, *Chinese Women of America: A Pictorial History,* University of Washington Press, 1986.

Credits

Grateful acknowledgment is made to the following sources whose works appear in this volume. Every effort has been made to trace copyright, but if omissions have been made, please contact the publisher.

Hwang, David Henry. From a lecture delivered on April 15, 1994, at the Abramowitz Lecture Series, at Massachusetts Institute of Technology. Reprinted by permission of the author.

Inouye, Daniel K. *Vital Speeches of the Day,* v. 34, September 15, 1968. Reprinted by permission of the author and publisher.

Mink, Patsy Takemoto. From "Seeking a Link with the Past," in *Representative American Speeches: 1971-1972.* Edited by Waldo W. Braden. H. W. Wilson, 1972. Copyright © 1972 by The H. W. Wilson Company. Reprinted by permission of the author.

Natividad, Irene. "Proceedings of Specializing in the Impossible: Women and Social Reform in America, 1890-1990

Irene Natividad

Conference," 1991, from a keynote address delivered on March 7, 1991, at the symposium of the National Museum of American History Smithsonian Institution in Washington, D.C., by Irene Natividad. Reprinted by permission of the author.

Uyeda, Clifford I. From a speech delivered on January 20, 1979, at the Twin Cities JACL Chapter Installation Dinner in Minneapolis, Minnesota. Reprinted by permission of the author.

Zia, Helen. From a keynote address delivered on August 27, 1992, at the Annual Convention of Asian American Journalists Association. Copyright © 1992 by Helen Zia. Reprinted by permission of the author.

The photographs and illustrations appearing in *Asian American Voices* were received from the following sources:

Cover: AP/Wide World Photos: Bette Bao Lord.

Timeline: UPI/Corbis-Bettmann: Kamehameha IV; U.S. flag over the Hawaiian Royal Palace; Syngman Rhee; U.S.S. *Arizona* wreckage after Pearl Harbor; soldiers of Japanese ancestry at Iolani Palace, WWII; Koreans identifying their dead; Spark M. Matsunaga; Iva Toguri ("Tokyo Rose"); Vincent Chin; **courtesy of Hiram Leong Fong; AP/Wide World Photos:** Robert Matsui.

Text: UPI/Corbis-Bettmann: pp. 6, 17, 26, 29, 32, 35, 72, 77, 81, 86, 89, 92, 113, 122, 125, 128, 131, 134, 143, 145, 147, 151, 158, 162, 169, 171, 173, 179, 181, 185, 190, 193, 195, 199, 200; **Corbis-Bettmann:** pp. 8, 50, 84; **Courtesy of Hiram Leong Fong:** p. 10; **Courtesy of David Henry Hwang:** p. 44; **AP/Wide World Photos:** pp. 57, 65, 75, 96, 102, 107, 113, 117, 176, 207; **Courtesy of Daniel K. Inouye:** p. 63; **Reuters/Corbis-Bettmann:** pp. 101, 104, 231; **Courtesy of Helen Zia:** p. 222.

Timeline of Important Asian American Events
1765–1997

(Boldface indicates speakers featured in this volume)

1765 Filipino sailors from the Spanish Manila Galleon trade between Mexico and the Philippines jump ship to escape brutal treatment. They settle around New Orleans, Louisiana.

1806 Eight shipwrecked Japanese sailors become the first Japanese to arrive in the kingdom of Hawaii.

1820 The first Christian missionaries arrive in Hawaii, introducing the native population to Western-style education, government, and laws.

The first recorded Chinese immigrant arrives in United States. For the next thirty years the few Chinese settlers in the country are to be found only on the West Coast.

1833 Filipino settlers gather in the fishing village of St. Malo in Louisiana.

1841 Japanese fisherman Manjiro Nakahama, also known as John Mung, is rescued at sea and brought to Hawaii. Making his way to the mainland United States, he is educated in Massachusetts and later returns to Japan.

Kamehameha IV, King of Hawaii (1834-63)

1790
First U.S. Naturalization Act allows only "free white persons" to become citizens

1791
Bill of Rights ratified

1803
Louisiana Purchase

1812–15
War of 1812

European and "Asiatic" laborers complete the last mile of the Pacific Railroad (sketch by A. R. Ward)

1850–52 Large numbers of Chinese immigrants arrive in California after news of the gold rush reaches Canton, China. Most work as indentured servants or low-paid laborers. Chinese miners are soon heavily taxed to discourage them from panning for gold.

1860 First Japanese diplomatic delegation visits the Unites States.

1862 Congress passes a law allowing "any alien" who is honorably discharged from the military to apply for naturalization.

1868 Two hundred thirty years of Japanese isolationism ends with a political shift in Japan from the Tokugawas to the Meiji clan. Since the seventeenth century, the Japanese imperial government had expressly forbidden travel to or from Japan and instilled in its people a sense of fear of all that was foreign. The penalty for violating the isolationist policy was death.

About 150 Japanese contract workers arrive in Hawaii to work on the sugar plantations.

1869 With a workforce consisting primarily of Chinese immigrants, the first transcontinental rail route across the United States is completed.

1870 Congress passes a Naturalization Act that excludes Chinese from citizenship and prohibits the wives of Chinese laborers from entering the country.

Angry mobs in California and other western states lash out violently against Chinese immigrants, who are blamed for taking away jobs from unemployed whites.

1876 A treaty between the United States and Hawaii allows Hawaiian-grown sugar to enter the country duty-free.

Continuing economic instability in the United States touches off a new round of racial violence against Chinese immigrants in San Francisco, California, and elsewhere.

1848–49
California
gold rush

1861–65
U.S. Civil War

1870
15th Amendment
grants all male citizens
the right to vote

• • 1840 • • 1850 • • 1860 • • 1870 • • 1880 • •

1880	The United States restricts the immigration of Chinese laborers through a treaty with China.
1882	The Chinese Exclusion Act prohibits Chinese laborers from entering the country and denies citizenship to those already in the United States.
	Japanese immigrants begin to replace the Chinese as laborers on the U.S. mainland. Many of them arrive from Hawaii, where they had been working on sugar plantations.
1891	**Liliuokalani** becomes queen of Hawaii.
1892	The Chinese Exclusion Act is extended for another ten years.
1893	In Hawaii, American businessmen and their European supporters overthrow Queen **Liliuokalani,** set up their own government, and apply to the United States for annexation.
1898–99	In the Treaty of Paris, which ends the Spanish-American War, Spain cedes Puerto Rico and Guam to the United States, and the United States agrees to pay Spain $20 million for the Philippines.
1898	Hawaii is annexed to the United States.
1901	Congress indefinitely extends the provisions of the Chinese Exclusion Act.
1903	Korean laborers begin to arrive in Hawaii.
1906	The San Francisco (California) School Board orders the children of Asian residents to attend a segregated public school.
1907	President Theodore Roosevelt issues an executive order prohibiting Japanese immigrants from entering the mainland via Hawaii, Mexico, or Canada.
1908	The United States and Japan reach an agreement restricting the immigration of Japanese laborers.

The homes of Chinese immigrants are attacked by angry mobs, Chinatown, California, c. 1880

The U.S. flag waves over the Hawaiian Royal Palace, 1898

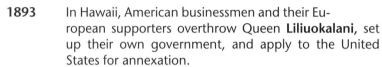

1884	**1890**			
Belva A. Lockwood is first woman to run for U.S. presidency	Soldiers kill 250 Sioux in Wounded Knee massacre	**1898** Spanish-American War	**1904–05** Russo-Japanese War	**1905** Japan unofficially occupies Korea

Syngman Rhee, 1932

1910 Angel Island Immigration Station, in San Francisco Bay, California, is set up to serve as a processing center for Asian immigrants. It soon becomes known for its long waiting periods and inhumane conditions.

The Supreme Court broadens the 1870 Naturalization Act to exclude Asians other than the Chinese from citizenship.

1913 California passes the Alien Land Act, which prohibits anyone who is ineligible for U.S. citizenship from buying land for agricultural purposes. Similar laws are later adopted in twelve other states.

1917 Congress passes the Immigration Act, which imposes a literacy requirement on all immigrants.

The Asiatic Barred Zone Act takes effect. It prohibits immigration from Asia and India.

1919 **Syngman Rhee** establishes a Korean government-in-exile in Hawaii after fleeing from the Japanese occupiers of his country.

1922 The Supreme Court upholds the Naturalization Law prohibiting Asian immigrants from becoming citizens.

Congress passes the Cable Act, which revokes the U.S. citizenship of any woman who marries an alien who is ineligible for U.S. citizenship.

1924 The Immigration Act of 1924 (also known as the Quota Immigration Act or National Origins Act) is signed into law. It prohibits the immigration of all Asian laborers (except Filipinos, who were already considered U.S. nationals).

1929 The Japanese American Citizens League (JACL) is founded with a focus on educational issues and civil rights.

1912
Republic of China founded by Sun Yat-sen

1914–18
World War I

1919
March 1 Movement against Japanese rule in Korea

1929
U.S. stock market crashes; Great Depression begins

1942   The U.S. War Department classifies Japanese American men of draft age as "enemy aliens."

President Roosevelt issues Executive Order 9066. It authorizes the evacuation of more than 120,000 Japanese Americans from designated areas of the West Coast to detention camps. Some Hawaiians of Japanese descent are also sent to camps on the mainland.

1943   Thousands of Japanese Americans volunteer to serve in the armed forces.

The Supreme Court rules that the curfew law imposed on all Japanese Americans is constitutional.

In a goodwill gesture toward China, an ally against Japan, Congress repeals the Chinese Exclusion Act; allowing Chinese immigrants to become naturalized citizens and establishing a quota of 105 Chinese immigrants per year.

1944   Two all-Japanese American military units, the 100th Battalion and the 442nd Regimental Combat Team, are united and go on to serve with distinction in Europe as the most decorated unit in United States history. Future U.S. Senators **Spark M. Matsunaga** and **Daniel K. Inouye** are among those who receive citations for their battlefield heroics.

1945   Japanese Americans held in detention camps are allowed to return to the West Coast.

1948   The Japanese American Evacuation Claims Act is signed into law. It enables former detention camp prisoners to file claims against the government for their financial losses, but many people have lost the documentation required and those who are able to file a claim receive less than ten cents for every dollar of lost property.

The independent Republic of Korea is proclaimed following United Nations-supervised elections. **Syngman Rhee** is named president.

Wreckage of U.S.S. Arizona after Japanese attack on Pearl Harbor, December 7, 1941

Three thousand American soldiers of Japanese ancestry assemble at Iolani Palace, Hawaii, World War II

1936
Congress of Industrial Organizations (CIO) admits non-white workers to the U.S. labor movement

1939–1945
World War II

1947
India and Pakistan win independence from Great Britain

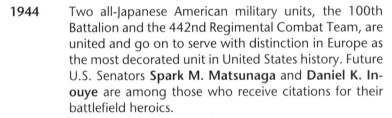

•• **1935** •• **1937** •• **1941** •• **1944** •• **1947** •• **1950** ••

Survivors weep over dead in Korean War, 1953

Hiram L. Fong

1952 The McCarran-Walter Immigration and Naturalization Act establishes immigration quotas for Japanese and other Asians and grants naturalization and citizenship rights to Asians not born in the United States.

1953 The Refugee Relief Act allows Chinese political refugees to enter the United States through 1956.

1959 Hawaii becomes the 50th state of the Union. Elected to represent Hawaii in the U.S. Congress are **Hiram L. Fong** (the first Chinese American elected to the Senate) and **Daniel K. Inouye** (the first Japanese American elected to the House of Representatives).

1962 **Daniel K. Inouye** becomes the first Japanese American elected to the U.S. Senate, and **Spark M. Matsunaga** is elected to the U.S. House of Representatives.

Patsy Takemoto Mink becomes the first Asian American woman elected to the U.S. House of Representatives.

1965 The Immigration Act of 1965 allows for much higher levels of non-European immigration to the United States, primarily from Latin America, the Caribbean, and Asia.

Rapid population growth and an increasingly authoritarian political system prompt an increasing number of South Koreans to immigrate to the United States.

1967 The Supreme Court rules unconstitutional all laws prohibiting interracial marriage.

1968 San Francisco State College president **S. I. Hayakawa** attracts national attention for taking a strong stand against student demonstrators on his campus.

1950–53
Korean War

1964
Civil Rights Act
prohibits employment
discrimination

1965
U.S. troops
participate in
Vietnam War

1968
Student protest
demonstrations hit
221 U.S. campuses

•• **1950** •• **1954** •• **1958** •• **1962** •• **1966** •• **1970** ••

1971 **Norman Y. Mineta** is elected mayor of San Jose, California, making him the first Japanese American mayor of a major U.S. city.

Urged on by Representative **Spark M. Matsunaga,** Congress repeals the Emergency Detention Act, which had legalized the imprisonment of Americans merely suspected of espionage or sabotage during a national security emergency and authorized holding prisoners in detention camps similar to those established for Japanese Americans during World War II.

Spark M. Matsunaga

In California, the Manzanar detention camp is designated a state historical landmark. Over the next few years, other camps that formerly housed Japanese American prisoners are granted similar status.

1974 Equal Educational Opportunity Act provides for bilingual education for non-English speakers in public schools.

Norman Y. Mineta becomes the first Japanese American from the United States mainland to be elected to the U.S. House of Representatives.

1975 After the fall of South Vietnam, Cambodia, and Laos, more than 140,000 refugees flee Southeast Asia. Many settle in the United States.

1976 Executive Order 9066, which authorized the evacuation and detention of Japanese Americans during World War II, is officially cancelled.

Iva Toguri, "Tokyo Rose"

1977 President Gerald Ford pardons Iva Toguri ("Tokyo Rose") nearly thirty years after she was convicted of trying to undermine the morale of U.S. troops during World War II.

1978 Under the leadership of **Clifford I. Uyeda,** the Japanese American Citizens League (JACL) launches its national redress campaign.

1969–1972	**1973**	**1974**
Humans walk on moon in Apollo missions	U.S. military participation in the Vietnam War ends	President Richard Nixon resigns after Watergate investigation

Vincent Chin

Robert T. Matsui

1982 In Detroit, Michigan, two unemployed autoworkers beat to death a young Chinese American man named Vincent Chin. **Helen Zia** subsequently cofounds and serves as national spokesperson for American Citizens for Justice, a group dedicated to seeking justice for Chin and combatting anti-Asian prejudice.

1983 The Commission on Wartime Relocation and Internment of Civilians (CWRIC) issues a report criticizing the government's treatment of Japanese Americans during World War II. It recommends that each person who had been detained in a camp receive a payment of $20,000.

1985 **Irene Natividad** becomes the first Asian American to be elected head of the National Women's Political Caucus.

1987 After impassioned speeches by Congressman **Robert T. Matsui** and others, the U.S. House of Representatives votes in favor of redress for Japanese Americans imprisoned by the U.S. government during World War II.

The Immigration Reform and Control Act is signed into law. Intended to curb illegal immigration, it allows aliens who can prove that they were in the United States before January 1, 1982, to apply for temporary status and then become citizens seven years after filing their applications.

1988 With Senator **Spark M. Matsunaga** leading the way, the U.S. Senate votes in favor of redress for Japanese Americans imprisoned by the U.S. government during World War II.

President Ronald Reagan signs into law the Civil Liberties Act of 1988. It grants redress to Japanese Americans imprisoned by the U.S. government during World War II.

1989 **David Henry Hwang** wins a Tony Award for his play *M. Butterfly*.

Helen Zia becomes executive editor of *Ms.* magazine.

1979–81
Fifty-two hostages are held at U.S. Embassy in Iran

1989
German reunification; Berlin Wall falls

1989
Tiananmen Square demonstration results in massacre, Beijing, China

•• **1980** •• **1982** •• **1984** •• **1986** •• **1988** •• **1990** ••

1990   **Daniel K. Akaka** becomes the first U.S. Senator of Native Hawaiian ancestry.

The first redress checks, in the amount of $20,000, are presented to Japanese Americans who were interned during World War II, along with a signed apology from President George Bush, at a ceremony in Washington, D.C.

First redress checks are presented to Japanese Americans interned during World War II by Attorney General Dick Thornburgh, Washington, D.C., 1990

1992   Racial violence involving blacks, whites, and Asians (mostly Korean Americans) erupts in Los Angeles, California, after four white police officers are acquitted in the beating of black motorist Rodney King.

U.S. troops leave the Philippines, ending nearly a century of U.S. military presence there.

An economic downturn in the United States results in a new round of Japan-bashing.

1994   California voters pass Proposition 187. It denies state education, medical, and welfare services to undocumented immigrants.

1995   Inspired by California, activists in more than a dozen other states mount efforts to end state affirmative action programs. The Supreme Court also issues a decision in favor of sharply limiting federal affirmative action programs.

1996   The National Asian Pacific Consortium reports that racially-motivated violence against Asian Pacific Americans is on the increase, especially in California and New York.

Participants in a special election called the Native Hawaii Vote overwhelmingly approve the idea of holding a convention to organize some form of independent government. They are among some 200,000 descendants of Hawaii's native population who resent the involvement of the United States in the 1893 overthrow of their last queen, **Liliuokalani.**

1990–1991
Persian Gulf War

1994
Republicans gain majorities in both the House and the Senate

1995
Million Man March, Washington, D.C.

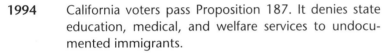

• • **1991** • • **1992** • • **1993** • • **1994** • • **1995** • • **1996** • •

Daniel K. Akaka

1924–

Chinese American/Native Hawaiian member
of the U.S. Senate

Daniel K. Akaka has been a member of the United States Senate since 1990, during which time he has earned a reputation as one of its hardest-working members. He is also regarded as one of its most modest, for he does not seek public praise or recognition for his dedication and efforts. A quiet, low-key man known for avoiding confrontations, he is totally devoted to advancing the interests of his fellow Hawaiians.

Generous Spirit of Family Fosters a Public Servant

A native of Honolulu, Hawaii, Akaka was the youngest of eight children in a family that had to struggle to make ends meet. Still, he recalls that his parents never hesitated to reach out and help others in need, regardless of their own shaky financial situation. In fact, Akaka believes that the generosity of spirit they displayed formed the basis of his own lifelong commitment to public service.

"TODAY, WE KNOW MORE ABOUT THE SURFACE OF PLANETS LOCATED MILLIONS OF MILES FROM EARTH THAN WE KNOW ABOUT MUCH OF THE OCEAN FLOOR, WHICH IS THE EARTH'S OWN BASEMENT."

1

Akaka also credits his parents with instilling in him a love of learning and a desire for a solid educational background. At the time he was growing up, the Hawaiian Islands offered little in the way of employment opportunities, except for the backbreaking work required on the coffee and sugar plantations. Akaka wanted more. After graduating from a private boys' school in 1942, he set out to earn some money for college. For several years during the mid-1940s he worked as a welder, first for the Hawaiian Electric Company and then for the U.S. Army Corps of Engineers. When his stint in the service ended in 1947, he enrolled in the University of Hawaii, earning a bachelor's degree in education in 1953 and a secondary school teaching certificate the following year.

Throughout the rest of the 1950s, Akaka gained valuable experience as an educator. He taught in a variety of rural and urban schools as well as in a military school. In 1960 he moved from the classroom into administration, serving several years as a vice principal and then as a principal. During this same period, Akaka returned to the University of Hawaii and obtained his master's degree in education.

From Education to Politics

Akaka's growing reputation as a leader in his field eventually led to his involvement in state politics. From 1969 until 1971, he was a program specialist for Hawaii's Department of Education. He followed that with a three-year term as director of the Hawaii Office of Economic Opportunity. Then he tried elective politics as a candidate in the 1974 Democratic primary election for lieutenant governor (the second in command in state government). Akaka lost that race, but the next year he went to work for newly elected Governor George R. Ariyoshi as his special assistant for human resources.

In 1976 Akaka decided to take another stab at elective politics, this time as a Democratic candidate for the United States House of Representatives. He captured some eighty percent of the vote and easily won reelection seven more times. Then, in early 1990, he was appointed to fill the U.S. Senate seat left vacant by the death of fellow Hawaiian **Spark M. Matsunaga** *(see entry). Later that same year, Akaka was reelected to the Senate in his own right.*

Hawaii's Voice in Washington

Since moving over to the Senate from the House of Representatives, Akaka has continued to promote a **liberal** point of view on the issues despite facing strong opposition from more **conservative** lawmakers. This has occasionally put him at odds with some of his colleagues—Republicans and Democrats alike. But Akaka quietly yet firmly sticks to his guns while using what he calls "the spirit of Aloha" to create an atmosphere that will bring people together rather than drive them apart.

As the first U.S. senator of Native Hawaiian ancestry, Akaka has taken a strong interest in issues of particular importance to Hawaii. Most notably, he has backed sugarcane growers by opposing efforts to cut federal sugar **subsidies.** And in the wake of the extensive damage caused by Hurricane Iniki in 1992, he urged the Federal Emergency Management Agency (FEMA) to create a field office on the islands.

Akaka has also tried to right some historical wrongs. In 1993 he successfully persuaded his fellow legislators to sign a joint congressional resolution admitting the U.S. government's role in overthrowing Hawaii's native government in 1893. (See entry on Queen **Liliuokalani** for more information.) As part of that resolution, the United States formally apologized to the Hawaiian people. In addition, Akaka's efforts have led to official recognition of Hawaiian civilians for their heroism in the days after the Japanese attack on the naval base at Pearl Harbor in December 1941—an attack that provoked American involvement in World War II.

Champions Environmental and Scientific Concerns

The environment is also of great concern to Akaka, who serves on the Senate Committee on Energy and Natural Resources. He is especially eager to preserve his homeland's delicate **ecosystem.** To that end, he has won passage of strict legislation safeguarding the Hawaiian Islands against the introduction of potentially destructive plant and animal species. He has also succeeded in establishing a tropical forest recovery program for Hawaii and has worked to eliminate U.S. territories in the Pacific as potential sites for nuclear waste disposal.

liberal: tending to be tolerant of different views, to embrace changes for the better, and to support government reform when necessary.

conservative: more inclined to follow tradition rather than seek change.

subsidies: money given by the government to farmers in support of their efforts to grow certain important crops.

ecosystem: the order of natural relationships between organisms and their environment.

In his role as chairman of the Subcommittee on Mineral Resources Development and Production of the Committee on Energy and Natural Resources, Akaka took a special interest in the use of technology to explore and mine the oceans. On November 4, 1993, he brought together numerous experts for a discussion of the issue. His goal was to gather facts that could prove helpful when he and his Senate colleagues tackled a general overhaul of mining laws that was scheduled to begin the following year.

Akaka opened the meeting with a brief statement outlining why he felt it was time to increase people's understanding of what lies beneath the sea—from both a scientific and a commercial, or business-related, standpoint. His remarks are reprinted here from Ocean Mining Technology: Hearing Before the Subcommittee on Mineral Resources Development and Production of the Committee on Energy and Natural Resources, United States Senate, *103rd Congress, 1st Session, U.S. Government Printing Office, 1994.*

Aloha, and good morning. The Energy Subcommittee on Mineral Resources Development and Production is in order, and today we will hear testimony on the status and future of ocean mining. In particular, we are interested in learning more about the development of technologies that could make ocean mining commercially **feasible.**

Such technologies would also have direct application in other disciplines, such as monitoring the ocean environment, pollution control, seafloor exploration, evaluation, and mapping, and other fields of scientific research and technology commercialization.

I should also point out that this technology will have direct application to undersea **ordnance** detection and removal. This is a major environmental problem for Kahoolawe, an island in Hawaii. Ever since the research vessel, H.M.S. *Challenger*, hoisted the first **manganese nodules** from the deep ocean during its epic voyage in 1873, there has been persistent and underlying curiosity about seabed minerals.

feasible: possible.

ordnance: weapons or ammunition.

manganese: a hard, grayish, metallic element.

nodules: lumps.

One hundred ten years later, another dramatic development occurred which will forever affect seabed research. In 1983, President [Ronald] Reagan established the 200-mile Exclusive Economic Zone [EEZ]. The U.S. EEZ is the largest territorial expansion in our history, larger than the Louisiana Purchase or the purchase of Alaska from Russia.

Our EEZ covers more than 2.5 billion acres, an area slightly greater than that of the United States. The U.S. EEZ is the largest under any nation's **jurisdiction**, and contains a resource base estimated in the trillions of dollars. It is a vast, new ocean frontier.

Because eighty-five percent of these waters are in the Pacific, Hawaii will play a central role in EEZ research and development. Unfortunately, our new frontier remains largely unexplored. After ten years, the United States has performed a detailed **reconnaissance** of less than five percent of our EEZ.

Every American schoolchild can recite President [John F.] Kennedy's famous challenge to reach the moon before the decade of the 1960s ended. The success of our country's space program has become a source of great national pride. Far less attention—far less—has been given to the speech Kennedy gave that same year which challenged Americans to tap the ocean depths.

Well, we have reached the moon and our spacecraft have explored our solar system. Today, we know more about the surface of planets located millions of miles from Earth than we know about much of the ocean floor, which is the Earth's own basement. Our map of Venus is better than the map of our own EEZ.

Competitiveness is the **buzzword** of the moment in Washington. Perhaps the greatest field of opportunity for enhancing U.S. competitiveness lies in our oceans, but like any area of economic opportunity, the payoff will only come if we commit adequate resources and attention to the task.

Today's hearing will examine the current status and future potential of technology used to explore and mine the ocean. Mineral-rich **oxides** found as nodules and crusts on the deep seabeds and on **seamounts** are one important EEZ resource.

jurisdiction: control, authority.

reconnaissance: survey.

buzzword: an important-sounding word or phrase.

oxides: blends of oxygen and other elements.

seamounts: mountains rising above the deep-sea floor.

A marine botanist prepares to explore the ocean depths off the shores of Hawaii with minisubmarine and a diving suit, 1979

Compared to land-base operations, mining of seabed minerals is not currently economical.

Investment in seabed exploration and the development of technologies to permit the efficient exploration of the oceans must be pursued as a long-term venture. Ocean technology continues to advance, but at an extremely slow pace, even though the potential payoffs associated with ocean technology development will be vast.

The Deep Seabed Hard Minerals Resources Act expires September 30, 1994. **Reauthorization** of this act offers an opportunity to examine the current state of technology necessary to survey, map, probe, sample, and monitor the deep seabed.

reauthorization: approval or okay given a second time.

Daniel K. Akaka

The availability of this technology will directly affect the pace, location, and cost of EEZ exploration and development.

In addition to seabed mineral resources, the hearing will focus more broadly on advances in technology which can improve U.S. competitiveness and **facilitate** the ... development of ocean resources in an environmentally responsible manner. The testimony and recommendations received today will be used to craft legislation which applies to many areas of ocean resource development other than fisheries.

I welcome all of our distinguished witnesses and would like to express my sincere gratitude for their efforts to help educate Congress—and this is a major endeavor, and this is the beginning of it—to educate Congress about the importance of ocean technology development....

I am pleased to welcome a witness [Dr. Robert Ballard] whose many accomplishments include the discovery of deep ocean hot vents which are host to previously unknown life systems, where creatures flourish without sunlight and feed on chemicals and heat generated by the Earth's **magma**.

He also founded the Jason Project, which has brought high-tech ocean adventure to millions of students, and I also understand that Dr. Ballard ... is one of the few that has seen so much mud in a lifetime on the bottom of the ocean in his ventures. [Laughter.] Dr. Ballard, welcome to the committee.

[After a morning of testimony from Dr. Ballard and more than a half-dozen other expert witnesses, the hearing came to an end with some additional thoughts from Akaka.]

Let me close with a few observations.

Japan and the European Community appear to be outpacing us with their **aggressive** programs in ocean technology development. If this continues, we will lose important opportunities that could lead to new ocean industries, technology advances and job creation.

To avoid this, the United States needs to refocus its ocean policy toward technologies that are critical to the future ocean research and development. Effective management of our EEZ depends upon having better tools to survey, map, probe, sample, and monitor the seabed in an environmental-

facilitate: encourage, make easier or simpler.

magma: molten rock (within the Earth).

aggressive: marked by energetic, forceful action.

Woods Hole Oceanographic Institution's DSV Alvin surfaces from a dive

R & D: research and development.

ly sound manner. At the same time, we must also get much more aggressive about establishing partnerships ... among industry, government and academia, which concentrate on ocean **R & D.**

Other nations, and particularly Japan, have employed this technique with great success. Such partnerships are our best hope of restoring the United States to a position of leadership in the use and protection of our ocean resources....

I will review the information gathered today, and will continue to closely follow the developments related to ocean technologies. With this information in hand—and thanks for all of your help—I will draft legislation to reauthorize the Seabed Mining Act in a way that fosters the technologies necessary to promote ocean research and development. We must provide our engineers and scientists with the tools and resources necessary to explore and economically develop our ocean resources.

99

On August 11, 1995, Akaka introduced Senate bill 1194 to amend the Mining and Mineral Policy Act of 1970. The amendment called for the promotion of research, identification, assessment, and exploration of mineral resources on the ocean floor. On September 28, 1996, after being evaluated by various committees, S. 1194 (renamed the Marine Mineral Resources Research Act of 1996) was passed by the U.S. Senate.

Sources

Books

Notable Asian Americans, Gale, 1995.

Ocean Mining Technology: Hearing Before the Subcommittee on Mineral Resources Development and Production of the Committee on Energy and Natural Resources, United States Senate, 103rd Congress, 1st Session, U.S. Government Printing Office, 1994.

Hiram L. Fong

1907–

Chinese American attorney, businessman, and former member of the U.S. Senate

During his long and productive life, Hiram L. Fong has played a role in more than a few important historical "firsts." He was, for example, the founder of the first multiethnic (made up of people who belong to different ethnic groups) law firm in Honolulu, Hawaii. He was also one of the first three legislators to represent Hawaii when it was proclaimed the fiftieth state of the union in 1959. And he was the first Chinese American to serve in the United States Congress. These achievements seem even more remarkable considering the poverty he faced as a child and his struggle to obtain the best education possible. But as one of his Senate colleagues once noted, Fong's life is a true rags-to-riches story that "exemplifies those deeply held, genuinely American beliefs in hard work, perseverance, and opportunity."

From Hardship to Harvard Law School

Fong was born and raised in a tough slum neighborhood of Honolulu. He was the seventh of eleven children of parents who had immigrated to Hawaii from China to work as indentured servants on a sugar plantation. (Indentured servants are people who pledge to work for someone for a specified time, often immigrants who work in return for their travel expenses, food, and shelter.) The family was so poor that little Yau, as he was known then, started picking beans at the age of four to help boost their finances. He continued doing odd jobs throughout his entire childhood, including shining shoes, selling newspapers, catching fish and crabs, and caddying at a local golf course.

Despite these hardships, Fong attended school regularly. A very good student who showed considerable promise, Fong had to put off going to college until he could earn enough money to pay his way. For three years he worked as a clerk at the Pearl Harbor Naval Shipyard. He then enrolled at the University of Hawaii. Fong completed the course work necessary for his bachelor's degree in only three years and earned highest honors in the process. This he managed to do while holding a variety of part-time jobs and pursuing many outside activities such as editing the school newspaper, participating in meets for the debate team, and competing in various sports.

It was also around this time that Fong changed his given name from Yau to Hiram in honor of the Reverend Hiram Bingham. Bingham was the leader of the first group of Congregational missionaries who arrived in Hawaii from New England in 1820. In addition to providing instruction in the Christian religion to the Hawaiians, the missionaries were responsible for setting up the first public schools on the islands. In fact, Fong—who became a Congregationalist himself— credits Bingham and the missionaries with bringing stability and advancement to Hawaii.

Following his graduation from college in 1930, Fong went back to work full-time as an employee of suburban Honolulu's water department. His goal was to make enough money to finance his next step up the ladder—law school. In 1932 he went off to Harvard University in Massachusetts. Three years later, he returned home completely broke— but with his law degree in hand.

Hawaii's Road to Statehood

For more than a hundred years before it officially became America's fiftieth state, Hawaii had strong religious, political, and economic ties to the West, especially Great Britain and the United States. The first contact came in 1778, when England's Captain James Cook "discovered" Hawaii and opened it up to foreign traders. The British continued to dominate the islands until 1790, when Native Hawaiians banded together politically under King Kamehameha I. Kamehameha I was the first of five native kings with the same name who held power until 1872. For the most part, the kings were friendly and cooperative to the white traders and settlers.

Merchants interested in Hawaii's sandalwood were among the first Americans to arrive on the islands around 1810. Ten years later groups of Congregationalist missionaries (mostly from New England) arrived. By this time disease and alcohol introduced to the islands by white newcomers had started to take their toll on the native population. On top of this, the missionaries were so zealous in their attempts to convert natives to Christianity and western-style education, government, and laws that they became a threat to the preservation of traditional Hawaiian ways. Opposition to their rules grew quite strong at times among the Hawaiians. Occasionally this led to minor revolts, but the missionaries maintained a very strong influence on Hawaii's affairs.

Beginning in the 1830s sugar emerged as an important export crop for Hawaii. The missionaries established the first plantations and brought in Chinese and Japanese laborers to work in the fields and in the

Establishes Honolulu's First Multiethnic Law Firm

Fong worked briefly as a municipal clerk in Honolulu before forming a partnership with several other local attorneys of Japanese, Korean, and Caucasian ancestry to establish Honolulu's first multiethnic law firm. It proved to be extremely successful, enabling Fong to make a series of profitable investments in real estate, insurance and finance firms, shopping centers, and a plantation. Within just a few years, the man who had once picked beans to help support his family was a millionaire.

Becoming financially independent made it possible for Fong to turn his attention to another interest—public service. He started out by working as deputy attorney for both the city and county of Honolulu until 1938. That year he won election as a Republican to the territorial House of Representatives.

mills. This concentrated even more economic and political power in the hands of the Americans.

In the late 1800s King Kalakaua and his successor, Queen **Liliuokalani** (see entry), tried to establish more self-government in Hawaii. But in the 1890s a committee made up mostly of foreign businessmen supported by the U.S. government overthrew Queen Liliuokalani and set up a temporary government headed by Sanford B. Dole, a lawyer and the son of an American missionary. In 1894 the Republic of Hawaii was created, and Dole was named president. The United States then annexed Hawaii in 1898 and officially made it a territory in 1900 with Dole as its governor.

Hawaii was generally overlooked by the American public until the United States entered World War II in 1941. The islands were then placed under military control until 1944. As a result, hundreds of thousands of Americans became familiar with Hawaii's charms while they were stationed there or passed through on their way to other bases in the Pacific.

The increased American presence in Hawaii, greater overall awareness of its strategic importance, and its potential as a tourist spot helped fuel a renewed push for statehood. There were obstacles, however, including strong prejudice against the many people of Japanese descent living in Hawaii. There were also fears of a **communist** influence in the islands' labor unions. Supporters of statehood kept up the pressure throughout the 1950s, however, and Hawaii became the fiftieth state in 1959.

There he served for the next fourteen years, including three terms as speaker and two as vice speaker.

Represents the Newest State in the U.S. Senate

One of Fong's top priorities as a territorial legislator was achieving statehood for Hawaii. (See box for more information.) His efforts were finally rewarded on June 27, 1959, when islanders voted to join the United States. A month later, on July 28, they elected Fong to one of the new state's two seats in the U.S. Senate.

As a legislator, Fong was a self-described **liberal** on social issues and a **conservative** when it came to military matters and the national budget. He supported major civil rights and antidiscrimination legislation, including the landmark Civil Rights Act of 1964. The following year he played a key role in drafting immigration reform laws that eliminated the old quota system based on race and national origin. The new

communist: following a system of government in which the state controls the means of production and the distribution of goods; communism clashes with the American ideal of capitalism, which is based on private ownership and a free market system.

liberal: tending to be tolerant of different views, to embrace changes for the better, and to support government reform when necessary.

conservative: more inclined to follow tradition rather than seek change.

laws opened the door for larger numbers of Asians to enter the United States. Fong also worked hard to make sure the country's newest state received fair and equal treatment from the federal government.

Promoted Understanding Between Two Cultures

Perhaps most notably, however, Fong served as a living bridge between two very different worlds—Asia and the United States. Throughout his entire Senate career he supported numerous cultural and economic exchanges between countries of the Asia-Pacific region and the United States. One of his greatest accomplishments was helping to establish and obtain financial backing for the East-West Center, an internationally respected **think tank** *based at the University of Hawaii. Fong has always been extremely proud of Hawaii's multiracial and multiethnic mix of residents. He frequently points to his beloved home state as an example of how harmony and brotherhood can exist in a diverse population.*

In 1960 Fong's devotion to this ideal prompted members of the National Conference of Christians and Jews to present him with their National Brotherhood Award for his outstanding service and leadership. He formally accepted the honor at a special gathering held in Providence, Rhode Island, on May 5th of that year.

In the speech he delivered to mark the occasion, Fong shared his thoughts on the factors that had contributed to Hawaii's uniqueness. On May 11, 1960, a colleague of Fong's stood up in the Senate and asked that the senator's remarks be entered into the Congressional Record. *The following version of Fong's speech is therefore excerpted from the* Congressional Record, *86th Congress, 2nd Session, Volume 106, Part 8, U.S. Government Printing Office, 1960.*

It is indeed a great honor and a great privilege for my wife Ellyn and me to be with you this evening—to sit down with you and to break bread with you and to make your friendship.

To receive from you, friends I have just come to know, ... this bronze award signifying service to the cause of brotherhood,

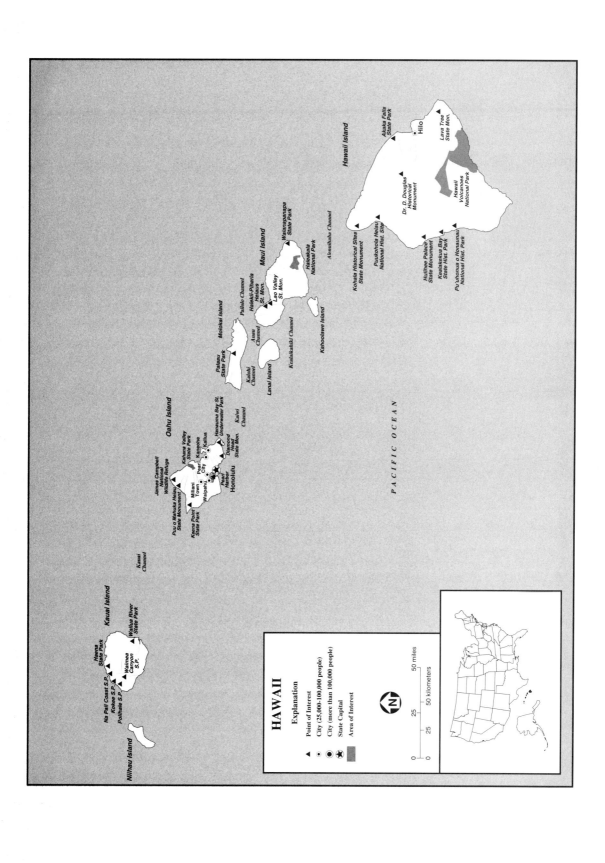

Nihau Island

Kauai Island

Na Pali Coast S.P.
Haena State Park
Kokee S.P.
Palihale S.P.
Waimea Canyon S.P.
Wailua River State Park

Kauai Channel

Oahu Island

James Campbell National Wildlife Refuge
Puu o Mahuka Heiau State Monument
Kahana Valley State Park
Milliani Town
Pearl City
Waipahu
Keena Point State Park
Pearl Harbor
Kaneohe
Kailua
Hanauma Bay St. Underwater Park
Diamond Head State Mon.
Honolulu
Kaiwi Channel

Molokai Island
Palaau State Park

Kalohi Channel
Lanai Island

Auau Channel

Maui Island
Waianapanapa State Park
Haleki-Pihana Heiau St. Mon.
Iao Valley St. Mon.
Haleakala National Park

Pailolo Channel

Kealaikahiki Channel

Kahoolawe Island

Alenuihaha Channel

Hawaii Island
Akaka Falls State Park
Hilo
Lava Tree State Mon.
Dr. D. Douglas Historical Monument
Hawaii Volcanoes National Park
Kohala Historical Sites State Monument
Puukohola Heiau National Hist. Site
Hulihee Palace State Monument
Kealakekua Bay State Hist. Park
Pu'uhonua o Honaunau National Hist. Park

PACIFIC OCEAN

HAWAII

Explanation

▲ Point of Interest
● City (25,000–100,000 people)
◉ City (more than 100,000 people)
✪ State Capital
▒ Area of Interest

N

0   25   50 miles
0   25   50 kilometers

moves me very, very deeply. I am doubly thankful for your kindness and for selecting me for this honor which I know I do not deserve....

Your regional director ... has asked me to discuss Hawaii's role in human relationships and I am happy to **accede** to her wishes....

Essential to a deeper understanding of Hawaii is a knowledge of its history, its geographical location, and of the peoples who settled there. Situated in the vast Pacific Ocean which covers one-third of our globe, the Hawaiian Islands number just eight out of the thousands of islands comprising Malaysia, Melanesia, Micronesia, and Polynesia. Archaeologists, anthropologists, and historians of these oceanic people and their culture virtually agree that stone-age Caucasian people in successive waves of migration from the Indochina Peninsula pushed eastward into Malaysia, then from there to Melanesia, then to the islands off and surrounding Tahiti, the heart of Polynesia. From Tahiti in great single and double canoes, they **dispersed** 2,500 miles north to Hawaii, southwest to New Zealand, and southeast to Mangareva, Pitcairn, and Easter Island....

It is generally **conceded** that the first Polynesians landed on Hawaii some 1,200 years ago.

Little is known of the history of Hawaii until Captain James Cook, of Great Britain, discovered the islands in 1778, and brought to a close the period of Hawaiian isolation which had existed for ten centuries. Thereafter, fur traders of the Northwest and California, on their way to sell their furs in China, together with the demand for Hawaiian sandalwood and the outfitting of whaling fleets, made Hawaii an important port of commerce.

The strategic significance of Hawaii as a Pacific outpost became apparent in the middle of the nineteenth century, when a power struggle for dominance of the islands took place between England, France, and the United States.

Hawaii today could easily have been an English colony by right of discovery or by **cession**, or a French colony by force of arms.

A British naval force seized Hawaii and for five months the British flag flew over the islands in 1843. However, by that

accede: give in.
dispersed: spread out.
conceded: acknowledged, recognized.
cession: the act of giving something up to someone else.

time, the influence of Americans in the islands and the gaining strength of the United States in the Pacific assured the Hawaiian kingdom of its independence.

From 1795 when Kamehameha, a Hawaiian chieftain, took control of Hawaii, Maui, and Oahu, to 1893, a period of almost 100 years, the Hawaiian Islands were under the rule of seven kings and one queen. In 1893, Queen **Liliuokalani** [see entry] was dethroned and a **provisional** government was formed. The Republic of Hawaii was established the following year.

Hawaii was **annexed** by the United States in 1898 and from 1900 to nine months ago, it was an incorporated territory of the United States with a representative legislature elected by the people but with an appointed governor.

Entrance hall and staircase of Iolani Palace, in Honolulu, Hawaii—the only royal palace in the United States

provisional: temporary.
annexed: acquired.

Hiram L. Fong | 17

Ethnically, Hawaii is composed of many nationalities. The early settlers were the Polynesians. Caucasian sailors, adventurers, whalers, traders, and missionaries were second comers. Then followed Chinese contract laborers recruited to work the sugar plantations....

With the annexation of the islands to the United States in 1898, Chinese labor immigration was completely prohibited as ... laws ... excluding Chinese laborers to the United States ... were made applicable to Hawaii.

Japanese contract laborers in great numbers were also imported from 1885 until their exclusion in 1924.

Portuguese, Swedes, Germans, Koreans, South Sea Islanders, Puerto Ricans, and Filipinos also comprised immigrant groups brought in for the cultivation and the processing of sugar.

From these **heterogeneous** and diverse ethnic groups has evolved a **homogeneous** community—a community which has been termed by students of **sociology** as a "twenty-first-century society" where racial harmony and cooperation are normal and accepted conditions of life. This spirit of working together **pervades** civic, business, political, and cultural endeavors. There is sincere respect for, rather than mere toleration of, each other's nationality, traits, characteristics, and cultures.

Living in an island paradise, tropical and balmy, with high standards of health and livelihood; with a good, free educational system; a stable, democratic government; where no group constitutes a racial majority; with peoples on one hand steeped in Christian **Puritan** outlook and justice, and on the other, **imbued** with **Buddhist** and **Confucian** philosophies stressing human and moral conduct; cemented together and mellowed by the generous open-heartedness and carefree *aloha* spirit of its native Hawaiian people, we in Hawaii would like to believe that we are giving life to a community approaching the ideal of a world at peace....

President [Dwight D.] Eisenhower said to the people of India during his recent trip, "Hawaii cries insistently to a divided world that all our differences of race and origin are less than the grand and indestructible unity of our common

heterogeneous: mixed, assorted.

homogeneous: unified; consistent.

sociology: the study of human society, social institutions, and social relationships.

pervades: spreads throughout.

Puritan: a Protestant reform group in England and New England during the 1500s and 1600s that followed an extremely rigid moral code.

imbued: filled.

Buddhist: in the way of Buddhism, a religion of eastern and central Asia centered on the importance of high moral standards, meditation, and the seeking of wisdom.

Confucian: in the way of Confucianism, a philosophy based on the teachings of the Chinese thinker Confucius, who stressed the importance of tradition, social reform, and respect among all peoples.

brotherhood. The world should take time to listen with [an] attentive ear to Hawaii."

Hawaii is indeed a showcase for true brotherhood. Elsewhere, even as in ancient days, massive discrimination continues to **blight** human relationships. Our news media carry daily evidence of man's inhumanity to man, evidenced by oppression, fear, hatred, bias, and discrimination in all quarters of our globe.

Behind the **Iron and Bamboo Curtains,** religious and political persecution persist. In Tibet, the Red Chinese regime continues mass **genocide** of the civilian population. Large numbers of people still flee East Germany and Red China, at risk of life and limb, to seek **sanctuary** in more tolerant oases. Anti-Semitism and anti-Christianity erupt as **atheistic** communism seeks to wipe out religious worship.

Belligerent **nationalism** is more the rule than not in modern struggles to throw off the **yoke** of **colonialism.** Too often such nationalism provokes wholesale bloodletting, with guns replacing ballots as the means of **attaining parity** and settling disputes.

Unmindful of man's growing yearning for equal status, many cling to senseless **caste** systems of the discredited past. As in South Africa, the ruling race shocked the world with its brutal methods to enforce **apartheid.**

There is something **barbaric** in today's repression of man's natural passion for **equity.**

Here in the United States we are not yet **purged** of intolerance and prejudice. Denial of voting rights; **desecration** of churches, schools, and public buildings; discrimination in employment and in public accommodations point up the urgent need for further progress in learning to live peaceably together. In connection with recent sit-down demonstrations at lunch counters, it is significant to note that many whites who object to Negroes sitting as customers on one side of the counter do not object to Negroes on the other side of the counter cooking and serving the food they eat. **Irrational** from a standpoint of logic, this attitude is bewildering from a standpoint of emotion as well.

blight: cause to fall apart; destroy.

Iron and Bamboo Curtains: the Iron Curtain refers to the barrier of ideas, politics, and military force that shut off eastern Europe and the Soviet Union from the rest of the world from the late 1940s through the late 1980s; the Bamboo Curtain describes the same concept in relation to Communist China.

genocide: the deliberate and organized destruction of a particular racial, cultural, or political group.

sanctuary: a place of protection.

atheistic: Godless.

nationalism: the belief that a particular nation or its culture is better than all others.

yoke: ties.

colonialism: one country or power taking control of another territory.

attaining parity: gaining equality.

caste: rigid social divisions.

apartheid: racial segregation.

barbaric: uncivilized, vicious.

equity: fairness, equality.

purged: freed.

desecration: the act of treating with contempt or disrespect.

irrational: lacking reason or understanding.

In our glass house that is America, our discrimination and bigotry are in full view of a critical world. We receive considerable **adverse** comment for our shortcomings—and perhaps not enough recognition for the undeniable progress we are making. Unlike some of our critics, we are not sweeping our problems of civil rights under the rug. We are facing up to them.

This year, in the Senate of the United States, 100 representatives of 179 million Americans aired our civil rights disagreements in public over a period of eight weeks. If ever opinions were thoroughly ventilated, these were. And when all the smog had lifted, what was the outcome?

Of the 100 senators, 82 supported passage of corrective and progressive civil rights legislation. Only 18 voted for the status quo.

In school, we usually consider 70 a "passing" grade. While 82 may not elevate us to honor roll, it certainly is a very respectable score.

In terms of public sentiment, the 82 percent of the Senate favoring this year's civil rights bill represents a sizable majority of American people. Without such widespread approval, this civil rights milestone would not have been achieved. Although the bill does not go far enough to suit some people and goes too far to suit others, it does **denote** real progress.

To those who are impatient with our speed in achieving true brotherhood, let me point out that, until 1957, more than eighty years elapsed without passage of a single significant civil rights law. Now, just three years later, we have enacted a second major civil rights statute. Unquestionably, this reflects significant transformation in American attitudes.

In many areas of the United States, of course, we still have not matched the tolerance found in Hawaii where acceptance, without regard to race, color, or creed, and based on individual merit and standing is the general rule—the unwritten rule. Acceptance comes from the heart. It is not **superimposed** by such means as legislation, judicial process, or promotional campaigns.

For example, discrimination does not exist in government employment [here in Hawaii]....

adverse: negative.
denote: indicate.
superimposed: placed over or on top of something.

Intermarriage between members of different ethnic groups has been and is common and has produced fine, outstanding people, many of whom are leaders in the business, professional, political, and religious life of the Islands.

In the matter of voting, Dr. Andrew W. Lind, professor of sociology at the University of Hawaii, states that "racial **bloc** voting, in the mainland sense of the vigorous control over an entire bloc of voters of a common race, does not occur in Hawaii, and even in the more restricted sense of voting exclusively for members of one's own ethnic group, it is so slight as to be inconsequential." He observed that "any politician of the slightest **sagacity** soon learns, if he does not already know, that the surest route to political suicide is an appeal on a racial basis."

I must confess there is some racial discrimination practiced by some social groups in Hawaii but in recent years, more and more private groups are opening their memberships to persons of all races. It may not be too long before racial bars are lifted altogether.

In the field of public accommodations, all of our restaurants, theaters, hotels, public parks, public beaches, public swimming pools, golf courses, tennis courts, and transportation facilities are free of any discrimination based on race, color, religion or national origin.

Justice is **dispensed** with equity. There has been no reported case in which any question of discrimination in the administration of justice appears to have been raised.

Even though racial harmony prevails in Hawaii, there are groups dedicated to furthering interracial relations such as the Hawaii Chapter of World Brotherhood, the Honolulu Council of Churches, and the Pacific and Asian Affairs Council. While we do not have a chapter of the National Conference of Christians and Jews in Hawaii, efforts in behalf of racial and religious understanding are carried on by the Council of Churches and World Brotherhood.

In addition, business organizations such as the Chamber of Commerce, Board of Underwriters, Commercial Club, Employers Council, Home Builders Association and the Retail Board are comprised of individuals of varying racial extractions.

bloc: a group united by a common interest.
sagacity: wisdom.
dispensed: measured out.

This is also true of civic, political, educational, fraternal, health, medical, veterans, and welfare groups.

Again this is true of the more than one dozen service organizations for young people.

The Honolulu Symphony Orchestra and the Community Theater include in their membership individuals of many races....

To bridge the gap between the two hemispheres, Hawaii has done many things. For instance, Hawaii sponsored an Afro-Asian student leader seminar where three dozen talented young college men and women from nearly as many countries on three continents **conferred** for four weeks on the place of higher education in society today.

Hawaii held an International Conference on Race Relations to discuss the conflicts and tensions which exist throughout the world between **imperialistic** powers and peoples imbued with the spirit of self-determination, with emphasis on the effect of economic change and nationalism on race relations in Africa, Asia, and the Western Hemisphere.

Hawaii held three East-West [philosophy] conferences where an Asian conferee remarked that these meetings were the only ones in which Asians had felt free to express themselves frankly and did so.

For six years, the University of Hawaii has conducted an Asian Orientation Center for [students] headed for graduate study at mainland U.S. universities.

Last month, three prominent citizens of Hawaii accompanied by their wives began a tour of southeast Asia and India. Their mission is to meet and mingle informally with the peoples of the Pacific area. Each of the group represents a different race of the Pacific. Each has prospered through his individual merit in Hawaii's climate of racial understanding and harmony. In turn, each has contributed to Hawaii's growth and stature....

As representatives of the State of Hawaii, they have vital information to **impart** on their tour. They can speak from personal experience of America's growing feeling of racial understanding so well in evidence in Hawaii. They can cite specific accomplishments in Hawaii resulting from this understanding.

conferred: compared opinions and ideas.

imperialistic: displaying the characteristics of imperialism, which is the practice of expanding a nation's authority by acquiring new territory or gaining control over the people of another country.

self-determination: freedom to choose one's own political future.

impart: share.

Hiram L. Fong

A group of three University of Hawaii students, one a mother of three, last week launched a statewide fund-raising campaign to finance scholarships for Asian students. They hope to expand the program eventually to include an undergraduate student exchange program....

Nearly two thousand elementary schoolchildren are participating in a "neighbor" language program to promote understanding through better communication. They are learning languages of the Far East under a program sponsored and conducted by the Hawaii Department of Public Instruction.

To promote better relations and understanding among the United States and the nations of Asia and the Pacific, the Senate of the United States last week authorized a three-year expenditure of $30 million to establish in Hawaii a Center for Cultural and Technical Interchange between the East and the West. I hope that the House of Representatives will **concur** and make it a reality....

The reason cited for the establishment of the Center in Hawaii was the uniquely favorable atmosphere there; a physical and a cultural climate in which students from the Orient can be at their ease; a community eager to participate in the program by opening its offices and homes to these students; and a community which itself displays the best qualities of East and West.

It is therefore manifestly evident that Hawaii, with its rich multiracial human resource, long and **amicable** history of ethnic integration, happy cultural interchange and strategic geography, has not ... withdrawn herself into her own island sanctuary, but has diligently pursued numerous ways to contribute her good fortune and know-how to bring closer cooperation among her neighbors.

Clothed with the dignity of a **sovereign** state, she is confident that her people, few as they are, can effectively help to hasten the **millennium** of the brotherhood of man.

This we have accepted as the ultimate unfolding of our destiny, our great contribution to America. This we know is our **transcendent** mission. We live brotherhood, we believe in it, and we know it has real prospect for success nationally and internationally, for it satisfies the soul and has the force of logic.

concur: agree.

amicable: showing peace and goodwill.

sovereign: independent, free.

millennium: a period of great happiness.

transcendent: above all else, surpassing all limits.

We in Hawaii do feel a sense of history—not just of a dramatic past, great as it may be, but of a dynamic future with its promise of richer achievement benefiting humanity and **auguring** peace.

What we have accomplished in Hawaii in so short a period can well be duplicated by all communities. Many and **propitious** may have been the factors for Hawaii to so quickly attain a happy homogeneous community. Yet the lack of some of these factors should not render that attainment impossible elsewhere. It may perhaps take longer.

All communities are endowed with the substantive factors for success in human relationship. All they need is to **catalyze** and to **synthesize** them. In Hawaii we have found it. You, I know in a great measure, have also found it. Surprisingly so, it is everywhere in some measure. In the Old Testament [of the Bible], a book so dear to Christians as well as to Jews, third chapter of First Kings, we are told that the Lord appeared to Solomon in a dream and asked him what he would want and Solomon replied, "O Lord, my God, give thy servant therefor an understanding heart to judge thy people, that I may **discern** between good and evil; for who is able to judge this thy so great a people?"

It pleased the Lord that Solomon had asked this thing and God said unto him, "Because thou hast asked this thing and hast not asked for thyself long life or riches or the life of thine enemies but hast asked for thyself understanding to discern what is right, behold, I have done according to thy words. Lo, I have given thee a wise and an understanding heart and I have also given thee that which thou hast not asked, both riches and honor."

I thank you.

99

Fong was reelected to the U.S. Senate two more times, once in 1964 and again in 1970. He retired from public office in January 1977. Since then, Fong has devoted himself to his many business interests and charitable activities. As a gift to the people of Hawaii he established a 725-acre plantation

auguring: predicting.

propitious: lucky, favorable.

catalyze: bring about change through inspiring some kind of action or reaction.

synthesize: combine different things into a whole.

discern: discover or understand the difference between two things.

and botanical garden so that everyone has a "place of fragrance and tranquility" to visit. In recognition of Fong's business success and generous contributions to making life better for others, Junior Achievement of Hawaii named him to the organization's "Hall of Fame" in 1995.

Sources

Books

Congressional Record, 86th Congress, 2nd Session, Volume 106, Part 8, U.S. Government Printing Office, 1960, pp. 9971–74; 94th Congress, 2nd Session, Volume 122, Part 25, U.S. Government Printing Office, 1976, pp. 32817–38.

Notable Asian Americans, Gale, 1995.

Periodicals

Hawaii Business, "Hall of Fame," January 1995.

S. I. Hayakawa

1906–1992

Japanese American educator, university administrator, and member of the U.S. Senate

One of the most colorful—and controversial—public figures in recent American history was noted educator Samuel Ichiye Hayakawa. He first emerged on the national scene in the early 1940s as the author of a bestselling book that examined how language can be used to influence thought and behavior. During the late 1960s Hayakawa made a name for himself as a university administrator who would not tolerate the student unrest then raging on college and university campuses across the country. Later he entered politics and again generated headlines for his outspoken conservatism.

An Interest in Words and Language

Known as "Don" to family and friends, Hayakawa was born in Vancouver, British Columbia, Canada, to parents who had immigrated there from Japan. His father ran an import-export business and frequently moved his wife and four children from one Canadian city to another. Hayakawa finished his high school education in Winnipeg, Manitoba. He then earned his bachelor's degree from the University of

Manitoba in 1927 and his master's in English literature from McGill University in Montreal, Quebec, three years later. Heading off to the United States to continue his education, he obtained his doctoral degree in English and American literature from the University of Wisconsin in Madison in 1935.

Unable to find a teaching job in Canada, Hayakawa remained in Madison after completing his degree. There he taught adult students in the university's extension division. He left Wisconsin in 1939 to take a job as an instructor in English at the Illinois Institute of Technology in Chicago. Hayakawa remained at the school throughout the 1940s, moving up the academic ranks to associate professor of English in 1942.

At the same time, Hayakawa was making a name for himself outside the classroom. Over the course of several years he had observed with great interest how Nazi leader Adolf Hitler and others like him in Europe had skillfully manipulated words and symbols to seize and maintain political control. During the late 1930s Hayakawa began assembling his thoughts on the subject into a book he hoped would explain this deliberate misuse of language to students as well as to a general audience.

Publishes Landmark Study of Language Use

His findings were based on the theories of Polish-born scholar Alfred Korzybski, who is considered the founder of general semantics (the study of how people evaluate words and how that evaluation in turn influences their behavior). Hayakawa published the first edition of his Language in Action (later Language in Thought and Action) in 1941. Its blend of humor and clear explanations of a difficult yet fascinating subject was a hit with the American public. The book became a bestseller and has been required reading in many high school and college courses from the 1940s through the present day.

Hayakawa was quickly recognized as one of the leading experts in the field of general semantics. He went on to establish the International Society for General Semantics and served for nearly thirty years as editor of its quarterly journal, ETC. He later wrote a total of seven other books on language *and communication. All were written in a way that enabled a popular audience to understand the complex concepts. Hayakawa's work met with some criticism in the academic community for not being "scholarly" enough, but he continued trying to find ways to relate the things he taught to everyday situations.*

In 1955, after spending five years as an instructor in semantics at the University of Chicago, Hayakawa joined the faculty of California's San Francisco State College (later University) on a part-time basis. His position allowed him the freedom to lecture and write. Near the end of 1968, however, growing student unrest on the San Francisco State campus suddenly thrust him into a new and unexpected role—that of college president.

President of San Francisco State College

Hayakawa's sudden promotion came at a time when American college campuses were in turmoil, hit hard by demonstrations, sit-ins, protest rallies, and strikes. San Francisco State was no exception. In 1968 a relatively small group of radical students there started making demands of the school. They insisted on getting rid of the school's ROTC program, a military training program that prepares young people for service in the Army Reserve. They also pushed for the admission of more minority students into the school. In addition they sought a black studies department and to reinstate a suspended black instructor.

When school officials refused their demands, demonstrators disrupted classes, vandalized buildings, and launched a strike. Local police were called in to restore order, but the unrest continued for weeks. Two San Francisco State presidents resigned in the space of seven months.

Into this chaotic atmosphere stepped Hayakawa. He sympathized with some of the demonstrators' demands, including the need to expand and improve the black studies program and take a new look at admission standards. Yet he felt the school's most important obligation was to the vast majority of students who were not on strike. In fact, he was one of the few faculty members who supported the idea of

starting classes again by any means necessary—even if it meant resorting to force.

Standing Up to Student Radicals

Hayakawa's feistiness and no-nonsense attitude soon caught the attention of California Governor Ronald Reagan. He named the outspoken professor acting president of San Francisco State in late November 1968. Hayakawa immediately banned all student demonstrations and speeches. He also announced that classes would begin again right after the Thanksgiving break.

When school reopened on December 2, angry students responded with violent attacks on classroom and administration buildings in an attempt to shut everything down again.

Hayakawa, as acting president of San Francisco State College, examines the fire damage to a colleague's office during campus disruptions, 1968

An equally outraged Hayakawa then confronted the protesters, climbed up on their sound truck, and ripped out the wires connected to their loudspeaker. That evening, after reports of his reaction hit the national news, Hayakawa became known as a man who would stand up to the growing turbulence on American campuses.

By mid-December Hayakawa's firmness and the presence of hundreds of police officers on campus seemed to have brought some peace to the campus. The majority of students had returned to school, and many protesters had been arrested or suspended. But in January 1969 new troubles surfaced. The local chapter of the American Federation of Teachers union, which represented some San Francisco State faculty members, called for a strike that again halted classes and increased tensions.

On February 3, 1969, Hayakawa testified before members of the U.S. House of Representatives in connection with the San Francisco State situation. Concerned about the problem of student unrest, legislators had begun to discuss ways of dealing with it. Members of the House were very interested in hearing from the man who had taken such a strong stand against protesters and welcomed him warmly to the halls of Congress. An excerpt from Hayakawa's testimony that day is reprinted here from the official report Campus Unrest: Hearings Before the Special Subcommittee on Education of the Committee on Education and Labor, House of Representatives, *91st Congress, 1st Session, U.S. Government Printing Office, 1969.*

liberal: tending to be tolerant of different views, to embrace changes for the better, and to support government reform when necessary.

incentive: a source of motivation or encouragement.

militancy: being engaged in fighting or combat.

....San Francisco State College has long been known for its **liberal** and interesting faculty.... Academic freedom has been a way of life and an **incentive** to attract exciting students and professors. This atmosphere may have had something to do with the rise of faculty **militancy** and the close relationship between some extremely liberal faculty members and students who became leaders of militant or ultraliberal groups....

S. I. Hayakawa

Generally, administrative control over the faculty cannot be described as **dictatorial** in the least.... The faculty has **autonomy** in essential matters.... The president cannot even fire a faculty member. He can only recommend action to the chancellor....

A relatively small segment of the faculty is close to the small segment of the students who are the militant or **dissident** leadership. This is a strange **alliance**. I believe that some faculty may be radicals and may develop close association with radical students because of professional inadequacies. For example, a faculty member who is not considered to be a strong scholar among his peers may seek recognition from students. Then there are at least a few, I am sure, who are dedicated revolutionaries. We do know that there is a certain amount of coaching of radical students by radical faculty but I think we have reached the point where the students have much to teach their tutors.

The relationship of the faculty to the administration is one of those strange **bureaucratic** arrangements. Some teachers are professional politicians within the institution, very close to administrators at all levels, influencing decisions, carrying messages, and frequently contributing worthwhile feedback of general faculty opinion. Then there are some on our campus, and every other campus, who ignore the administration completely as they come and go from home to the classroom, laboratory, and library....

A portrait of student unrest groups: We have several white radical or ultraliberal groups. Their numbers total something around 300.... Their central control is probably **vested** in less than 50 people. These 50 or so are dedicated, experienced, and effective in the field of organizing or disruption....

Of our 800 or 900 black students, I would estimate that less than 100 have been involved in the recent disruptions, although many more attend rallies under pressure from their leaders. The bravest young people on our campus are the nonviolent young black students who keep on attending classes at the risk of physical attack from black militants and in the face of distrust on the part of the majority of white students. I have praised these young people before in public and

dictatorial: absolute, unreasonabley severe.

autonomy: independence; freedom.

dissident: in disagreement with established powers.

alliance: association, union, bond, or connection.

bureaucratic: official.

vested: rooted or established.

A police officer draws his revolver as students and police clash at San Francisco State College, 1969

appreciate the opportunity to repeat my feelings of admiration for them today.

There is an important difference between black and white activists. Generally speaking, the black students are fighting for a place in society. White activists, such as the Students for a Democratic Society [SDS], are fighting to destroy the society, even though they have nothing better to propose as a substitute. It is only during periods of particular kinds of **strife** that both groups find enough in common to join forces as they have on our campus this year. And when they do join together the bonds are weak. The alliance [fails] to achieve common **objectives**.

The Third World Liberation Front is relatively new. It was meant to include all the nonwhite and nonblack minorities. It

strife: struggle, conflict.
objectives: aims or goals.

is supposed to unite the oppressed peoples of the world.... Since its formation on our campus last April, the Third World has been dominated by a handful of Spanish-speaking students who claim to represent the much larger Latin and Oriental population of the campus and the community. There is little evidence to **substantiate** this claim.

We have some off-campus **agitators** involved in the present affair. But actually our home-grown brand need little outside help, except in numbers at those senseless rallies and endless marches. We have all the militant leadership that is needed for a first-class revolt and I understand that we have also exported some talent for disruptions at other campuses on both coasts.

Dissidents of all colors have worked exceedingly hard to build sympathy in ethnic communities throughout the year, with the objective of turning a campus problem into a much larger community problem. But their efforts have failed miserably. They have been able to attract as many as 100 students from other campuses for a one-day rally and march. But they have failed completely to attract any large numbers of citizens from the Spanish-speaking, black, or Oriental communities of San Francisco. From these facts, it is clear that the majority of the ethnic minority population is more interested in education as conducted or proposed by the college than in the wild plans for education by mob rule as proposed by our dissident students.

Some militants are genuine in their desire to improve the educational system. But it is also clear that some militants, especially in the Black Students Union [BSU], are more concerned with personal power than with education.... What is unfortunate is that so many well-meaning supporters of increased opportunity for black students have attached different meanings to the struggle. The people on the fringes are the ones saying the noble things about opportunity and progress. The BSU leaders keep saying they want absolute control, with no **accountability** to anyone except their **constituents**, constituents ruled by force, intimidation, and gangster tactics.

The white militants are as **explicit** as the blacks. Their story is now familiar on every major campus. They believe our society is so corrupt that there is no hope except to destroy the entire structure and rebuild from the ground up. But their idea of

substantiate: support.

agitators: troublemakers, rabble-rousers.

accountability: responsibility for explaining or justifying something.

constituents: supporters.

intimidation: being bullied or threatened.

explicit: perfectly clear (in meaning).

S. I. Hayakawa   **33**

rebuilding along the lines of a **participatory democracy** is to deny the very freedoms they claim are sacred. We have seen them in action....

We are asked frequently whether channels of communication are open to students. I cannot think of a college or university in this country where the channels are more open. Many imaginative proposals for changes in education and administration have resulted from the ability of our students to present new ideas to their professors, departments, schools, and presidents. We have supported a large experimental program for years....

The people we are forced to deal with in the present crisis—people trying to seize power or to destroy the institution—have used every device to corrupt the channels of communication. Their style of **confrontation** to achieve ends does not allow for free and open communication because communication in that sense might lead to reason and **negotiation**, which are the last things they want.

Our present difficulties were not triggered by a specific event, even though the temporary suspension of Black Panther George Murray, part-time instructor and graduate student, is often cited as the reason for the BSU action. The crisis was not triggered at all. It was planned very carefully over a long period of time. To illustrate, the strike started on the anniversary of the date in 1967—November 6—when nine black students attacked the campus newspaper editor and his staff in their offices. Many of those nine are the present student strike leaders. Many are out [of prison] on parole.

From the very first day, our present strike has been characterized by planned violence. The objective was to cripple instruction. There was no attempt to seize buildings or to disrupt the administration. The first actions were directed toward the classroom. At first, bands of black students entered academic buildings to terrorize instructors and students by shouting, overturning furniture, and just pushing people around. Then we had a rash of minor bombing attempts and arson intended to frighten rather than to damage. For example, on one day we had fifty fires, all in waste baskets, on desk tops or in rest rooms, so the results would disrupt classes rather than to destroy buildings.

participatory democracy: government by the people.

confrontation: opposition; a face-to-face challenge.

negotiation: solving a problem through discussion and compromise.

S. I. Hayakawa

After the white and Third World militants joined the BSU, which was only a matter of a few days, the action took on more massive proportions and for a time we had a combination of **guerrilla** tactics and mob action. Every midday in December there was an outdoor rally, usually resulting in attacks on one or more of the classroom buildings.

The people who **deplore** the use of police on campus seem to forget that the first days of this strike saw violence introduced by the students themselves as essential to their plan. The college use of police was a response to violence, not the cause. What we have succeeded in doing is to move the action from the classroom to the space between buildings and from there to the streets surrounding the campus. For weeks now the classrooms and the inner campus have been quiet and safe.

National Guardsmen move in on protesters in Berkeley, California, 1969

guerrilla: independent acts of warfare, harassment, and destruction.

deplore: disapprove of strongly or condemn.

I believe that we have introduced something new to this business of preserving order on campuses. At most institutions the use of police is delayed as long as possible and when assistance is finally requested, the force is usually too small to handle the situation and new troubles develop. I went the other way. I had **ample** force available and demonstrated a willingness to use it quickly to protect people and property from attack. The opposition has received my message. I think we have communicated successfully.

During my eight weeks in office, my principal action has been to restore order. But I would not want anyone to believe that I think this is the solution for campus unrest. It is merely a first step. This is where my beliefs vary from those of many of the conservative supporters who have communicated with me. Several things must be accomplished if we are to end the present trend toward confrontation and violence. First, we must **reassess** many of our educational objectives and administrative systems. We must modernize quickly and on a vast scale to make the entire system more responsive to the times and to the needs of our young people.

Second, we must look realistically at problems of discipline and devise systems that will work without resorting to outside help. We must eventually put campus discipline in the hands of responsible faculty and student groups who will work cooperatively with [the administration] for the greater good of institutions. Our faculty and student disciplinary systems are not geared for today's problems.

In a sense, the issues behind most present troubles are **valid**. As a nation, we have said that education is vital for success for every citizen. Yet we still have an overwhelming number of elementary and secondary school systems that are crippling the poor and the minorities educationally. What we see now is a body of Negro, Spanish-speaking, and other young hammering on the door for an opportunity to obtain the education we have told them is so important to their future.

If we were dealing with hunger instead of education—you can imagine what would happen if we had a walled city in which the citizens had all the food they needed while outside there were **hordes** of starving people. We could not open the gates just a little to admit handsful of the starving and expect

ample: enough; plenty of.

reassess: to look at again; reconsider.

valid: real, reasonable, and accepted as true.

hordes: huge crowds.

the rest to remain patiently outside. No. We would have to be prepared to open the gates wide and admit everyone, or be prepared for a riot. That is the situation now with higher education. We have opened the doors just a little with special programs that serve hundreds while thousands are **clamoring** for education. I believe we should open the gates fully, even at enormous expense, to provide educational opportunity at every level—in high schools, adult schools, junior colleges, state colleges, and the universities—for our entire minority and poor populations. We should **mobilize** the best brains available, just as we did when the nation attacked our problems of modern science.... [Solving] an educational crisis ... means as much to our national welfare as our efforts in outer space....

Prognosis: It is not easy at this point to predict the course of events on our campus or elsewhere. I feel that the danger to the nation and to higher education has been vastly underestimated by a majority of people. Most of the news and much of the commentary deals with the action rather than the underlying causes of dissent and the methods to correct obvious ills.

If we are to end campus rebellion without destroying the educational institutions, we must redirect our energies. We must look beyond the day-to-day combat to the reasons underlying this deadly attack on higher education. We must learn to deal both with the dedicated revolutionary leaders and the unsolved problems that enable those leaders to enlist followers. The solution to these problems will take time, brains, and money. This nation is amply **endowed** with those resources. But we must act promptly and decisively.

In March 1969 San Francisco State officials, students, and faculty finally settled their disputes—mostly on Hayakawa's terms—and the college slowly returned to normal. Although some who disagreed with him left the university, many others in California and around the country cheered his willingness to get tough with rebellious militants. Supporters began urging him to seek political office. Hayakawa declined, however, explaining that he wanted to stay on at San Francisco

clamoring: shouting loudly.
mobilize: gather for action.
endowed: furnished or provided.

The English-Only Movement

During Lyndon Johnson's presidency in the 1960s, bilingual education (the approved use of more than one language in the classroom) was a hot issue. As a result of immigration reforms passed in 1965, many newcomers from Latin America, the Caribbean, and Asia entered the United States. Some school districts suddenly found themselves with a significant population of children who could not speak English. Meanwhile, in the southwestern United States civil rights activists lobbied for bilingual education programs. They wanted to combat the high dropout rates in Mexican American communities by helping Spanish-speaking students with limited English skills compete with their classmates. The idea was to continue teaching the Mexican American students in Spanish while helping them master English as quickly as possible. In 1968 Congress passed the Bilingual Education Act, which required school districts to offer such programs.

But support for language minorities within the United States has been decreasing since the early 1980s and disagreement about bilingual education has grown. Supporters insist that without it, immigrant children will not get enough education to compete in American society. Opponents maintain that bilingual education only slows down students' transition to English and separates them into "language ghettos" that undermine their efforts to succeed. Furthermore, bilingual education can create a heavy financial burden for school districts with large and diverse immigrant populations.

State to finish what he had started. In July 1969 he was named permanent president of the college.

In 1973, feeling that he had accomplished his goals, Hayakawa retired from the presidency of San Francisco State. He then officially switched his political party affiliation from Democrat to Republican and announced his intention to run for the U.S. Senate. Under California law, however, he turned out to be ineligible because he did not change parties at least twelve months before becoming a candidate. So Hayakawa waited until the 1976 elections and tried again. His support for conservative measures such as decentralized government (redistributing power held by the federal government, with more decision-making power to the states), lower taxes, and fewer regulations on business proved popular with voters, and he won the race.

S. I. Hayakawa

Those in favor of declaring English the official language of the United States fear that by accepting or encouraging multilingualism, the United States is heading down a potentially self-destructive path that may divide people into conflicting minorities. Their aim is to uphold the idea of the United States as a "melting pot" of many cultures. Learning English, they say, is part of the process of shedding one's immigrant past and becoming American.

In the mid-1990s, several pieces of legislation came up for consideration dealing with the English-only issue. In February 1995, Representative Peter King of New York proposed the National Language Act. In addition to declaring English the official language of the United States, it called for the repeal of the Bilingual Education Act and the closing of the Office of Bilingual Education within the U.S. Department of Education. It also sought to eliminate provisions in the Voting Rights Act of 1975 that require election officials to offer ballots in foreign languages to non-English-speaking citizens who want to vote. In addition, the National Language Act was supposed to override state laws involving the government in multilingualism or bilingual education. At least four other bills were introduced in 1995 on these issues.

In August 1996, the House of Representatives passed the English Language Empowerment Act, which proposed making English the official language of the United States and forbidding the federal government from conducting most of its business in any other language. However, President Bill Clinton announced that he would veto such a bill if it passed in the Senate. A Supreme Court ruling dealing with an English-only law in Arizona was expected in 1997.

Makes Waves as U.S. Senator

Once in Washington, Hayakawa quickly revealed himself to be one of the most conservative members of the Senate. He opposed busing to achieve racial integration in public schools, for example, and he tried to withhold public funds from universities with affirmative action programs. (Affirmative action programs promote educational, employment, and economic opportunities to women and minorities in an effort to make up for past and present discrimination.) Business owners applauded his backing of a measure to reduce the minimum wage for younger workers.

Hayakawa was equally well known for his sometimes unusual behavior, most notably his habit of falling asleep during Senate meetings. (He claimed that it only happened when a speaker took twenty minutes to say something that could have been said in two.) What was not generally known, however, was that Hayakawa suffered from a sleeping disorder known as narcolepsy. This condition quite suddenly and unexpectedly plunges its victims into brief periods of deep sleep.

By the time he was up for reelection in 1982, Hayakawa had lost the backing of wealthy California conservatives. Without their support, he could not win, so he quickly withdrew from the race. But he did not give up politics completely. From 1983 until 1990 he served as special advisor to the U.S. Secretary of State for East Asian and Pacific Affairs.

Speaks Out Against Redress and Bilingualism

*Hayakawa continued to stir up controversy during the 1980s. Members of the Japanese American community were angered when he spoke out against **redress** for people of Japanese descent who had been imprisoned in special camps during World War II because they were believed to be a threat to national security. (Hayakawa was a Canadian citizen at the time and living in Chicago, Illinois, so he did not share in the fate of many Japanese Americans on the West Coast.) He argued that because Japan had bombed Pearl Harbor and their soldiers had a reputation for being ferocious, the U.S. government had acted in a reasonable manner when it decided to uproot Japanese Americans from their homes and imprison them. Hayakawa said that he was "embarrassed" by the "ridiculous" attempts of some of these former prisoners to demand an apology and money for what they had endured.*

Many people, especially other Japanese Americans, regarded Hayakawa's opinions on such issues as puzzling if not infuriating because he had experienced racial prejudice himself. Until the early 1950s, for instance, he and other Asian Americans were denied U.S. citizenship because of their race. And Hayakawa's longtime marriage to a white woman was not considered legal in many states.

Although Hayakawa later changed his mind and came out in favor of redress, he caused more uproar with his English-only views. Hayakawa was once quoted as saying, "The most rapid way of getting out of the ghetto is to speak

redress: compensation; a way of righting a wrong done to someone.

good English." On April 23, 1982, he appeared before the Subcommittee on Education, Arts and Humanities of the Senate Committee on Labor and Human Resources to explain why he was against encouraging bilingualism in the United States. He used the occasion to urge support for his proposed constitutional amendment making English the country's official language. He also lobbied for a bilingual education bill he had just introduced in the Senate, the Bilingual Education Improvement Act (S. 2412).

As he declared in his opening statement, the goal of his constitutional amendment was to legally recognize "what is already a social and political reality: that English is the official language of the United States." Regarding his bilingual education bill, he hoped that it would "clarify the confusing signals we have given in recent years to immigrant groups.... Our immigration laws already require English for citizenship. The role of bilingual education is then to equip immigrants with the necessary English language skills to qualify them for this requirement. The problem is that all too often, bilingual education programs have strayed from their original intent of teaching English."

In the same speech before the Senate, Hayakawa expressed his ideal of the American melting pot.

We all grew up with the concept of the American melting pot, that is the merging of a multitude of foreign cultures into one. This melting pot has succeeded in creating a vibrant new culture among peoples of many different cultural backgrounds largely because of the widespread use of a common language, English. In this world of national strife, it is a unique concept.... In light of the growing emphasis on maintaining a second culture and instruction in the native languages, I ask myself what are we trying to do? Where do we want to go? **Demographic** research tells us that in some of our states, ten or twenty years from now there will be a majority of individuals with Spanish background. It seems to me that we are preparing the ground for permanently and officially bilingual states. From here to

demographic: relating to the statistical characteristics of the human population.

separatist movements à la [the French-speaking province of] Quebec [Canada, which has engaged in an ongoing battle for independence] would be the final step. Is this the development which we want to promote?...

I want to avoid a similar situation here in America where use of another language is encouraged to the point that it could become an official language alongside English. This would **perpetuate** differences between English-speaking and non-English-speaking citizens and isolate one group from the other. There can be no doubt that recent immigrants love this country and want to fully participate in its society. But well-intentioned transitional bilingual education programs have often **inhibited** their command of English and retarded their full citizenship....

The issue of English as our official language and bilingual education for immigrants is especially timely in light of [recent] Census Bureau figures.... The 1980 census found that 23 million people in the United States aged 5 or older speak a language other than English at home. We as Americans must reassess our commitment to the preservation of English as our common language. Learning English has been the primary task of every immigrant group for two centuries. Participation in the common language has rapidly made the political and economic benefits of American society available to each new group. Those who have mastered English have overcome the major hurdle to participation in our democracy. Passage of my English language amendment, as well as my bilingual education proposal, will insure that we maintain a common basis for communicating and sharing ideas.

99

Hayakawa helped establish a private lobbying organization called U.S. English and served as its honorary chair. Its goals include making English the country's official language and abolishing bilingual education programs in public schools. In addition, Hayakawa founded a group known as the California English Campaign, which in 1986 succeeded in persuading voters to have English declared the official lan-

separatist: pushing for cultural separation.

perpetuate: continue, encourage.

inhibited: restricted, discouraged.

guage of California. Since then, several other states—mostly those with large Hispanic populations—have approved similar measures.

Sources

Books

Campus Unrest: Hearings Before the Special Subcommittee on Education of the Committee on Education and Labor, House of Representatives, 91st Congress, 1st Session, U.S. Government Printing Office, 1969.

Hayakawa, S. I., and Alan Hayakawa, *Language in Thought and Action,* 5th edition, Harcourt, 1989.

Notable Asian Americans, Gale, 1995.

Periodicals

America, "Echoes of Nativism," December 10, 1988, p. 483.

Chicago Tribune, "Justices to Weigh Language: Court Will Consider Whether English Can Be Official Tongue of U.S.," March 25, 1996; "House Clears English-Only Measure After Emotional Debate," August 2, 1996.

English Journal, "From Pearl Harbor to Watergate to Kuwait: *Language in Thought and Action,*" February 1991, pp. 28–35; "A Conversation With the Hayakawas," February 1991, pp. 36–40.

Forbes, "Do We Want Quebec Here?" June 11, 1990, pp. 62–64.

Fortune, "The Comeback of English," April 3, 1995, p. 141.

New York Times, "S. I. Hayakawa Dies at 85; Scholar and Former Senator," February 28, 1992, p. B6.

Time, March 9, 1992, p. 64.

U.S. News and World Report, "One Nation, One Language? Would Making English the Nation's Official Language Unite the Country or Divide It?" September 25, 1995.

Vital Speeches of the Day, "Bilingual Education Improvement Act: A Common Basis for Communication," June 15, 1982, pp. 521–23.

David Henry Hwang

1957–

Chinese American playwright and screenwriter

David Henry Hwang was only twenty-three when his first play was performed in a New York City theater. He was barely past thirty when he picked up his first Tony Award for the year's best Broadway play. Since then he has continued to write a number of plays, screenplays, and even a multimedia dramatic piece. Hwang's thought-provoking dramatizations of the cultural clash between the East (Asia) and the West (Europe and the United States) and his own experiences as a Chinese American have earned him praise as one of the late twentieth century's most talented playwrights.

Grandmother's Stories of China Inspire Early Writing

Hwang was born in Los Angeles, California, and grew up in the well-to-do suburban community of San Gabriel. Both of his parents were immigrants who had arrived in the United States during the early 1950s. His father, who was from Shanghai, China, established the first Asian American-owned bank in the States. His mother, who was also of Chinese ancestry but who grew up in the Philippines, was a pianist and music teacher.

All the time they were growing up in their very westernized household, the three Hwang children—David was the oldest and the only boy—were strongly encouraged to "be American." As a result Hwang hardly ever gave much thought to his Chinese heritage. He considered it an interesting yet unimportant personal characteristic, "like having red hair," as he once remarked in a New York Times Magazine interview. But the many hours he spent as a little boy listening to his grandmother's stories made a strong impression that later influenced his own work. When he was about twelve years old, Hwang began writing down what he had heard from her—ancient Chinese myths and fables as well as tales of their own family. He then copied the finished work and passed it around to other relatives.

After graduating from a local college prep school in 1975, Hwang entered California's Stanford University with the intention of earning a law degree. Before long, however, he found himself drawn to other interests, including music and writing. He was particularly fascinated with drama as a means of expressing his ideas, so he began studying the art of writing plays, first at Stanford and then at a special workshop held during the summer of 1978 in Claremont, California.

His First Play: the Clash of Two Cultures

Those college years proved to be a time of self-discovery in other ways for Hwang. For the first time he began to think about what it meant to be Chinese American, and at the Claremont workshop he wrote about it in a play he titled FOB. The play examined the cultural conflicts between a newly arrived immigrant from China—known by the insulting term "FOB" for "Fresh Off the Boat"—and his very westernized Chinese American cousin. Hwang continued revising and polishing the text of his play once he returned to school that fall. In March 1979 he directed a cast of fellow students in the first performance of FOB, which was held in a Stanford dormitory lounge.

Hwang received his bachelor's degree in English that same spring. Shortly afterward, he left for Waterford, Connecticut, where FOB *was being featured at the prestigious National Playwrights Conference. At this annual workshop, Hwang was able to watch professional actors perform his play in front of an audience of theater critics and other playwrights. They then offered their suggestions for changes and improvements.*

First Effort Captures an Obie Award

Back home in California, Hwang taught creative writing at a Los Angeles-area high school. He also continued his writing whenever he could. Meanwhile, FOB *had captured the interest of Joseph Papp, the artistic director of the New York Shakespeare Festival. Papp staged a full-scale production of Hwang's work Off-Broadway at the famous Public Theater during the 1980-81 season. It received fairly good reviews and went on to win an Obie Award for best play of the year.*

By then Hwang had moved east to attend the Yale University School of Drama in Connecticut. While there he wrote his second play, The Dance and the Railroad. *This story of Chinese railroad workers in the United States during the mid-nineteenth century is told from the point of view of two of the workers, both of whom dream of returning to China one day to perform in the Beijing Opera. Like* FOB, *Hwang's second work was also staged Off-Broadway in New York City, where it enjoyed a long and successful run.*

Hwang soon followed up with another play, Family Devotions, *which takes a comical look at a very prosperous Chinese American family—one very much like the author's own. Despite his lighthearted approach to the subject, Hwang makes serious points in his play, particularly showing how a mother's Christian beliefs make it difficult for a son to learn about his Chinese heritage.*

*Hwang wrote two more plays—*The House of Sleeping Beauties *and* The Sound of a Voice—*before the burdens of being a successful young playwright and an unofficial spokesperson for Asian Americans became too much for him to bear. Unable and unwilling to turn out work that he feared might just be "repackaging the old stereotypes in more intellectually*

The Story of *Madame Butterfly*

In Hwang's play *M. Butterfly*, the lead character, an opera singer, performs the title role in one of the most beloved operas of all time, *Madame Butterfly*, written by noted Italian composer Giacomo Puccini in 1900. The opera is based on a play by American writer David Belasco. Also titled *Madame Butterfly*, Belasco's play was taken from the supposedly true story of an American naval officer named Pinkerton who becomes romantically involved with a young Japanese geisha girl named Butterfly. Pinkerton does not take their affair very seriously, but Butterfly does. Over the objections of her family, she marries Pinkerton, who soon returns to the United States. Meanwhile, Butterfly gives birth to their son and remains faithful to her absent husband despite offers of marriage from other men.

Three long years pass with no word from Pinkerton. Eventually, Butterfly hears that he is on his way to Japan—with an American wife. She refuses to believe such news and waits patiently for him to arrive. When he does show up with his wife, Butterfly is forced to face the fact that Pinkerton never really loved her. As for Pinkerton, at first he cannot bring himself to face Butterfly after realizing how badly he had treated her. When he finally works up the courage to go to her and their son, he is too late—the grief-stricken Butterfly has killed herself.

Hwang incorporated *Madame Butterfly* into his own play to help underscore the points he wanted to make about racism and sexism. He was especially interested in its stereotyped view of the submissive Asian woman allowing herself to be dominated by a white (western) man.

---

hip forms," as he put it, he stopped writing, traveled extensively, and once again considered enrolling in law school.

Within a couple of years, however, Hwang returned to playwriting. His first effort from this period, titled Rich Relations, *did not do well. But its lack of success finally left the author feeling free to tackle other kinds of projects, including some work for films and television.*

Meanwhile another play was slowly taking shape in Hwang's mind. In 1986 he heard about the true story of a French diplomat who had carried on a twenty-year-long love affair with a beautiful and mysterious Chinese opera singer. In a bizarre twist to the tale, the Frenchman insisted that during the time he and the singer were together, he had no idea she was really a spy—and a man.

M. Butterfly

Hwang took this idea and created a play around it called M. Butterfly. *The work explores the nature of **imperialism** and how racism and sexism can blind people to the truth.* M. Butterfly *opened on Broadway in 1988. Critics gave it somewhat mixed reviews, but audiences were very enthusiastic. It went on to win a number of awards, including a Tony for best play. It was also nominated for a 1989 Pulitzer Prize.*

Hwang later wrote a movie adaptation of M. Butterfly, *which was released in 1993 under the same title. However, he was not entirely pleased with the results on screen. One of his future goals, in fact, is to move into directing the films of his screenplays so that he can have more control over the finished product.*

Since the success of M. Butterfly, *Hwang has been involved in a variety of creative projects. In addition to writing more plays, including* Bondage *and* Face Value, *he has completed several screenplays. His play* Golden Gate *was made into a movie in 1994. Two others are adaptations of novels written by other people—A. S. Byatt Booker's* Possession *and Caleb Carr's debut* The Alienist.

Along with music composer Philip Glass and stage designer Jerome Sirlin, Hwang created a multimedia drama titled 1000 Airplanes on the Roof. *In this work a single character tells the story of his terrifying abduction by visitors from outer space. Hwang has also worked with Glass on a number of other things, including the libretto (words) for Glass's opera* The Voyage.

Struggles to Define "Asian American"

While he has branched out to try his hand at these and other "non-Asian" projects, Hwang nevertheless continues to explore what it means to be Asian American. On the one hand, he observes, everyone in the United States is encouraged to assimilate (blend in with the main culture) to help create a common "American" identity out of many different cultures. On the other hand, many people would like to maintain a sense of their own cultural identity, too, by celebrating their social, racial, ethnic, and religious differences (known as multiculturalism).

imperialism: the practice of expanding the power of a nation by taking over other areas of land or by gaining indirect political and/or economic control over other people.

*One part of this debate that is of special interest to Hwang concerns the notion of "**authenticity**" in connection with creative works by or about minorities, women, or homosexuals. In the theater, for instance, raising the issue of authenticity sparks discussions about casting decisions, such as having a non-Asian play an Asian role. In education, disagreements arise over how to interpret history or literature.*

Hwang addressed these and other related topics during a talk he gave on April 15, 1994, while serving as artist-in-residence at the Massachusetts Institute of Technology (MIT) in Cambridge. His appearance as the 1994 William L. Abramowitz Lecturer came at the end of his stay on campus. Over a three-day period, he had watched a rehearsal of his play FOB, *worked with students in MIT theater classes, and spoken to high school students in the Cambridge Public Schools. An excerpt from his lecture is reprinted here from a copy provided by the MIT Office of the Arts.*

“

....Most of us know that in another thirty, fifty years, Caucasians, European Americans—whatever you want to call them—will be a **plurality** rather than a majority. In other words, this country will not have a single majority race, and that leads to a great number of cultural and societal changes. The very definition of what it means to be an American is changing, and therefore the culture of America also is being re-examined. Two places where this battle is felt very strongly are one, in the arts, and two, in academia.

In the arts there is, for instance, the whole issue of what's called nontraditional casting—that is, who should get to play what parts, of what races....

In **academia**, of course, the battle's over curriculum—what works are in the **canon**, what constitutes quality in literature as well as history, how ... we [should] interpret history.... The whole notion of history as **objective** has always been somewhat doubtful, but it's particularly being called into question now as it relates to the experiences of different cultural groups—women, gays, whatever—and there is the charge that all this is

authenticity: not false or an imitation of the real thing; like the original; real.

plurality: a large number; numerous.

academia: the world of education or learning.

canon: the group of writings accepted as standard or authoritative.

objective: based on fact and not on a person's own opinions, emotions, or interpretations.

Warner Oland in The Mysterious Dr. Fu Manchu. *Hwang recalls: "Even as a boy, I think I began to try to search for some sort of authenticity behind the Fu Manchus and the Vietnamese generals that I saw on television."*

compromise: endanger by conceding to other standards.

leading to a lowering of standards, that by the inclusion of the voices of diverse groups, we **compromise** some sort of objective standard of excellence which previously had existed....

So today I've chosen to address the subject of authenticity, because a lot of these debates come down to some sort of struggle over whether we can reach a definition of objective truth, whether or not we can define a universal standard of excellence. I think that those of us who write about minorities, women, gays, whatever, are often criticized for being inauthentic by our own group and in turn, some of us (like myself) also go and criticize other people for being inauthentic. So I feel like I've been on both sides of that fence, and I'm going to frame this a little bit in terms of my own artistic journey....

I look at myself now, and I'm not exactly the same person as I was ten years ago, and I don't exactly have the same beliefs that I had ten years ago, and I don't expect that I will ten years from now. When I was younger, I used to feel that it was important to be completely consistent. Now I feel that it's a good idea to be consistent at least at any given time, but that I may **contradict** myself from the past....

Some of my earliest memories about being Asian American have to do with a certain **aversion to** Asian American characters in movies and television, and perhaps this was the beginning of why I ended up doing what I do today.... I remember feeling ashamed and changing the channel or not going to a particular movie. We'd talk about these sort of **blatantly** evil Asian American characters like Fu Manchu or the various soldiers in Japanese or Vietnam war movies, or we'd talk about sort of the **benign, obsequious** version, the [fictional Asian detective played throughout the 1930s and 1940s by various white actors] Charlie Chan or the [dishwasher] guy in the Calgon [dish soap] commercial that said "ancient Chinese secret." All of those were a source of great embarrassment to me, and I think that, in the final analysis, I felt that these people were not me. And yet because of the way we looked, I was expected to have some sort of identification with them....

That leads to a discussion of the whole issue of the **tyranny** of appearances and how it is that the way we look establishes to a large extent the way that we're perceived, at least on first notice. Every minority group, I think, and every group in general, has their particular burden to bear. I think that among Asians, we have to deal with the idea of being **perpetual** foreigners. One's family can have been in this country five or six generations, but people still go, "Oh, you speak really good English," whereas it's not necessarily assumed that someone of Swedish descent speaks Swedish....

contradict: do or suggest the opposite of.

aversion to: dislike of.

blatantly: obviously.

benign: mild-mannered.

obsequious: groveling, fawning, or overly attentive to the point of being subservient.

tyranny: enslavement, oppression.

perpetual: eternal, everlasting.

The perpetual-foreigner idea was especially ironic given my parents' desire to be Americans.... They were very interested in blending into or assimilating into this culture, and they were trying to really create a new identity for themselves. In that sense, they were, in their own way, saying that their appearance was not an authentic representation of who they were inside.

Even as a boy, I think I began to try to search for some sort of authenticity behind the Fu Manchus and the Vietnamese generals that I saw on television. The only experience that I really had with writing before I got to college was when I was about twelve. We thought that my grandmother was going to die, and she was the only one who knew all of the family history. I thought it was really important that this sort of stuff be preserved, so I spent a summer with her and did a lot of oral histories and eventually wrote this into a kind of one-hundred-page nonfiction novel which was Xeroxed and distributed among my family and got very good reviews. I think that what I was trying to do was find a context for myself, find some way in which my identity, my existence as an Asian American could be **validated**, could be made authentic. I was trying to find something more real than the images that were around me.

Writing for me continued to be a search for authenticity. When I began wanting to write plays in college, I didn't actually have any idea I was going to focus on Asian American subjects. I was merely interested in the theater and in trying to become a playwright. I wrote a lot of plays about a lot of other subjects. I found a professor at Stanford [University] who told me they were really horrible (which they were) and that my problem was I was trying to write theater in a vacuum—that is, I didn't know anything about the theater.

So I spent the next couple years trying to read as many plays and see as many plays as I could.... As I began to write [again] ..., I found that my work was leading me in a very unexpected place. It was leading me back to when I was twelve years old, back to the stories of my grandparents, things that I would hear as a child, back to the images that haunted me of [stereotypical characters like] Fu Manchu and Charlie Chan and all those things that I'd turn off on the television.

validated: confirmed.

This was happening within a larger political **context.** There was an Asian American "yellow power" movement which was a child of the black power movements that had begun in the '60s. I lived in an Asian American theme house [at Stanford] for a year and began to absorb various literary influences that were also Asian American. When I read *The Woman Warrior* by Maxine Hong Kingston, for instance, it was sort of a personal and artistic revelation to me, because the **juxtaposition** of almost a hyper realistic view of growing up Chinese American in Stockton, California, with the ghosts of some imagined or mythological past seemed to feel very real to me....

At the same time, I was also very drawn to Frank Chin's work.... He was the first Chinese American to be produced Off-Broadway professionally, and he inspired me to think that this was possible. There's a character in one of his plays, Gwan Gung, who represents a sort of Chinese American spirit, as it were, the spirit of the early immigrants.

I began to think about the juxtaposition of Fa Mu Lan, the woman warrior character from Maxine's book, and Gwan Gung, the [fighter] character from Frank Chin's plays, and I began to think what would happen if they met in a Chinese restaurant in Torrance [California]. Was there a way to **synthesize** these two traditions?

That led to my first play, *FOB*.... In it, Dale, who's the ABC, or American Born Chinese character, is trying to deal with his own identity and the irritation he feels from Steve, an FOB, or Fresh Off the Boat immigrant. Steve is the sort of nightmare version of Dale's self. Dale has spent a lifetime trying to fit in, trying to be hip, trying to be white, basically, and Steve brings out the fact that he may be something different.... Steve and [Dale's cousin] Grace, who were born in Asia and have immigrated to the States, are relative newcomers to America, but they have access to dramatic sequences where they **metamorphose** into Gwan Gung and Fa Mu Lan [through a] sort of unconscious treasure trove of memories and cultures. Dale may also have these myths buried somewhere in his genes, but he's really alienated from them and can only watch kind of in silent confusion while his cousin and her friend [Steve] play out stories that he either doesn't know or won't learn.

context: setting, background.
juxtaposition: the act of placing two (or more) things side by side.
synthesize: combine, blend.
metamorphose: change.

I think the idea of this rich cultural treasure trove, for instance, that's **inherent** in *FOB* is an interesting place to start looking at the notion of authenticity. Clearly, I was trying to search for something authentic beyond the stereotypes. And I was reaching out to a Chinese American literature as well as a root-culture Chinese tradition, and through this I thought that I was touching something authentic. Now was I touching something authentic? I think [there] are arguments to be made both ways. The argument can be made, for instance, that *FOB* is not historically accurate, that Fa Mu Lan and Gwan Gung, in Chinese literature, exist in different times and there's just no way that they would have met. Besides the fact that they're in a Chinese restaurant in Torrance, there's no way that they would have met even in the original literature.

Similarly, I think the question can be raised, are Gwan Gung and Fa Mu Lan really part of my past? These aren't stories that I grew up listening to. In order to find out who Gwan Gung was, I had to go to read *The Romance of the Three Kingdoms* [an ancient work of Chinese literature], in which Gwan Gung appears. To what extent does the **appropriation** of these mythical figures really constitute some sort of authenticity? To what extent can we say there is a rich cultural unconscious treasure trove?...

During this period I began what I was calling my "**isolationist/nationalist** phase." I think that when you begin to deal with your ethnicity when you haven't all your life, there's almost kind of a religious conversion quality to it, and you realize that certain things that you might have felt that are painful are not necessarily unique to you. For instance, if you're completely isolated and you don't know a lot of other Asian Americans and you don't share the experience, then if you're walking down the street and someone goes "Ching Chang Chong" or whatever, you might think, was I doing something too Oriental? Whereas if you are with a number of other people and you realize that this is a fairly common occurrence, then you realize that it's not you that is the problem, that there are certainly difficulties in the society itself. Your anger becomes refocused on change for the society.

And so it was a very exciting time. I wrote a lot of Chinese American plays.... [For example,] *Family Devotions* was a play

inherent: inborn, natural.

appropriation: the act of taking or making use of something.

isolationist: withdrawn from society.

nationalist: a devotion to one's nationality over all other nationalities or groups.

David Henry Hwang

that was largely autobiographical, and in it there's a character named Chester who is a violinist who's about to go off and play (with the Boston Symphony, as a matter of fact). He meets an uncle, Di-Gou, who's just arrived from the PRC [People's Republic of China] and is not part of the **fundamentalist** Christian tradition that he [Chester] was brought up in.

They have a discussion which I think is very much about the issue of authenticity. Chester says, "I'm leaving here. Like you did." And Di-Gou says, "But, Chester, I've found that I cannot leave the family. Today—look!—I follow them across an ocean." Chester says, "You know, they're gonna start bringing you to church." Di-Gou, "No. My sisters and their religion are two different things.... There are faces back further than you can see. Faces long before the white missionaries arrived in China. Here. Look here. At your face. Study your face and you will see—the shape of your face is the shape of faces back many generations—across an ocean, in another soil. You must become one with your family before you can hope to live away from it.... Chester, you are in America. If you deny those who share your blood, what do you have in this country?"

... We who are born in America absorb our images of self and culture basically through western eyes, through the mainstream point of view, and even if we decide to, say, read original Chinese literature, we're often looking at translations that were made by western scholars with their own sets of **idiosyncrasies** or prejudices or **preconceptions**.

Under such circumstances, how can we possibly discover who we really are? How can we discover the reality or the authentic Asian or Asian American culture? The questions of authenticity continue to haunt me....

Because of all these questions, I ... didn't write anything for two years. I hit a period of writer's block.... I looked at my work, and some of it had more dragons and gongs and stuff, and some of those seemed to be the more popular. I was wondering if I was repackaging the old stereotypes in more intellectually hip forms.

Authenticity is an extremely heated debate among Asian Americans and among people in general. The most common criticism an Asian American author hears is that his or her work reinforces stereotypes. I criticized *Miss Saigon* for

fundamentalist: from a movement stressing strict adherence to a literal translation of the Bible.

idiosyncrasies: unique characteristics.

preconceptions: ideas a person forms about someone or something before he or she actually has direct knowledge.

reinforcing the stereotype of submissive Asian women. *M. Butterfly* was criticized for reinforcing the stereotype of Asian men being **effeminate**. [Amy Tan's novel] *The Joy Luck Club* was criticized for reinforcing the notion that Asian men are not very nice. Frank Chin criticized both *The Woman Warrior* and *FOB* for inauthentic use of mythology. And Frank Chin's own plays, when first staged in Seattle, were picketed by Asian Americans for reinforcing stereotypes of broken-English-speaking Chinatown tour guides.

Now by and large, I have to say that I think these are really healthy debates. I mean, I don't like being criticized. Who does? But to some extent, it's a **corollary** for what I call the official Asian American Syndrome: when there's only one [of us] who's in the spotlight at a given time, everything we say is expected to represent the entire culture....

Essentially of course, one has to come to the conclusion that only the community of artists can represent the community, that no one artist can speak for an entire people as if those people were completely **monolithic**. But it does lead to what's called the **"political correctness"** debate right now. I think, personally, that political correctness has been a bit overplayed by the media.... Critics, **aesthetic** critics, are free to blast works of art for being **banal** or poorly put together ... without being accused of **censorship**.

The question is, therefore, do criticisms become ... more dangerous when they focus on a work of art's content as opposed to the aesthetics? Personally, I think not. I think that as Americans we should be intellectually **rigorous** enough to promote healthy debate on both fronts. I think it's particularly true at a time in our history like now, when the definition of who is an American and what does it mean to be an American is in **flux**, because art has always served as one means by which people define themselves and define their vision of themselves. I don't think that political criticism necessarily equals censorship.... If anything, the debates over political correctness usually, from a practical standpoint, just increase the number of people who decide to go see the work.

I do think, though, that there's an argument to be made that traditional criticism or traditional correctness, if you will, has existed as a type of censorship. I think it was [playwright]

effeminate: displaying qualities more typical of a woman than a man.

corollary: something that naturally follows something else.

monolithic: exhibiting a single point of view.

"political correctness": a certain way of thinking, speaking, or acting that very carefully avoids any word or behavior that might offend or insult others.

aesthetic: focused on defining and appreciating the beauty of something.

banal: ordinary.

censorship: the practice of keeping from the general public any material thought to be objectionable, inappropriate, or harmful.

rigorous: strict.

flux: a state of change.

Arthur Miller who once said that there is no single person in the old Soviet Union who has more authority over what people do or do not see in the theater than does the head critic of the *New York Times*. I think also if you look at, for instance, Bruce Lee, who developed the "Kung Fu" series but was replaced by David Carradine [in the U.S. television version] because the executives felt that an Asian American actor couldn't carry the lead in a series ... that this is not an example of the best man for the job. Therefore, to me, the people who are very hysterical over political correctness seem to be a little **disingenuous** and a little **nostalgic**....

I think ethnic isolationism also runs the risk of reinforcing a larger prejudice in society—that ethnic minorities are defined primarily by their race. This can lead to the **ghettoization** of writers. Certainly those who choose to write about a particular ethnic group are really falling into a great literary tradition of writers like Tennessee Williams or [F. Scott] Fitzgerald or August Wilson, whose work stems from its cultural **specificity**. That's certainly legitimate.

But there is this notion in Hollywood oftentimes that, okay, we should hire some African American, but they basically would write African American stuff. And women would write romantic comedies. Whereas in reality, if you look at, for instance, England—Kazuo Ishiguro, an Anglo-Japanese writer, wrote a beautiful novel, *Remains of the Day,* about an English butler. I think that we see that the ability of art to cross racial lines exists....

I came out of this period by writing a play called *Rich Relations* which had no Asian characters.... I basically wrote an autobiographical play about my family and then just made them all white. That wasn't the way to do it.

Then I was at a party and somebody told me the story of the French diplomat who had a twenty-year affair with a Chinese actress who turned out to be A) a spy and B) a man. I thought that was interesting. I began to think of the real diplomat (whose name is Bernard Bouriscot) and what did he think he was getting when he met the spy. The answer came to me—he probably thought he was meeting some version of *Madame Butterfly*....

In some sense, [my play] *M. Butterfly* allowed me to explore the very issues of authenticity which had caused the writer's block. I created a French diplomat who was caught up in an Orientalist fantasy, and in so doing, I was exploring both the **pervasiveness** and the seductiveness of these stereotypes. Through the juxtaposition of fantasy and reality that's in the play, I'm asking whether it's really possible to see the truth, to see the authenticity about a culture, a loved one, or even our-

disingenuous: lacking in fairness or honest expression.

nostalgic: sentimental about a time in the past (especially a time that is supposedly better than the present in some way).

ghettoization: isolation, as if placing in a ghetto.

specificity: distinctiveness.

pervasiveness: extensiveness; widespread nature.

selves. Are we always going to be imprisoned within the realm of our own **subjectivity** and forced to perceive meaning through our own prejudices?...

And so I'm bringing into the discussion of authenticity the question of subjectivity. There is a certain point where I felt that political activism would rescue me from subjectivity, that trying to see things from a point of view that took into account sociological perspective [and] history would therefore allow me to look at culture and look at identity in an objective fashion.

I question whether that's the case.... The political sometimes gets wrapped up in the personal....

[My play] *Face Value*.... was a lot about this.... The plot basically hinged off of the *Miss Saigon* affair. It was about two Asian Americans who go in whiteface to disrupt the opening night of a musical in which the lead actor is a Caucasian playing an Asian. The plot is complicated with the arrival of two white supremacists who then kidnap the Caucasian actor, believing he actually is Asian and is stealing jobs from white people....

To some extent, what *Face Value* is about, and what I will try to make it more about in future rewrites, is the value or the lack of value of faces. True, we all come from different cultures, or many of us come from different cultures. There are, therefore, certain behavioral **predispositions** that exist with culture, but the face, the race, the skin color, does not necessarily equal the culture....

I think that in the future we are going to be seeing more and more examples of how it is not possible to predict behavior simply from race. Therefore the **disunion** of face and culture becomes more and more **pronounced**. So when I go back to some of my early work and the issues that I was exploring ... I ask myself, what is the power in faces? Is there an inherent spiritual or identity objectivity that we can hold on to from looking into the mirror? At this point in my life, I think the answer for me is no, there is not....

I think it's important to envision futures which are more just and inviting. I guess I'm arguing for a **non-fundamentalist** approach to the issue of authenticity—that authenticity should be flexible enough to encompass change. What is au-

subjectivity: the inclination to base one's reactions to something on feelings and emotions rather than on facts.

predispositions: tendencies, preferences.

disunion: separation.

pronounced: strongly marked.

non-fundamentalist: more moderate; not bound by strict rules.

David Henry Hwang   59

thentic in 1960 is not necessarily authentic in 1990 and will not necessarily be authentic in 2020.

What this means is we will have to write about each other and about ourselves, and we will continue to expect criticism and be subject to criticism. We will learn from one another, and that is simply the socialization process which I think is going to be taking place as the country struggles to redefine itself. Those of us who are minorities often talk about this change—Caucasians will no longer be a majority. White males, in particular, need to get it together and realize that the world is changing....

Now we have polls which show a sharp increase in the number of African Americans who characterize Asians as the most racist of all ethnic groups. Even the term "Asian American" itself ... faces some degree of redefinition, I think, in the light of intermarriage and the wide **diversity** of new immigrants. So we can't rest on the assumptions of the past. We have to realize that as America changes, all of us are going to be involved in change and all of us are going to be involved in investigating the authentic.

I've been quoted as saying that to have an honest discussion about race between people of different races is more intimate than sex. It was a little flip but I believe that, because to some extent it's very difficult for us to believe one another right now. It's very difficult for us to trust one another enough to be honest. It's easier to be defensive or not communicate or be polite—anything but really express whatever anger or frustrations that it is that we feel.

I think that if there is a certain degree of subjectivity to the debate over authenticity, then a corollary of that is that we may not necessarily have to like one another. We may not necessarily have to trust one another at this stage. But I think it might be nice to take the step to believe one another....

If a white man says, "I feel that I didn't get into X University because of quotas, reverse racism, and I feel that I'm qualified"—well, I have to believe that that's how he feels. I may then try to have a discussion and point to statistics and whatever, but I have to start with the assumption that he actually does have that feeling. That's somewhat more complicated than it sounds, because I think it's just as easy for us to slip into

diversity: variety.

David Henry Hwang

denial from all sides and to want to tell the white man, "You're crazy. Don't you realize that you're one of the most privileged people that ever walked the face of the planet?"

But I don't know that that's actually going to help us figure out what kind of society we're going to have in the future. So, in the final analysis, authenticity to me is a debate over the quest to validate the humanity of various peoples, of all the people in this country.

I know a couple who's—gosh, he's Irish and Jewish and Japanese and she's Haitian and Filipino and something else. Anyway, they had a child, and someone whose business it is to know such things informed them that their child had never existed before. I began to wonder if this child grows up and becomes a writer—let's say it's a woman—what do we call her? Is she an African American writer or an Asian American writer, European American or is she basically a woman's writer, or etc.? And I think that when the day comes that we can simply call her an American writer, then we will have gone a long way to claiming the humanity and the authenticity of all our experiences as Americans....

Sources

Books

Hwang, David Henry, *Broken Promises: Four Plays,* Avon, 1983.

Hwang, David Henry, *M. Butterfly,* New American Library, 1989.

Notable Asian Americans, Gale, 1995.

Street, Douglas, *David Henry Hwang,* Boise State University Press, 1989.

Periodicals

Boston Globe, "Hwang's Political Stage," April 15, 1994.

Christian Science Monitor, "For Playwright Hwang, Mediums Change While Themes Stay the Same," April 13, 1994, p. 15.

New York Times Magazine, March 13, 1988.

People, January 9, 1984, p. 88.

U.S. News & World Report, March 28, 1988.

Daniel K. Inouye

1924–

*Japanese American member
of the U.S. Senate*

Democrat Daniel K. Inouye has served the people of Hawaii since their island home became the fiftieth state in 1959. He began as a member of the U.S. House of Representatives—he was, in fact, the first Japanese American in Congress. In 1962, he was elected to the U.S. Senate. Since then, Inouye has enjoyed considerable power and influence. In his typically low-key fashion, however, he has always emphasized compromise over confrontation. This approach has brought Inouye the respect of his colleagues within the government as well as the support of Hawaii's voters, who have re-elected him to national office a total of seven times.

Red Cross Volunteer during High School

In the Japanese American community, Inouye is a member of what is called the nisei generation. Nisei is a Japanese word that describes the U.S.-born children of parents who had immigrated from Japan. (The immigrants themselves are known as issei.) Inouye's father was just a young boy when he arrived in Hawaii with his own parents. Later, as an

"ALTHOUGH WE WERE SEPARATED BY A VAST OCEAN AND MOUNTAIN RANGES, WE FROM THE MAINLAND AND HAWAII SHARED ONE DEEP-SEATED DESIRE— TO RID OURSELVES OF THAT INSULTING AND DEGRADING DESIGNATION, 'ENEMY ALIEN.' WE WANTED TO SERVE OUR COUNTRY."

adult, he worked in Honolulu as a file clerk to support his wife and four children, earning barely enough for the family to get by. But as his son Dan later recalled, the Inouye household was a happy one despite the fact that money was always in short supply. And more important, he grew up with the feeling that a better future awaited him if he were willing to work for it.

By the time he had reached his senior year of high school, Inouye's dream was to become a surgeon. But those plans changed forever on the morning of December 7, 1941, as he and his family were getting ready to go to church. Over the radio came news of the Japanese air raid then in progress at the U.S. Navy's nearby Pearl Harbor base. Inouye, who taught first aid at the local Red Cross station, immediately took off to help and stayed on duty for almost a week. In fact, because he felt so guilty that the attack had been carried out by the Japanese, he ended up spending much of the rest of his senior year going to school during the day and working a twelve-hour shift for the Red Cross at night. Meanwhile, in the streets of Honolulu, he and other Hawaiians of Japanese descent encountered taunts and insults from angry whites.

In the fall of 1942, Inouye enrolled in the pre-med program at the University of Hawaii. He also added his voice to those of many other young nisei men who were asking the U.S. government to allow them to serve in the armed forces. More than anything, these men wanted to demonstrate their loyalty to their country. Finally, in January 1943, the War Department announced that it would accept fifteen hundred nisei volunteers for a new unit, the 442nd Regimental Combat Team. Inouye quit school and immediately joined up.

Critically Injured During World War II

The 442nd became the most decorated unit in U.S. military history. Its four thousand members—who adopted "Go for Broke!" as their motto—received more than eighteen thousand medals for bravery. Inouye earned fifteen of them himself as one of the 442nd's most heroic leaders. During the last few months of the war, he was critically wounded in Italy while directing a difficult uphill assault against a

heavily-fortified German position on a high ridge. Inouye spent the next two years in the hospital recovering from multiple bullet wounds to his abdomen and leg and the amputation of his right arm.

Upon returning home in 1947, Inouye resumed his education at the University of Hawaii. But he was no longer able to be a surgeon, and he decided he was no longer interested in a medical career. After receiving his bachelor's degree in 1950, Inouye headed to George Washington University Law School in Washington, D.C. Following his 1952 graduation, he returned to Honolulu and became involved in politics. He won election to the Territorial House in 1954 and served two terms as majority leader. In 1958, he made a successful bid

Inouye reenacts his oath-taking after he was sworn in as a member of the House of Representatives, August 1959

*for a seat in the Territorial Senate, and there, too, he as-
sumed the role of majority leader.*

Represents Hawaii in Congress

*By the time Hawaii was admitted to the union as the fifti-
eth state in 1959, Inouye was so popular with his fellow islanders that he easily captured the new state's first seat in
the U.S. House of Representatives. Three years later, he decided to run for the U.S. Senate. He ended up beating his Republican opponent by more than a two-to-one margin.*

*From the very beginning of his congressional career, In-
ouye has tended to have a liberal opinion on social issues but
a more moderate or even conservative view on economic and
defense issues. For example, he has consistently supported
civil rights legislation through the years and backed the
"Great Society" social welfare programs of President Lyndon
Johnson. As a loyal Democrat, he also supported Johnson's
handling of the Vietnam war. Once Republican Richard Nixon
took office as president in 1969, however, Inouye joined forces with other Democrats who called for an end to the war.*

*Inouye's party loyalty was rewarded during the 1960s
with his appointment to a number of high-ranking positions.
He served as assistant majority whip in the Senate and vice-
chair of the Democratic Senatorial Campaign Committee. He
was also mentioned several times as a possible vice-presiden-
tial candidate, especially after he delivered the following keynote address to delegates attending the Democratic
National Convention in Chicago on August 29, 1968. (See
box for more information.) Inouye won widespread acclaim
for a stirring speech in which he criticized the forces then
threatening to tear apart the United States and urged concerned citizens to take positive steps to solve the nation's political and social problems. An excerpt from his remarks that
evening is reprinted here from* Vital Speeches of the Day,
September 15, 1968.

My fellow Americans: This is my country. Many of us have
fought hard for the right to say that. Many are struggling today

from Harlem to Danang [the site of an important U.S. military base in Vietnam] so that they may say it with conviction.

This is our country.

And we are engaged in a time of great testing—testing whether this nation, or any nation conceived in liberty and dedicated to opportunity for all its citizens, can not only endure but continue to progress. The issue before all of us in such a time is how shall we **discharge**, how shall we honor our citizenship.

The keynote address at a national political convention traditionally calls for rousing oratory. I hope to be excused from this tradition tonight. For I do not view this occasion as one for either flamboyance or **levity.**

I believe the real reason we are here is that there is a word called "commitment," because we are committed to the future of our country and all our people, and because for that future, hope and faith are more needed now than pride in our party's past.

For even as we emerge from an era of unsurpassed social and economic progress, Americans are clearly in no mood for counting either their blessings or their bank accounts.

We are still embarked on the longest unbroken journey of economic growth and prosperity in our history. Yet we are torn by **dissension**, and disrespect for our institutions and leaders is **rife** across the land.

In at least two of our greatest universities, learning has been brought to a halt by student rebellions; others of the student revolution have publicly burned draft cards and even the American flag.

Crime has increased so that we are told one out of every three Americans is afraid to walk in his own neighborhood after dark.

Riot has **bludgeoned** our cities, laying waste our streets, our property and, most important, human lives. The smoke of destruction has even shrouded the dome of our Capitol [in Washington]....

Voices of angry protest are heard throughout the land, crying for all manner of freedoms. Yet our political leaders are

discharge: fulfill.
levity: making light of something; frivolousness.
dissension: disagreement, conflict.
rife: widespread; common.
bludgeoned: beaten, pounded.

The 1968 Democratic National Convention

As Democrats from all over the country met in Chicago, Illinois, in August 1968 to choose their candidates for president and vice president, political, social, and cultural rebellion was in the air all over the United States. Race riots had exploded in many major cities resulting in hundreds of deaths, thousands of arrests, and millions of dollars in property damage. In addition, people were still reeling from two assassinations in the weeks just prior to the convention—that of civil rights leader Martin Luther King, Jr., in April, followed in June by that of Democratic presidential candidate Robert F. Kennedy. And as more and more U.S. troops were sent off to fight in Vietnam, antiwar demonstrations were erupting on university and college campuses across the nation.

Some of that summer's dramatic moments occurred right outside the convention hall itself. There, in the streets of Chicago, about 10,000 antiwar protesters and radical activists battled with police in full view of television cameras and reporters from all over the world. Protests also occured in city parks.

picketed and some who cry loudest for freedom have sought to prevent our president, our vice president and cabinet officers from speaking in public.

None go so far as publicly to **condone** a politics of assassination. Yet assassins' bullets have robbed our country of three great leaders within the last five years. [Inouye is referring here to the deaths of Martin Luther King, Jr., and Robert F. Kennedy earlier in the year as well as the 1963 assassination of Robert Kennedy's brother, President John F. Kennedy.]

Why?... Why—when we have at last had the courage to open up an attack on the age-old curses of ignorance and disease and poverty and prejudice—why are the flags of **anarchism** being hoisted by leaders of the next generation? Why, when our maturing society welcomes and appreciates art as never before, are poets and painters so preponderantly hostile? Some conveniently blame all our ills and agonies on a most difficult and unpopular commitment overseas. The Vietnam war must end, they say, because it is an immoral war.

Of course, the war in Vietnam must be ended. But it must be ended, as President Johnson said last March, by patient political negotiation rather than through the victorious force of

condone: approve.

anarchism: belief in a state without laws or government.

Chicago Mayor Richard Daley took strong—many say brutal—action. Around 20,000 city and state police officers teamed up with about 4,000 National Guard troops and used teargas, nightsticks, and firearms to crack down on demonstrators and clear out the parks. Reporters and other bystanders were roughed up in the process, as were some convention delegates.

Meanwhile, inside the convention hall, another struggle was under way among liberals, moderates, and conservatives within the Democratic party. Most of the controversy was over the issue of U.S. participation in the Vietnam war, but there were also conflicts regarding the direction of the party on other issues such as crime and civil rights. In the end, after several days of turmoil, Hubert Humphrey, then vice president in the administration of Lyndon Johnson, easily won the nomination over antiwar candidates Eugene McCarthy and George McGovern.

The fight left the party in shambles. Many disillusioned liberals, intellectuals, and young people simply refused to support the Humphrey ticket. In a three-way race that fall featuring Humphrey, Alabama Governor George Wallace (a Democrat who ran as an independent), and Republican Richard Nixon, Nixon was elected president.

arms—even though this may be **unpalatable** for those raised in the tradition of glorious military victories.

But like our other complex problems, this one must also be solved responsibly. Just as we **shun** irresponsible calls for total and devastating military victory, so must we guard against the illusion of an instant peace that has no chance of permanence....

But when young people have rioted in China and Czechoslovakia as well as at Columbia [University in New York City], and in Paris [France] and Berlin [Germany] as well as in Berkeley [at the University of California], I doubt that we can blame all the troubles of our time on Vietnam.

Other critics tell us of the revolution of rising expectations. They charge that it has reached such proportions that men now take it as an insult when they are asked to be reasonable in their desires and demands.

If this is too often true as a generalization, it is all too frequently aimed particularly at our fellow citizens of African ancestry, whose aspirations have burst full-blown on us after more than one hundred years of systematic racist **deprivation.**

unpalatable: distasteful, unpleasant.

shun: reject, avoid.

deprivation: having been denied the necessities of life.

Daniel K. Inouye | **69**

As an American whose ancestors came from Japan, I have become accustomed to a question most recently asked by a very prominent businessman who was concerned about the threat of riots and the resultant loss in life and property. "Tell me," he said, "why can't the Negro be like you?"

First, although my skin is colored, it is not black. In this country, the color of my skin does not ignite prejudice that has smoldered for generations.

Second, although my grandfather came to this country in poverty, he came without **shackles;** he came as a free man enjoying certain constitutional rights under the American flag.

Third, my grandfather's family was not shattered as individual members of it were sold as **chattel** or used as security on loans.

And fourth, although others of my ancestry were **interned** behind barbed wires during World War II, neither my parents nor I were forced by covenants and circumstances to live in ghettos.

Unlike those of my ancestry, the Negro's unemployment rate is triple the national average. The mortality rate of his children is twice that of white children.

He often pays more for his miserable tenement than comparable space will cost in the white suburbs. He is likely to pay more for his groceries, more for his furniture, more for his liquor and more for his credit.

And, my fellow Americans, today many thousands of black Americans return from Vietnam with medals of valor, some of them have been crippled in the service of their country. But too often they return to economic and social circumstances that are barely, if at all, improved over those they left.

Is it any wonder that the Negro questions whether his place in our country's history books will be any less forgotten than were the contributions of his ancestors? Is it any wonder that the Negroes find it hard to wait another one hundred years before they are accepted as full citizens in our free society?

Of course, expectations are rising—and they are rising faster than we in our imperfect world can fulfill them.

shackles: cuffs used around the wrists or legs to restrain a person.

chattel: property.

interned: imprisoned.

Daniel K. Inouye

The revolution we in the United States are experiencing was born of Democratic processes that not only **accommodate** economic progress and social mobility, but actively encourage them.

But it is important to remember that these expectations are the children of progress and that today's restlessness has been nurtured by our very real achievements. Out of these should emerge a brighter and better society than we have known.

Nowhere is this clearer than in the situation of our young people today. The success of our economic system has freed them in ever-increasing numbers from the tragedies of **premature mortality** and early labor.

It has built the schools in which they are being educated to higher levels than ever in our nation's history. And this progress has been achieved in a political system that not only admits but safeguards the right of **dissent.**

So it should hardly surprise us when the children of such progress demand to be heard when they become aware of **inequities** still to be corrected. Neither should we fear their voices. On the contrary, whether we know it or not, the marching feet of youth have led us into a new era of politics and we can never turn back.

But what should concern us is something far more fundamental. The true dimension of the challenge facing us is a loss of faith. I do not mean simply a loss of religious faith, although this erosion is a major contributor to our unease. I mean a loss of faith in our country, in its purposes and its institutions. I mean a retreat from the responsibilities of citizenship.

The plain fact is that in the face of complexity and frustration, too many Americans have drifted into the use of power for purely destructive purposes. Too many Americans have come to believe it is their right to decide as individuals which of our laws they will obey and which they will violate.

 I do not mean to say that all our laws are just. They're not, and I don't mean to suggest that protest against unjust laws is not proper. Performed in an orderly manner, the right to protest is a cornerstone of our system.

accommodate: allow for; make room for.

premature mortality: early death.

dissent: disagreement, protest.

inequities: inequalities, injustices.

A rally in New Haven, Connecticut, in support of Bobby Seale and the Black Panthers, 1970. Inouye declared: "Whether we know it or not, the marching feet of youth have led us into a new era of politics and we can never turn back."

disengagement: a state of withdrawal.

abdication: the act of giving up or abandoning.

Men must have the opportunity to be heard even when their views are extreme and in a lesser democratic country, dangerous. I, too, have spoken against laws which I considered wrong and unjust, and I am sure I will speak—and vote—against many, many more.

But my fellow Americans, I have not burned my birth certificate, and I will not renounce my citizenship.

Those who would do such things are relatively few. But there is a much larger number who in the face of change and disorder have retreated into **disengagement** and quiet despair. Less destructively but not less surely, such men are also retreating from the responsibilities of citizenship.

Now let us not deceive ourselves about the consequences of such **abdication.** It is anarchy. It is a state in which each indi-

Daniel K. Inouye

vidual demands instant **compliance** with his own desires, and from there it is but a short step to the assumption by each individual of the right to decide which of his neighbors shall live and which shall not, and so accelerate the sickening spiral of violence which has already cost us our beloved John F. Kennedy, our great leader Martin Luther King, Jr., and the voice of this decade, Senator Robert F. Kennedy.

We have been told that the revolts are against the system, and that the Establishment must be torn down. But my fellow Americans, in Paris recently, students cut down hundred-year-old trees to erect temporary street barricades. Those trees had lived through two world wars. Some of them had even survived the revolution of 1848.

Were the goals of these students served by the destruction of those trees? How long will it take for their beauty and the vitality they symbolized to grow again? What trees did the students plant in their place?

If we cut down our institutions, public and private, and with indifference starve the systems which have given us our achievements, who will feed the hungry? Who will train the unskilled?

Who will supply the jobs that mean opportunity for the generation whose voices are not yet heard? And who will launch the much-needed ... plan to rebuild our cities and open opportunity for all Americans? These undertakings are too great for individuals going their separate ways....

Fellow Americans, this is our country. Its future is what we, its citizens, will make it.

And as we all know, we have much to do. Putting aside hatred on the one hand and timidity on the other, let us grow fresh faith in our purpose and new vigor in our citizenship.

Let us welcome the ideas and energies of the young and the talents and participation of all responsible people.

Let us plant trees and grow new opportunity. And, my fellow Americans, let us build not only new buildings but new neighborhoods and then let us live in them, all as full citizens and all as brothers.

compliance: conformity; fulfilling.

In closing I wish to share with you a most sacred word of Hawaii. It is "aloha." To some of you who visited us it may have meant hello. To others "aloha" may have meant good-bye. But to those of us who have been privileged to live in Hawaii, "aloha" means "I love you."

So to all of you, my fellow Americans, aloha.

"

Throughout the administrations of presidents Richard Nixon, Gerald Ford, Jimmy Carter, Ronald Reagan, George Bush, and Bill Clinton, Inouye continued to favor liberal causes such as abortion rights, gun control, organized labor, and consumer protection laws. Yet he has also voted to support some conservative military measures, including funding for development of a neutron bomb.

Inouye's influence in a number of these areas has been considerable, due in large part to the high-ranking positions he has held on key Senate committees. These assignments have occasionally put him in the national spotlight. In 1973, for example, Inouye served as a member of the Senate Watergate Committee, the group in charge of investigating the political scandal in the administration of President Richard Nixon. The senator from Hawaii won many fans for his patient and persistent questioning of uncooperative witnesses in the Watergate affair. Inouye again found himself in the public eye in 1987 when he chaired the Iran-contra hearings, a Senate investigation into the questionable activities of some members of President Ronald Reagan's administration.

In 1976, Inouye served as chair of the Senate Select Committee on Intelligence. Under his leadership, the committee drafted new rules governing the secret operations of U.S. intelligence organizations at home and abroad. (The Senate's goal was to clamp down on potential abuses of power.) As a longtime member of the Senate Appropriations Committee and former chair of its Foreign Operations Subcommittee, Inouye helped determine which foreign countries will receive U.S. aid and how much they will receive. He also served as chair of the Science and Transportation Subcommittee on

Communications of the Senate Commerce Committee. In this role, he oversaw developments in cable television, telephone communications, and the "Information Superhighway."

Because of his own experience with racial prejudice during World War II, Inouye has always been especially sensitive to discrimination against minorities. The concerns of Native Americans in particular have always been of great interest to him. As the longtime chair of the Senate Committee on Indian Affairs, Inouye strongly supported tribal **sovereignty** and **self-determination.**

Since his days in combat in World War II, Inouye has maintained a very strong bond with his fellow members of the 442nd Regimental Combat Team. In March 1993, hundreds of the former soldiers met in Honolulu to mark the

Inouye with members of the Red Lake Band of Chippewa, of Minnesota, who thanked him for introducing legislation honoring their tribe, 1987

sovereignty: freedom from control by others.

self-determination: freedom to choose one's own political future.

fiftieth anniversary of the founding of their unit. Their thoughts often turned to the bravery they had displayed overseas and their triumph over bigotry at home. One of the two featured speakers at the reunion was Inouye, who delivered an especially moving keynote address on March 24. The senator supplied a copy of his speech, an excerpt of which follows.

This gathering is an important one—it will be a gathering of nostalgia ... a gathering of sad memories ... a gathering of laughter and fun ... a gathering of goodbyes, for this may be our last roll call of the regiment.

We have travelled vast distances—from every state and from many foreign lands—to be together in Honolulu. We have travelled a lifetime together for this meeting in Honolulu. When did this journey to Honolulu begin?

Although this is our 50th reunion, our journey began before that date. Our fate was decided 52 years, 3 months and 2 weeks ago on that tragic Sunday in December. Our journey began on December 7, 1941. [On December 7, 1941, the Japanese bombed the U.S. naval base at Pearl Harbor, Hawaii.]

Soon after that tragic Sunday morning, we who were of Japanese ancestry were considered by our nation to be citizens without a country. I am certain all of us remember that the Selective Service system of our country designated us to be unfit for military service because we were "enemy aliens." Soon after that, on February 19, 1942, the White House issued an extraordinary Executive Order—Executive Order 9066. [For more information, see entries on **Robert T. Matsui, Spark M. Matsunaga, Norman Y. Mineta**, and **Clifford I. Uyeda**.] This dreaded Executive Order forcibly uprooted our mainland brothers and their families and their loved ones from their homes with only those possessions that they were able to carry themselves....

Our mainland brothers were not charged or indicted or convicted for the commission of any crime—because no crime was committed. Their only crime, if any, was that they were born of Japanese parents and for that crime, they were incarcerated

Japanese Americans in Hawaii take the oath of induction to the Army after volunteering for combat duty, 1943

in internment camps surrounded by barbed-wire fences, guarded by machine-gun towers.... Although a few members of Hawaii's Japanese community were interned in Honouliuli (a rather well-kept secret), very few, if any of us in Hawaii, were aware of the mass internment of our mainland brothers and their families.

Although we were separated by a vast ocean and mountain ranges, we from the mainland and Hawaii shared one deep-seated desire—to rid ourselves of that insulting and degrading designation, "enemy alien." We wanted to serve our country. We wanted to demonstrate our love for our country.

After many months of petitions and letters, another Executive Order was issued with the declaration that "...Americanism is a matter of mind and heart; Americanism is not, and never was, a matter of race or ancestry." By this Executive Order, the formation of the special combat team made up of Japanese Americans was authorized.

More than the anticipated numbers volunteered; in fact, in Hawaii, about eighty-five percent of the eligible men of Japanese Americans volunteered. Those who were selected assembled in Schofield Barracks to prepare for our departure from Hawaii.... In early April [1943], we boarded railway flatbeds in Wahiawa and rode to Iwilei. There we got off the trains with our heavy duffel bags to march to Pier 7. But keep in mind that most of us had less than two weeks of military training and many of us were yet to be toughened and hardened. And so we found ourselves struggling with those heavy bags on a march of over a mile. This was the farewell parade of the 442nd. For many parents this was the last sight of their sons. I cannot understand why the Army did not place those duffel bags in trucks and permit us to march heads up and tall as we said goodbye to Hawaii. For many, the last look of their sons must have been a rather sad one....

But after several weeks, we from Hawaii and the mainland gathered in Camp Shelby in Hattiesburg, Mississippi, the home of chiggers and ticks, sweat and dirt.

All of us were of the same ancestry, but somehow our first encounter was an unhappy one. In a few days, violent arguments and fights erupted within our area and these fights became commonplace. The men of the regiment found themselves segregated into two camps, one from Hawaii and the other from the mainland. This relationship was so bad that senior Army officers seriously considered disbanding the regiment.

Many projects were initiated and many lectures were delivered to bring about unity, but all failed except the Rohwer experiment. [Rohwer was one of the internment camps where Japanese Americans were held during World War II. It was located in Arkansas.] Our regimental records will not disclose the name of the author of this experiment, but history will show that we owe much to him.

Whoever he was, [he] suggested that the internees of Rohwer send an invitation to the regiment inviting young enlisted men from Hawaii to join them for a weekend of fun and festivities in the camp. As I recall, each company selected ten enlisted men. I was fortunate to be one of those selected by E Company. On the appointed day, these men from Hawaii, all cleanly showered, smelling of after-shave lotion, with their guitars and ukuleles, boarded trucks for this journey to Rohwer....

From the time we left Shelby in the early morning hours, this special convoy was a convoy of laughter and music. All were anticipating happy times with the young ladies of Rohwer.

Suddenly, this fantasy was shattered. We came in sight of the Rohwer internment camp. In the distance, we could see rows of barracks surrounded by high barbed-wire fences with machine-gun towers. The music stopped and there was no laughter.

Keep in mind that very few, if any of us, were aware of these camps. Our mainland brothers never spoke of them, never complained, and so we did not know.

When we finally came to the gate, we were ordered to get off the trucks. We were in uniform and were confronted by men in similar uniforms but they had rifles with bayonets. For a moment, I thought that there would be a tragic encounter, but fortunately nothing happened as we were escorted through the gate. There we were greeted by the people of Rohwer who were all persons of Japanese ancestry—grandparents, parents, children, grandchildren. Although a dance was held that evening, I doubt if any of us really enjoyed ourselves. But it was an unforgettable evening.

When we left Rohwer the following morning, the singing and the laughter and music that filled our trucks when we left Camp Shelby was replaced by grim silence. The atmosphere was grim and quiet, and I believe that all of us, as we reflected upon that strange visit, asked ourselves the question, "Would I have volunteered from a camp like Rohwer?" To this day, I cannot give an answer because I really do not know if I would have volunteered to serve our nation if I had been interned in one of those camps.

So suddenly, our respect, admiration, and love for our ... brothers rose to phenomenal heights. They suddenly became our blood brothers and overnight a new, tough, tightly united military fighting machine was formed. It was a regiment made up of blood brothers and we were ready to live up to our motto, "Go for Broke." And thus the 442nd Infantry Regimental Combat Team was formed.

There are too many battles to recall.... But there is one we will never forget and one hopefully that our nation will always remember—the Battle of the Lost Battalion.

This battle began during the last week of October 1944. The members of the First Battalion of the 141st Infantry Regiment of the 36th Texas Division found themselves surrounded by a large number of enemy troops. This "lost battalion" was ordered to fight its way back, but could not do so. The Second and Third Battalions of the Texas Regiment were ordered to break through but they were thrown back, and so on October 26, the 442nd was ordered to go into the lines to rescue the "lost battalion." On November 15, the rescue was successfully concluded.

Two days later, we were ordered to assemble ... to personally receive the commendation of the 36th Division from the commanding general of the Texas unit. The men of the regiment assembled in a vast field of a French farm. I can still hear the company commanders making their reports—A Company, all present and accounted for; B Company, all present and accounted for; E Company, all present and accounted for. It was an eerie scene. It has been reported that General Dahlquist, who had ordered this formation, was at first angered by the small attendance and reprimanded our commander, who in reply is reported to have said, "Sir, this *is* the regiment." As a result of the Battle of the Lost Battalion, two thousand men were in hospitals and over three hundred had died. The price was heavy. Although we did not whimper or complain, we were sensitive to the fact that the rescuers of the Texas Battalion were not members of the Texas Division. They were Japanese Americans from Hawaii and from mainland internment camps. They were "enemy aliens."

I can still hear the proud and defiant voices of the company commanders as they made their reports. I can still see the company commander of E Company making his report. E Company had forty-two men, and though we were less than a quarter of the authorized company strength, E Company was the largest company [there].... K Company was led by a staff sergeant. K Company was made up of twelve men. When I heard the last commander shout out his report, "All present and accounted

Nearly 3,000 Japanese American soldiers gather at Iolani Palace, Honolulu, Hawaii, for farewell ceremonies before leaving for their posts, 1943

for," like many of you, I could almost feel the insulting and degrading designation that was placed on our shoulders long ago in December 1941—the designation of "enemy alien"—fall crashing to the ground in that faraway French farm. And we knew that from that moment on, no one could ever, ever, question our loyalty and our love for our country. The insulting stigma was finally taken away....

Over the years, many have asked us—"Why?" "Why did you fight and serve so well?" My son, like your sons and daughters, has asked the same question—"Why?" "Why were you willing and ready to give your life?" We have tried to provide answers to these questions and I hope that my answer to my son made sense.

I told my son it was a matter of honor. I told him about my father's farewell message when I left home to put on the uniform of my country. My father was not a man of eloquence but he said, "Whatever you do, do not dishonor the family and do not dishonor the country." I told my son that for many of us, to have done any less than what we had done in battle would have dishonored our families and our country.

Second, I told my son that there is an often-used Japanese phrase—*Kodomo no tame ni.* Though most of us who went into battle were young and single, we wanted to leave a legacy of honor and pride and the promise of a good life for our yet-to-be-born children and their children.

My brothers, I believe we can assure ourselves that we did succeed in upholding our honor and that of our families and our nation. And I respectfully and humbly believe that our service and the sacrifices of those who gave their all on the battlefield assure a better life for our children and their children.

Yes, I believe we can stand tall this evening in knowing that our journey together, a journey that began on that tragic Sunday morning, was not in vain. And so tonight, let us embrace with our hearts and minds the memory of those brothers who are not with us this evening and let us do so with all of our affection and gratitude. Let us embrace with deep love our loved ones for having stood with us and walked with us on our journey. Let us embrace with everlasting gratitude and Aloha the many friends and neighbors who supported us throughout our journey. Let us embrace with everlasting love our great nation.

And finally, let us embrace our sons and daughters with full pride and with the restful assurance that the story of our journey of honor will live on for generations to come.

And so, my brothers, let us this evening, in the spirit of our regiment, stand tall with pride, have fun, and let's "Go for Broke."

"

Sources

Books

Inouye, Daniel K., and Lawrence Elliott, *Journey to Washington,* Prentice-Hall, 1967.

Notable Asian Americans, Gale, 1995.

O'Neill, William L., *Coming Apart: An Informal History of America in the 1960s,* Quadrangle, 1971.

Periodicals

Congressional Quarterly Weekly Report, "The Quiet Insider: Hawaii's Daniel Inouye Wields a Private, Personal Power," April 16, 1988, p. 979.

Grand Rapids Press, "442nd Unit Marks 50th Anniversary," March 22, 1993, p. D11.

Newsweek, August 10, 1959, pp. 22–24; April 9, 1962, pp. 39–40.

Time, "New Faces in Congress," August 10, 1959, p. 13; August 27, 1973, p. 18.

Vital Speeches of the Day, "Commitment" (keynote address at 1968 Democratic National Convention), September 15, 1968, pp. 709–711.

Liliuokalani

1838–1917

Native Hawaiian leader and musician

> "ALL WHO UPHOLD YOU IN THIS UNLAWFUL PROCEEDING MAY SCORN AND DESPISE MY WORD; BUT THE OFFENCE OF BREAKING AND SETTING ASIDE FOR A SPECIFIC PURPOSE THE LAWS OF YOUR OWN NATION, AND DISREGARDING ALL JUSTICE AND FAIRNESS, MAY BE TO THEM AND TO YOU THE SOURCE OF AN UNHAPPY AND MUCH TO BE REGRETTED LEGACY."

A strong and determined woman who projected an air of quiet dignity, Liliuokalani was the last queen of Hawaii. When she began her rule in 1891, she was expected to serve mostly as a figurehead—someone who would allow the large and powerful community of American businesspeople to continue running life on the islands as they had for many years. But Liliuokalani resented the fact that the Americans had so much say in Hawaii's affairs. She believed that native Hawaiians had the right to decide their own future. Her stubborn insistence on winning independence for her island home eventually cost Liliuokalani her throne, but she will always have the love and respect of the native Hawaiian people for daring to rebel against the powerful forces of American business and government.

A Royal Childhood in Hawaii

Lydia Kamakaeha, as she was known at the time of her birth in Honolulu, was the third of ten children of two native Hawaiian high chiefs, Kapaakea and his wife, Keohokalole.

As was the custom in her native land, however, Lydia was not actually raised by her biological parents. To cement friendships between tribes and encourage harmony, children were often given to others to bring up as their own. So, right after she was born, Lydia was adopted by another chief, Paki, and his wife, Konia. She grew up regarding them as her parents and their daughter as her sister. Most of Lydia's own brothers and sisters were adopted by other chiefs. As a result she had limited contact with them, and they were never close.

Through her biological parents as well as her foster parents, Lydia had ties to Hawaii's King Kamehameha I. He was the first person to unite the islands under a single ruler back in the late 1700s. (See box for more information.) Because she was of royal blood, Lydia began attending a special school at the age of four. It was run by Christian missionaries from America and catered exclusively to the children of high chiefs. There she mastered written and spoken English and became a devout Congregationalist (a Protestant religion).

As a young princess Lydia took part in the social activities of the court of King Kamehameha IV and his queen, Emma. Lydia was also a talented poet and musician who enjoyed experimenting with the effects she could create by playing western melodies on Hawaiian instruments such as the ukelele. She even composed two of her country's best-known songs, "He Mele Lahui Hawaii," the islands' national anthem, and "Aloha Oe/Farewell to Thee," which was the first Hawaiian song to enjoy widespread popularity outside the islands.

But not long after her brother, David Kalakaua, became king in 1874, Lydia assumed a much more important role in the royal family. Kalakaua had no children, and his younger brother—the next likely choice as heir—died in 1877. That year Kalakaua declared that his sister was to become queen upon his death.

Prepares for Her Future Role as Queen

From then on Lydia was generally known by her royal name, Liliuokalani. To prepare for her future role she began

King Kalakaua of Hawaii

taking on more serious responsibilities. She regularly visited the other islands in the Hawaiian chain to show her concern for the people and to emphasize her rank in the new Kalakaua dynasty. She also made an official visit to England, where she was presented at the court of Queen Victoria, and to the United States, where she met with President Grover Cleveland. In addition, Liliuokalani became involved in setting up and supervising schools and other educational programs for Hawaiian children.

Meanwhile, tensions were on the rise throughout Hawaii between the native population and the growing community of American residents, most of whom had settled on the islands early in the 1800s as missionaries or businesspeople. Some native Hawaiians deeply resented the Americans and their insistence that the islanders abandon their own cultural traditions in favor of western-style religious beliefs and social customs.

Also alarming to some islanders was Hawaii's increasing economic dependence on the United States. The profitable sugarcane plantations were owned and run mostly by Americans, while Chinese and Japanese immigrants supplied much of the labor in the fields and in the mills. Thus, native Hawaiians had very little say in running the islands' affairs.

Even the monarchy itself was under attack. The generally friendly relations that had existed between various Hawaiian leaders and the Americans throughout the 1800s had made it possible for the newcomers to chip slowly away at the power of the king. Finally, in 1887, Kalakaua's American cabinet ministers (the group of people who advise a leader on major policies and programs) used threats and intimidation to force him to agree to a new constitution that transferred virtually all of his authority to them. They also removed from office the few remaining native Hawaiians serving in top government posts and replaced them with Americans. Their next aim was outright annexation—officially making Hawaii a territory of the United States.

Becomes Queen Upon Her Brother's Death

King Kalakaua died in January 1891 while on a trip to the United States. His sister Liliuokalani ascended to the throne as planned. But she soon showed that she had no intention of allowing the Americans to continue dominating life in Hawaii—in fact, she made it quite clear that she wanted to regain some of the power that previous rulers had already surrendered. Her goal was to give native Hawaiians more say in how business and government operated on the islands.

Not surprisingly, Liliuokalani's plans greatly upset the American businesspeople who had been accustomed to running Hawaii as they saw fit. Another blow to their way of life had occurred just the year before, in 1890, when a new U.S. trade law went into effect. Since 1875 Hawaiian sugar had enjoyed free and favored entry into the United States. But under the terms of the new law (known as the McKinley Tariff), these special advantages ended, and Hawaiian sugar was suddenly subject to duty, or taxation. The change plunged the islands into economic chaos and made the political situation there even more unstable.

But Liliuokalani continued with her attempts at reform, making widespread changes throughout all branches of government. In January 1892 she dismissed her cabinet, which included some holdovers from her brother's regime. But Hawaiian legislators—under pressure from the American business leaders—would not approve any of the new cabinets she tried to assemble.

Attempts at Reform Lead to U.S. Takeover

In January 1893 Liliuokalani took even bolder action. She proclaimed a new constitution that returned power to the throne, thus making the legislature and the cabinet answerable to her rather than the other way around. The Americans living in Hawaii (along with a handful of European supporters) responded promptly and with force. They organized a Committee of Public Safety and, with the approval of the U.S. government representative assigned to Hawaii, called on nearby U.S. Navy troops to help them "protect American life and property." Committee members quickly took charge of official buildings in Honolulu, abolished the monarchy, and

Hawaii's Kamehameha Dynasty

When England's Captain James Cook first "discovered" the Hawaiian Islands in 1778, he found a native population of around 300,000 people. At the time they were divided politically into four major competing kingdoms, each headed by a single chief. This made it fairly easy for the British to establish themselves as the dominant power as they and other foreigners began trading with the Hawaiians.

Beginning in 1782, however, a war broke out among the Hawaiians for control of the islands. With the help of white merchants from whom he obtained guns and ships, one particularly ambitious chief named Kamehameha emerged victorious after a ten-year struggle. By 1795 he held all of the main islands except two. By 1810 he had claimed even those two, thus uniting all of the islands politically under his leadership and launching the Kamehameha dynasty.

Under Kamehameha I, as he was known, Hawaii prospered as the center of the sandalwood trade. (Sandalwood is a beautiful yellowish wood of the sandalwood tree used for making ornamental carvings and fine furniture.) But the arrival of so many outsiders also led to problems. Pirates, sailors, adventurers, and others who flocked to the islands brought with them illnesses against which the Hawaiians had no defense. The newcomers also introduced them to liquor. Disease and alcoholism took a heavy toll on the native population.

Kamehameha I nevertheless remained on friendly terms with the whites while he fought to control the behavior of his own people. He banned the production of alcohol in the islands and tried to force Hawaiians to observe native religious customs more faithfully. But the foreigners' influence was strong, and slowly but surely it undermined the old traditions.

Kamehameha I died in 1819 and was succeeded by Kamehameha II, who abolished the Hawaiian religion within months of taking the throne. Less than a year later the first groups of Congregationalist missionaries (mostly from New England) arrived and began to establish a strong presence on the islands. They taught the Hawaiians that their traditional way of life was sinful and introduced them to Christianity and western-style education, government, and laws. (The chiefs, especially the female ones, were among their most devoted followers.) They also imposed a sense of peace and order by clamping down on the behavior of foreigners they felt were leading the local people astray.

What the missionaries failed to see was that their Eurocentric perspective—their tendency to interpret the world in terms of white, European, Christian values, customs, and experiences—contrasted sharply with Hawaiian ways. A number of Hawaiians and

set up a temporary government headed by a Hawaiian-born American lawyer (and missionary's son) named Sanford B. Dole. They then applied to the United States for annexation.

many foreigners deeply resented their strict rules. From time to time, these resentments touched off minor revolts, especially during the reign of Kamehameha III, who led Hawaii from 1825 until 1854. For the most part, however, the missionaries were able to maintain their influence on the islands' affairs. They served as advisors to the king and shaped Hawaii's growth and development.

In 1839, an American missionary named William Richards persuaded Kamehameha III to issue a "Declaration of Rights" and an "Edict of Toleration," followed a year later by Hawaii's first constitution. These documents were based on western-style concepts of government, including the division of responsibilities among legislative, executive, and judicial branches (separate branches that make, enforce, and interpret the laws of a nation) and the guarantee of certain personal and property rights.

Along with these political and social changes, the economic picture also took on a new look. Sugar became an increasingly important export crop for Hawaii. The missionaries established the first plantations and brought in Chinese and Japanese people to work in the fields and in the mills. This concentrated even more power in the hands of the Americans. In fact, a missionary named Gerrit P. Judd served as Kamehameha III's prime minister during the last dozen years (1842–54) of his long and eventful reign.

Kamehameha the Great

The dynasty continued under Kamehameha IV, who ruled from 1854 until 1863, and ended with Kamehameha V, who ruled from 1863 until 1872. Both of them were educated, well-traveled men who remained as committed as Kamehameha III had been to western principles of government. Unlike him, however, they were inclined to favor the British ways over those of the Americans. This led to a power struggle between the pro-British and pro-American forces in the royal family upon the death of Kamehameha V. Eventually the pro-American forces won out with the rise in power of King Kalakaua. But the monarchy itself was in trouble by this time, unable to maintain the power to rule Hawaii through the vast economic and political restructuring brought about by American business.

Liliuokalani did not offer any resistance during the overthrow and was placed under house arrest (confinement under guard at one's home rather than in a prison). Instead she protested to her friend President Cleveland and asked him to reinstate her as queen. It proved to be an impossible task, however. Using force to restore her to the throne was unacceptable to the U.S. president, and the Committee of Public Safety absolutely refused to give up control of the islands.

The next five years continued to be an unsettled time for Liliuokalani and for Hawaii. While awaiting word from Washington about her fate, the queen urged her people to remain calm and avoid any violent uprisings. But their patience and their faith in America went unrewarded. On July 4, 1894, the temporary government gave way to the newly created Republic of Hawaii, and Dole was named president.

Arrested and Tried for Treason

On January 6, 1895, a group of Hawaiians loyal to the monarchy tried unsuccessfully to launch a revolution against the Republic. Ten days later Liliuokalani was arrested for treason (attempting to overthrow the government) and told that all of her supporters would be executed or imprisoned if she did not agree to give up her throne. Thus, on January 24, she officially abdicated (resigned).

Despite their promises to Liliuokalani, officials of the Republic went ahead and sentenced some of the conspirators to death and others to prison. Only when the U.S. government protested—and strongly hinted that any executions would stand in the way of annexation—did the Republic agree to less severe punishment.

On February 5, 1895, Liliuokalani herself was brought to trial on charges that she had known about the plan to overthrow the Republic and failed to inform the proper authorities. She later wrote in her autobiography, Hawaii's Story by Hawaii's Queen, "The only charge against me really was that of being a queen; and my case was judged by ... my adversaries [opponents] before I came into court." After denying that she was guilty of concealing acts of treason, she handed her attorney the following statement to be read aloud in court. It is excerpted here from her autobiography, which was originally published in 1898 but reprinted in 1964 by Charles E. Tuttle.

In the year 1893, on the fifteenth day of January, at the request of a large majority of the Hawaiian people, and by and with the consent of my cabinet, I proposed to make certain changes in the constitution of the Hawaiian kingdom, which were suggested to me as being for the advantage and benefit of the kingdom, and subjects and residents thereof. These proposed changes did not **deprive** foreigners [any of the] rights or privileges enjoyed by them under the constitution of 1887, **promulgated** by King Kalakaua and his cabinet, without the consent of the people or **ratified** by their votes.

My ministers at the last moment changed their views, and requested me to **defer** all action in connection with the constitution; and I **yielded** to their advice as bound to do by the existing constitution and laws.

A minority of the foreign population made the action the **pretext** for overthrowing the monarchy, and, aided by the United States naval forces and representative, established a new government.

I owed no **allegiance** to the **Provisional** Government so established, nor to any power or to any one **save** the will of my people and the welfare of my country.

The wishes of my people were not consulted as to this change of government, and only those who were in practical rebellion against the constitutional government were allowed to vote upon the question [of] whether the monarchy should exist or not.

To prevent the shedding of the blood of my people, natives and foreigners alike, I opposed armed interference, and quietly yielded to the armed forces brought against my throne, and submitted to the **arbitrament** of the government of the United States the decision of my rights and those of the Hawaiian people. Since then, as is well known to all, I have pursued the path of peace and **diplomatic** discussion, and not that of internal **strife**.

The United States having first interfered in the interest of those founding the government of 1893 upon the basis of

deprive: deny or remove from.
promulgated: proclaimed.
ratificd: approved.
defer: postpone.
yielded: gave in.
pretext: excuse, reason.
allegiance: loyalty.
provisional: temporary.
save: except.
arbitrament: judgment.
diplomatic: using open-minded, give-and-take methods to handle difficult situations.
strife: conflict or struggle.

The U.S. flag waves over the Hawaiian Royal Palace, 1898

revolution, concluded to leave to the Hawaiian people the selection of their own form of government.

This selection was **anticipated** and prevented by the Provisional Government, who, [having] military and police power of the kingdom, so cramped the **electoral** privileges that no free expression of their will was permitted to the people who were opposed to them.

By my command and advice the native people and those in sympathy with them were restrained from rising against the government in power.

The movement undertaken by the Hawaiians last month was absolutely **commenced** without my knowledge, **sanction**,

anticipated: expected.
electoral: election.
commenced: started.
sanction: approval.

consent, or assistance, directly or indirectly; and this fact is in truth well known to those who took part in it.

I received no information from any one in regard to arms which were, or which were to be, **procured**, nor of any men who were induced, or to be induced, to join in any such uprising.

I do not know why this information should have been withheld from me, unless it was with a view to my personal safety, or as a **precautionary** measure. It would not have received my sanction; and I can assure the gentlemen of this commission that, had I known of any such intention, I would have **dissuaded** the promoters from such a venture. But I will add that, had I known, their secrets would have been mine, and **inviolately** preserved.

That I intended to change my cabinet, and to appoint certain officers of the kingdom, in the event of my restoration [to the throne], I will admit; but that I, or any one known to me, had, in part or in whole, established a new government, is not true. Before the 24th of January, 1895, the day upon which I formally abdicated, and called upon my people to recognize the Republic of Hawaii as the only lawful government of these Islands, and to support that government, I claim that I had the right to select a cabinet in **anticipation** of a possibility; and history of other governments supports this right. I was not **intimidated** into abdicating, but followed the counsel of able and generous friends and well-wishers, who advised me that such an act would restore peace and good-will among my people, **vitalize** the progress and prosperity of the Islands, and induce the actual government to deal leniently, mercifully, charitably, and **impassionately** with those who resorted to arms for the purpose of **displacing** a government in the formation of which they had no voice or control, and which they themselves had seen established by force of arms.

I acted of my own free will, and wish the world to know that I have asked no **immunity** or favor myself, nor plead my abdication as a petition for mercy. My actions were dictated by the sole aim of doing good to my beloved country, and of **alleviating** the positions and pains of those who unhappily and unwisely resorted to arms to regain an independence which they thought had been unjustly **wrested** from them.

procured: obtained.
induced: encouraged, urged.
precautionary: safeguarding.
dissuaded: advised against.
inviolately: without being disclosed or violated.
anticipation: looking forward to something.
intimidated: bullied or threatened.
vitalize: give life to.
leniently: mildly.
impassionately: with warmth and feeling.
displacing: removing.
immunity: protection.
alleviating: relieving, easing.
wrested: snatched forcibly.

As you deal with them, so I pray that the Almighty God may deal with you in your hours of trial.

To my regret much has been said about the danger which threatened foreign women and children, and about the blood-thirstiness of the Hawaiians, and the **outrages** which would have been **perpetrated** by them if they had succeeded in their attempt to overthrow the Republic government.

They who know the Hawaiian temper and disposition understand that there was no foundation for any such fears. The behavior of the rebels to those foreigners whom they captured and held shows that there was no **malignancy** in the hearts of the Hawaiians at all. It would have been sad indeed if the doctrine of the Christian missionary fathers, taught to my people by them and those who succeeded them, should have fallen like the seed in the **parable**, upon barren ground.

I must deny your right to try me in the manner and by the court which you have called together for this purpose. In your actions you violate your own constitution and laws, which are now the constitution and laws of the land.

There may be in your consciences a **warrant** for your action.... All who uphold you in this unlawful proceeding may scorn and despise my word; but the offence of breaking and setting aside for a specific purpose the laws of your own nation, and disregarding all justice and fairness, may be to them and to you the source of an unhappy and much to be regretted **legacy**.

I would ask you to consider that your government is on trial before the whole civilized world, and that in accordance with your actions and decisions will you yourselves be judged. The happiness and prosperity of Hawaii are henceforth in your hands as its rulers. You are commencing a new era in its history. May the divine Providence grant you the wisdom to lead the nation into the paths of **forbearance**, forgiveness, and peace, and to create and **consolidate** a united people ever anxious to advance in the way of civilization outlined by the American fathers of liberty and religion.

In concluding my statement I thank you for the courtesy you have shown to me, not as your former queen, but as [a] humble citizen of this land and as a woman. I assure you, who believe you are faithfully fulfilling a public duty, that I shall

outrages: acts of violence.
perpetrated: committed.
malignancy: evil.
parable: short story with a moral.
warrant: reason, justification.
legacy: something left by ancestors to new generations.
forbearance: patience.
consolidate: to join together into a whole.

never harbor any resentment or cherish any ill feeling towards you, whatever may be your decision.

Three weeks later Liliuokalani was found guilty of concealing the treasonable acts of her supporters and given the maximum penalty—a $5,000 fine and imprisonment at hard labor for five years. But the sentence was never carried out; instead, its purpose seemed to be to intimidate the native Hawaiians and humiliate their former queen. She continued to be held under house arrest until September 1895, at which time she was released on parole.

Liliuokalani was pardoned for her "crime" in February 1896. In December of that same year, eager for a change of scenery, she left Hawaii on an extended visit to the United States. While there, she went to Washington to plead her case directly with the president. By this time, however, Hawaii had taken on increased strategic importance for the United States as a result of growing conflicts with Spain over Spanish presence in the Pacific, namely in the Philippines. Independence for Hawaii was therefore no longer an option. In 1898 the United States formally annexed the islands.

Liliuokalani spent the rest of her days living quietly but comfortably in Honolulu, out of the public eye. She devoted most of her time to writing and to music. Besides composing her own songs, she made an effort to record and preserve examples of native Hawaiian music, including ancient chants detailing the creation of the world. She remains a beloved figure to her people, even after her death from a stroke in 1917.

Sources

Books

Allen, H. G., *The Betrayal of Liliuokalani*, 1983.

Liliuokalani, *Hawaii's Story by Hawaii's Queen* (autobiography; originally published in 1898), Charles E. Tuttle, 1964.

Stone, Adrienne, *Hawaii's Queen: Liliuokalani*, 1947.

Periodicals

New York Times, November 12, 1917.

Bette Bao Lord

1938–

Chinese American writer and prodemocracy/human rights activist

The path Bette Bao Lord traveled on her journey to becoming a bestselling author and respected activist has been marked by many unexpected twists and turns. She was born in Shanghai, China, to Dora and Sandys Bao. Sandys was an electrical engineer who worked for the Nationalist Chinese government. Shortly after the end of World War II, he left on an extended business trip to the United States. The Chinese government was in the market for equipment to help rebuild China, and Bao served as the nation's representative in the States. As his assignment stretched from months into a year, Bao grew lonesome for his family. In 1946 he was finally given permission to send for his wife and two of their three daughters, including eight-year-old Bette. An infant daughter, Sansan, stayed behind with relatives because her parents felt she was too young to make the long journey.

Civil War in China Exiles Family

The Baos first settled in Brooklyn, New York, where Bette was enrolled in public school. Soon after, they moved to

Teaneck, New Jersey. The family was still in the United States when civil war erupted in China between the nationalist government and communist rebels led by Mao Zedong. (The nationalists wanted to keep control of China in the hands of landowners and businesspeople; the communists wanted the country turned over to the peasantry.) By the time the communists claimed victory over the nationalists in 1949, the Baos knew that they could not return home. Mao was by that point suppressing opposition to his leadership with brutal punishments. An estimated one million—some say as many as two million—people were executed as counterrevolutionaries in the new government's first twelve months. The Baos also realized that trying to get little Sansan out of China would be dangerous if not impossible. So the rest of the family remained in New Jersey, and it was there that Bette Bao grew up.

Bao was an excellent student who was well-liked by her classmates. She graduated from high school in 1954 and went on to college at Tufts University in Boston, Massachusetts. As she once explained to a Chicago Tribune reporter, her original intention was to major in chemistry, because "every Chinese child is supposed to grow up to be an '-ist,' as in scientist." But both she and her professors agreed that she would probably be happier in another field. So she switched to history and earned her bachelor's degree in 1959. The following year she obtained her master's degree in international relations from the Fletcher School of Law and Diplomacy, which is part of Tufts.

Bao then headed to the University of Hawaii. There she served as an assistant to the director of the school's East-West Center. Within a short time, however, she had been named head of her own department. Bao left Hawaii in 1961 for a job in Washington, D.C., as an advisor to the director of the Fulbright Exchange Program (a scholarship program that encourages cross-cultural education). She then became reacquainted with a former Tufts classmate, Winston Lord, who was a member of the U.S. Foreign Service (the government's staff of diplomats). They were married in 1963.

Recounts Her Sister's Life Story in First Novel

Meanwhile, Sansan Bao—who had been separated from her family for more than fifteen years—was finally allowed to leave China when she convinced authorities that she had to visit her sick mother in Hong Kong. However, the "illness" was just a trick that enabled the Baos to help Sansan escape to America. Friends who were familiar with her story—a lifetime of hardship under the communist regime in China and her eventual reunion with her family—thought her biography could be the basis of a fascinating book. Bette agreed, and when she couldn't find anyone else to take on the project—the fact that her sister spoke no English was a major obstacle—she quit her job and tackled it herself. The result was Eighth Moon: The True Story of a Young Girl's Life in Communist China. *Published by Harper in 1964, it enjoyed tremendous success with both readers and critics.*

From 1965 until 1967 Bette Bao Lord taught and performed modern dance in Geneva, Switzerland, where her husband was posted as a member of a U.S. negotiating team discussing taxes on international trade. Not long after their return home, Winston Lord joined the administration of President Richard Nixon as a top aide to foreign policy advisor Henry Kissinger. He was very much involved in the events leading up to official U.S. recognition of communist China in 1972.

The following year Lord accompanied her husband on a journey to the land of her birth—her first visit since she had left there as a child. Her impressions of modern China eventually found their way into a historical novel entitled Spring Moon, *which she worked on during the late 1970s. Like her first book, it was a hit with both readers and critics and was nominated for a National Book Award.*

Returns to China as U.S. Ambassador's Wife

In 1985 the Lords returned to China when Winston was named U.S. ambassador. There Bette Bao Lord once again devoted herself to cultural activities. She became active in local theater and turned the American Embassy in Beijing into a meeting place for writers and artists.

Lord also provided valuable assistance to her husband as a sort of unofficial diplomat, guiding him through what proved to be an especially turbulent time in Chinese history. Just as his term was coming to an end during the spring of 1989, student-led **prodemocracy** demonstrations erupted in at least twenty major cities, including Beijing. Although Winston Lord had to return to Washington in April, his wife stayed behind and provided commentary on the unfolding events for CBS News and Newsweek magazine. She left China just days before the June 4 massacre in Tiananmen Square—a massacre that brought the protests to a sudden and violent end. (See box for more information.)

The horrors experienced by so many of those who shared dreams of a brighter future for China forced Lord to take action. Shortly after her return to the United States, she wrote the nonfiction book Legacies: A Chinese Mosaic. The work is a selection of oral histories she had gathered while living in China—histories she hoped would "put faces and stories with what happened there [in Tiananmen Square]." Like her previous works, it was very well received.

Allies Herself with Human Rights Movement

The events of Tiananmen Square also marked the beginning of Lord's involvement with the human rights movement. In 1991 she joined the board of directors of Freedom House, a New York City-based organization cofounded during the 1940s by Eleanor Roosevelt, the wife of President Franklin Roosevelt. It monitors and works for human rights around the world while promoting democracy as the key to preserving those rights. Two years after linking up with Freedom House, Lord became its chair.

Lord appeared in Washington, D.C., in connection with her role at Freedom House to speak before the Foreign Affairs Committee of the U.S. House of Representatives on March 10, 1993. There she offered her views on the role of U.S. foreign policy in strengthening human rights and democracy around the world.

In the written statement that accompanied her testimony, Lord makes it clear that she regards American-style democracy as "the most successful model for **nurturing** a **vibrant**

prodemocracy: favoring government by the people.

nurturing: developing, cultivating.

vibrant: full of life.

Tiananmen Square Massacre

For several weeks in the spring of 1989, the eyes of the world were focused on China as thousands of prodemocracy demonstrators peacefully challenged the country's leaders to end government corruption and allow freedom of speech and freedom of the press. The mass movement had begun to take shape in mid-April following the death on April 15 of former Communist party chairman Hu Yaobang. Many reform-minded Chinese (especially university students) looked upon him as a hero because he had always been sympathetic to their calls for change. But what started out as a series of memorial services and demonstrations soon turned to horror.

A few days after students began holding protests in Beijing and several other Chinese cities, on April 20, 1989, the government ordered the demonstrators to stop their marches and rallies. The students ignored the order, and before long workers and professionals from all walks of life were joining in the call for reform.

In mid-May, former Soviet president Mikhail Gorbachev—who was at that time leading the reform movement in his own country—arrived in Beijing on an official state visit. Chinese demonstrators hailed him as a political revolutionary. They held marches and launched a hunger strike that quickly attracted several thousand participants. By May 17, about a million people were packed into Beijing's massive Tiananmen Square, and similar antigovernment activities were taking place elsewhere across China. On May 20, Chinese officials responded to the growing unrest by declaring **martial law** and demanding that the students leave Tiananmen Square. But for two weeks, Chinese leaders argued over whether to take a hard-line approach or to negotiate with the demonstrators and showed little sign of aggression.

From the time that martial law was first declared, army troops from nearby bases had been moving into Beijing. By and large, their contacts with demonstrators in Tiananmen Square, whose number by early June had dropped to about ten thousand, and others living in the city were friendly and respectful.

martial law: a state in which law and order is maintained through the use of military forces rather than the police, usually in response to an emergency situation.

neo-isolationism: a country's new or revived policy of staying out of international economic and political affairs.

disengagement: withdrawal.

society, responsive government, a free press, effective unions, domestic harmony and global cooperation." At the same time, she condemns "**neo-isolationism** and **disengagement** from world affairs" now that communism no longer appears to be a worldwide threat. As Lord noted: "In the end, the true power of America is its ideas."

Lord's oral statement to the members of the House Foreign Affairs Committee is excerpted here from The Future of U.S. Foreign Policy (Part II): Functional Issues—Hearings

The students felt relaxed enough to build a 35-foot-tall replica of the Statue of Liberty, which they named the "Goddess of Democracy." She stood in Tiananmen Square as a powerful symbol of their struggle.

The hard-liners in the government won out, though. Local soldiers were quickly replaced by combat troops from a rural area of China's Mongolia region. They had no personal ties to the capital city—they didn't even speak the same dialect as Beijing's residents—and they showed little inclination to side with the protesters.

During the early morning hours of June 4, the combat troops crashed through student barricades into Tiananmen Square with tanks, armored personnel carriers, and automatic weapons. They opened fire on the panic-stricken crowd of demonstrators and charged others with bayonets, reportedly running over the bodies of the dead and wounded with their vehicles and setting fire to the remains. Moving from the square and into the streets of Beijing to follow those who had fled the massacre, the soldiers began randomly firing into buildings and shooting unarmed civilians.

Student leader on a hunger strike at Tiananmen Square, May 16, 1989

By the time the bloodshed ended later that day, some three to five thousand people were dead (the exact number will probably never be known) and thousands more were injured. Hundreds of students and workers were eventually arrested, and many were executed or imprisoned. Others were forced to go into hiding or flee the country.

Before the Committee on Foreign Affairs, House of Representatives, *103rd Congress, 1st Session, U.S. Government Printing Office, 1993.*

As an immigrant, I have a singular honor to testify before this committee. As the chairman of Freedom House, I have the opportunity to speak on behalf of a **bipartisan**, nonprofit

bipartisan: involving members of two political parties, in this case the Democratic and Republican parties.

organization ... on the subject that is our reason for being, promoting democracy and human rights.

While my written statement addresses your important questions in a more **orthodox** way, permit me to speak personally. I do so to provide a different perspective, one that native-born Americans cannot offer naturally. Taught to question every **premise**, they do not **flinch** from **dissecting**

orthodox: traditional.

premise: assumption.

flinch: withdraw.

dissecting: separating into pieces; analyzing.

Bette Bao Lord

America's failings. It is a most admirable trait. But such clinical probes overlook the **intangibles** through which people living in distant lands **discern** America. I know. I am able to disappear among them and **eavesdrop.**

To the masses denied dignity by their rulers America is not just another country with material goods that they **covet.** It is the **embodiment** of intangibles—liberty, conscience, hope....

I recall how curious my Chinese friends were watching our presidential debates, but what they viewed as an earth-shaking phenomenon totally escaped even me. They were awestruck by the fact that a lowly TV journalist—apologies to Dan [Rather of CBS], Tom [Brokaw of NBC], and Peter [Jennings of ABC]—could politely, but in no uncertain terms, tell the **paramount** leader of the most powerful nation in the world that his time was up.

How **confounding,** just when technology and humanity's newest trials **mock** walls, borders, and oceans, some **extol** the **efficacy** of withdrawing to our shores or, worse, ethnically correct **enclaves.** Just when human rights, however mislabeled or mangled, must be given **lip service** by even the most **repressive** regimes, some Americans **balk** at **invoking** them at all. Just when there is but one superpower left, some question America's need to stay **engaged.**

How ironic, just when **totalitarian** states have **imploded** and democracy holds sway among more peoples than ever before, Americans are losing faith in the wisdom of promoting freedom and human rights abroad.

Some wonder if certain peoples will always be incapable or **averse** to ruling themselves. They fail to acknowledge that no man or woman has ever aspired to be a **pawn.** On the contrary, regardless of culture and history, everyone yearns to be the master of his or her own fate.

Some consider it culturally **chauvinistic** to project our own values elsewhere. They fail to understand that freedom is not a matter of "Westernization," it is the core of modernization. They also fail to recognize that human rights are not made in America, that they are universal, that every nation belonging to the United Nations has pledged to honor them, that international organizations ... invoke them in their work.

intangibles: things that cannot be perceived through the senses (especially the sense of touch).

discern: understand.

eavesdrop: listen secretly.

covet: desire.

embodiment: representation in solid form.

paramount: supreme; chief.

confounding: puzzling, frustrating.

mock: scorn, make fun of.

extol: praise.

efficacy: effectiveness.

enclaves: culturally distinct areas within a larger territory.

lip service: a pledge of support or approval that consists simply of words and no action.

repressive: using force to curb people's natural rights, especially the right to self-expression.

balk: refuse abruptly.

invoking: calling upon, mentioning.

engaged: involved.

totalitarian: exercising unlimited power.

imploded: exploded inward, collapsed.

averse: opposed.

pawn: a person who can be used by others for their own purposes.

chauvinistic: inclined to feel excessively superior to something or someone else.

Some fret that promoting democracy and human rights is a luxury we can ill afford. They fail to understand that this pursuit not only serves our values but [our] interests. Spreading democracy not only warms American hearts but cools foreign threats. What hundreds of billions [of dollars] worth of arms failed to do, rallies of converts did. Gone, the Berlin Wall, gone, the Warsaw Pact. [The Berlin Wall stood for nearly thirty years in Germany as a barrier between communist East Berlin and democratic West Berlin. The Warsaw Pact refers to the alliance of nations of eastern Europe and the former Soviet Union created to oppose NATO, which was the alliance of nations of western Europe and the United States.] Democracies do not war against one another, democracies make better partners. Democracies do not ignore the environment, shelter terrorists, or **spawn** refugees. Democracies honor human rights.

Now, for the third time in this century, destiny calls. [The first two calls were for American involvement in World War I and World War II.] America must step forth. We must earn the right to enjoy our **myriad** blessings. I speak about only two. First, the **vitality** of Americans. Where does it come from? From everywhere.... We are the world. Second, the **stature** of America. Believe me, despite all the **venom** the most **arrogant** dictators may spew they care profoundly where Uncle Sam points a finger, shakes hands, or pats them on the back. They hate losing face, but they crave respectability.

Thus, vitality and stature **endow** America with extraordinary gifts for making a difference in the world. Like liberty, conscience [and] hope, they are intangibles. To be true to our legacy, to enrich our future, America must invest in freedom.

99

In 1996 Lord released a novel titled The Middle Heart, *published by Knopf. It focuses on events in modern China from the 1930s through the Cultural Revolution of the 1960s (the elimination of old culture, customs, and ideas from the Chinese way of life) and the events at Tiananmen Square in 1989.*

Sources

Books

Fox, Mary Virginia, *Bette Bao Lord: Novelist and Chinese Voice for Change,* Childrens Press, 1993.

The Future of U.S. Foreign Policy (Part II): Functional Issues—Hearings Before the Committee on Foreign Affairs, House of Representatives,

spawn: produce.
myriad: many different.
vitality: being full of life; the capacity to live and develop.
stature: position or rank in relation to others.
venom: poison; ill will.
arrogant: overly proud or self-important.

103rd Congress, 1st Session, U.S. Government Printing Office, 1993, pp. 260–61, 312–19.

Lord, Bette Bao, *Legacies: A Chinese Mosaic,* Knopf, 1990.

Newsmakers: 1994 Cumulation, Gale, 1995.

Notable Asian Americans, Gale, 1995.

Periodicals

Chicago Tribune, June 3, 1990.

Economist, "Battering at the Gate of Heavenly Peace," May 27, 1989, pp. 31–32.

Maclean's, "A Bloodbath in Beijing," June 12, 1989, pp. 22–23; "The Terror Now," June 19, 1989, pp. 24–27; "Legacy of a Massacre," June 18, 1990, pp. 32–33.

Nation, "Who Died in Beijing, and Why," June 11, 1990, pp. 811–22.

National Review, "China Devours Its Children," August 4, 1989, pp. 28–31.

Newsweek, "These People Have No Fear," May 29, 1989, p. 29; "Beijing Bloodbath," June 12, 1989, pp. 24–29; "'Warn Americans Not to Be Fooled,'" June 12, 1989, p. 28; "Reign of Terror," June 19, 1989, pp. 14–22; "Walking in Lucky Shoes," July 6, 1992, p. 10.

New York Times, February 5, 1993; "Leader of '89 Beijing Protest Faces Conspiracy Charges," October 13, 1996.

Time, "The Wrath of Deng," June 19, 1989, pp. 18–21.

Robert T. Matsui

1941–

*Japanese American attorney and member
of the U.S. House of Representatives*

Democrat Robert T. Matsui is one of the most powerful and respected politicians in Washington, D.C. He has represented his Sacramento, California-area district in the House of Representatives since 1978. An acknowledged leader in such areas as trade, taxes, social security, health care, and welfare reform, he also played a key role in obtaining justice for the thousands of Japanese Americans held prisoner in detention camps during World War II. For Matsui and his family, who were among those affected by the forced relocation, it was one of the most personally satisfying victories of his congressional career.

An Infant in the Internment Camp

Matsui was born in Sacramento to parents who were also American-born but of Japanese ancestry. He was only several months old when Japan and the United States went to war after the bombing of the naval base at Pearl Harbor, Hawaii, on December 7, 1941. Just a couple of months later, on February 19, 1942, President Franklin Roosevelt

"THE DECISION WE MAKE TODAY REALLY IS NOT A DECISION TO GIVE $20,000 TO THE 66,000 SURVIVING AMERICANS, THE DECISION TODAY IS TO UPHOLD THAT BEAUTIFUL, WONDERFUL DOCUMENT, THE CONSTITUTION OF THE UNITED STATES."

issued Executive Order 9066. (Also see entries on **Daniel K. Inouye, Spark M. Matsunaga, Norman Y. Mineta,** and **Clifford I. Uyeda.**) This controversial order called for the evacuation of some 120,000 Japanese Americans—supposedly for their own "protection"—from the West Coast to "relocation centers" in remote areas of nearly two dozen states, including Arizona, Arkansas, inland California, Colorado, Idaho, Utah, and Wyoming. (A number of smaller camps were also set up in fourteen other states.) About two-thirds of the people taken to those centers were U.S. citizens. Japanese Americans in other parts of the country were not affected by the order, and no similar action was taken against German Americans or Italian Americans, even though the United States was also at war with Germany and Italy.

Like most others in their situation, the Matsuis were given very little time to prepare for their evacuation—just two or three days. Mr. Matsui sold the family home for $50 and abandoned his small produce business so that he, his wife, and infant son could leave for their assigned camp in northern California. They were later transferred to Idaho and forbidden to return to Sacramento until World War II ended.

Although Matsui himself was too young to have any memories of that sad and difficult time, he vividly recalls the impact it had on his parents. They were always reluctant to discuss their experiences, and they felt a lasting sense of shame for having had their loyalty to the United States questioned. Seeing them so hurt and confused—even though they had done nothing wrong—later motivated their son to seek redress (repayment or compensation) for all who had been treated so unjustly by their own government.

Matsui's college years were spent at the University of California at Berkeley, from which he received a degree in political science in 1963. Inspired by the example of Clarence Darrow (1857–1938), an attorney famous for defending clients who supported unpopular or controversial causes, he then decided to become a lawyer so that he, too, could "protect the underdog." Matsui fulfilled his dream in 1966 upon his graduation from the Hastings College of Law. Before long *he had established a private practice in his hometown and was involved in various civic and cultural activities.*

Enters Politics

Ever since hearing John F. Kennedy's words in his 1961 inaugural address "Ask not what your country can do for you—ask what you can do for your country," Matsui had thought about running for public office. So in 1971 he ran for and won a seat on the Sacramento City Council. He was reelected in 1975 and became vice mayor of Sacramento in 1977.

A year later he decided to run for the U.S. House of Representatives. Matsui trailed two other Democratic candidates early in the race. But then he went into action, calling upon the networking skills and local, grassroots support that had earned him his city council position. In the end he was able to overtake his opponents in the primary. He later defeated his Republican challenger in the general election. By the late 1990s the voters had returned him to office eight more times by wide margins.

*Since arriving in Washington, D.C., Matsui has distinguished himself as one of the most respected and powerful legislators on Capitol Hill. In general, he takes a **liberal** stand on social issues and a more **conservative** approach to business issues. He is a member of the influential House Ways and Means Committee (specifically its subcommittees on trade and human resources), which helps decide how the government will raise and spend the money it needs to run. As such he has played key roles in drafting policies regarding U.S. trade negotiations.*

Matsui is also recognized as a champion of issues that have a particular impact on children, especially those living in poverty. He has, for example, fought to include money in the federal budget for programs designed to prevent child abuse and neglect and to help keep families together. In addition, he has introduced welfare reform legislation that encourages people receiving assistance to find work. And he has been outspoken on the need to make health insurance for children a national priority.

liberal: tending to be tolerant of different views, to embrace changes for the better, and to support government reform when necessary.

conservative: more inclined to follow tradition rather than seek change.

Leads the Clinton Administration's Fight for NAFTA

In 1993 President Bill Clinton picked Matsui to lead the administration's fight for the passage of the North American Free Trade Agreement (NAFTA). The goal of this controversial measure was to reduce trade barriers between the United States and its nearest neighbors, Canada and Mexico. Many people who were opposed to NAFTA feared it would lead to a massive loss of jobs in the United States. Others thought that U.S. environmental protection standards might be relaxed to accommodate different practices elsewhere, especially in Mexico.

To "sell" NAFTA to a doubt-filled Congress, Matsui pulled together a bipartisan (two-party) team of fellow legislators, past and present cabinet secretaries, scholars, business leaders, and environmentalists. The representative himself made numerous appearances on television news shows to present arguments in favor of the agreement to the American public. His efforts ultimately paid off when he was able to win congressional approval for NAFTA. It was a significant victory for the new Clinton administration and further confirmation of Matsui's political skills.

Before his high-profile position in the NAFTA debate, however, Matsui was already known for his staunch support of what was called the "redress movement." The aim of this movement was to obtain compensation for Japanese Americans whose constitutional rights were ignored in the rush to round up "enemy aliens" during World War II.

Introduces Bill Proposing a Study of Japanese American Internment

On September 28, 1979, along with fellow Japanese American congressional representative **Norman Y. Mineta** and others, Matsui became one of the cosponsors of H.R. 5499. This bill proposed creating a commission to investigate the wartime relocation of Japanese Americans and determine what, if any, compensation was owed to them for the losses they had suffered both emotionally and economically. A Senate version of the bill, S. 1647, passed in mid-1980 and was signed into law. A year later the new Commission on Wartime Relocation and Internment of Civilians

(CWRIC) began holding hearings to gather testimony. Eventually, more than seven hundred people went on the record with their recollections and opinions, including Matsui.

In 1983 the CWRIC published a report of its findings titled Personal Justice Denied. *In this report, members of the commission condemned the relocation of Japanese Americans as a measure undertaken not for military reasons but out of "race prejudice, war hysteria and a failure of political leadership." They later issued several recommendations for redress. For one, they suggested that Congress and the president apologize to Japanese Americans and acknowledge the injustice that had been done to them as a result of Executive Order 9066. They also advised paying $20,000 to each of the estimated sixty thousand survivors of the camps.*

Several years of debate followed. Most of the opposition centered on the notion of awarding monetary damages to former prisoners. Some questioned the fairness of holding present-day taxpayers responsible for wrongs committed decades earlier. They feared that approving such payments would open the door to similar claims from African Americans and other groups who had faced injustice at some time in U.S. history.

Matsui presented his case in support of redress on several occasions during the 1980s at various hearings. On June 20, 1984, he appeared before the Subcommittee on Administrative Law and Governmental Relations of the House Committee on the Judiciary. This particular subcommittee was considering legislation to adopt the CWRIC's recommendations. His testimony is excerpted from the official government transcript Japanese-American and Aleutian Wartime Relocation: Hearings Before the Subcommittee on Administrative Law and Governmental Relations of the Committee on the Judiciary, House of Representatives, 98th Congress, 2nd Session, U.S. Government Printing Office, 1985.

The topic before us is of tremendous importance for our system of constitutional liberty....

[Former President] William Howard Taft reminded us that "constitutions are checks on the hasty actions of the majority." Today we are faced with the memory of a time when our system failed to provide the necessary checks, when hasty actions trampled over the rights of 120,000 people, most of whom were citizens of this country.

But today we have the opportunity to restore the system to its proper balance. With legislative action, we can at last provide redress to Americans of Japanese ancestry who were deprived of their basic civil rights during World War II.

For me, and I know this is true for many others here, this issue is **endowed** with strong personal memories. I was a mere ten months old when I entered the internment camp at Tule Lake with my family. Like so many of those interned, my parents were proud citizens of the United States, a country they had known to be just and ruled by a reasoned constitutional law.

But with Executive Order 9066, my parents' citizenship and loyalty suddenly meant nothing. The exclusion and detention order recognized ancestry and only ancestry. That they were born in this country—my mother in 1920 and my father in 1916, in Sacramento, California—[that they] upheld its laws and were loyal to its principles, [these facts were] discarded as **irrelevant**.

What was the experience of that camp? It's interesting, because my parents, prior to the formation of the Commission that the Congress set up, refused to talk about it. I never could understand why. It was not until the last twenty-four months that I became appreciative of their own situation. For my parents, there was the discouraging loss of business, home, and other possessions.

My father had just begun a private **produce** business with his brother. Of course, that was lost. They had a home in which they had been living for about six months. That was lost. They sold their refrigerator and other worldly possessions for $5 or $10, whatever they could receive from the person who would knock on their door and say, "I know you have to leave within a short period of time and, therefore, I'll give you $5 for the refrigerator" or whatever it happened to be.

endowed: loaded.

irrelevant: having no bearing on the matter at hand; not applicable to the discussion.

produce: fresh fruits and vegetables.

They also have visions of barbed-wire fences and **sentry** dogs, of loss of privacy and lack of adequate sanitation, and memories of the heart-wrenching divisions that occurred as families were separated by physical distance and the emotional distress of the camps.

I might add, however, that my family was somewhat fortunate. After nine months at Tule Lake, we were able to move on to a farm labor area in Idaho. Although there were no soldiers or watchtowers, we remained within restricted boundaries, unable to return to our home in California for three more years.

But what is most striking about all of these internment camp stories … is the faith and hope that remained, faith in the law of the land, pride in this country, and most of all, a sincere desire to prove loyalty to this great nation and be allowed to

Elderly Japanese American men weeding onions at Tule Lake camp in California, 1943

sentry: guard.

serve its ideals and principles. All this, despite the fact that basic constitutional and civil rights were being denied to them and others in their position.

It is the spirit of this faith that brings me here before you today, for I firmly believe that our actions here are essential for giving credibility to our constitutional system and reinforcing our traditional sense of justice.

As you will hear today from the Commission on Wartime Relocation and Internment of Civilians, there is no question that basic, civil rights were denied. There was no review of individual cases and no exceptions or considerations of personal service. The basic concept of **habeas corpus** was forgotten....

As you hear more from the witnesses in the next few days, it will be clear that constitutional rights were just simply ignored. For my part, I would like to leave the subcommittee with one simple thought: because justice was denied, there certainly is a need for redress. The question before us must be to provide the most appropriate form of redress for this tragic episode in our nation's history.

As a lawmaker involved in framing the redress legislation, I will not [personally] accept monetary reparations, because to do so would lead some to suggest my actions are motivated by self-interest. They certainly are not. I am convinced that monetary compensation must be a part of any redress effort. Estimates of losses from income and property alone would account for the sum requested by the bill. Such estimates do not include disruption of careers, long-term loss of opportunity, and the tremendous personal losses from the denial of freedom and the **stigma** of being interned and being considered disloyal to one's country. These are the types of issues considered when awarding damages.

 But the logic of compensation goes far beyond simple economics.... [It] stress[es] the notion of accountability. If we make it absolutely clear that people will be held accountable for their actions, we can hope to deter such actions in the future. When the actions are taken by our government, it is particularly important to stress that we will hold it accountable....

Some will argue that there were **extenuating circumstances**, that our government acted in what is believed to be in

habeas corpus: a legal order that may be issued to bring a jailed person before a court or judge to determine if he or she is being held lawfully (intended to prevent people from being imprisoned without "just cause," or without good reason).

stigma: a mark of shame or disgrace.

accountability: responsibility.

extenuating circumstances: special conditions that can excuse certain behavior or actions or make them seem less serious.

Robert T. Matsui

everyone's best interest. But I must contend that nothing a government does is inherently above the law. All actions, including those of our leaders, must be subject to the **constraints** established by our U.S. Constitution.

War is a period of extreme national stress. It is during such periods of stress that the survival of liberty is at its most **fragile** point. We must try to tailor our safeguards to fit these **treacherous** moments.

Our task now is to provide the final legal redress and reinforce our system of justice and equity. We must remind future generations that such a tragic denial of rights must not and will not be tolerated ever again....

I personally would like to thank you for holding these hearings. I know, from some of the mail I have received, the kind of situation you have placed yourselves in just by merely holding these hearings—the fact that there are some people who have attempted to **equate** what happened to me and my family and others in my position with what happened at Pearl Harbor during World War II.... I know that you are probably receiving a lot of hate type mail. But the mere fact that you have decided to hold these hearings indicates to me that our system does work and that there are opportunities for all Americans, **irrespective** of our race, our color, creed, or religious background....

99

Although H.R. 4110 did not make it to the House floor in 1984, a revised version of it—known as H.R. 442—finally did come up for a vote on September 17, 1987. It proposed that the CWRIC's recommendations be adopted, including the provision for awarding monetary damages to Japanese Americans who were interned. This was a major sticking point for some legislators, especially Republican Dan Lungren of California, who had been a member of the CWRIC. He opposed the idea that the present generation of taxpayers should be held responsible for injustices committed decades earlier. He also felt that the approval of such payments might encourage similar demands from African Americans and other minority

constraints: limits.
fragile: delicate, breakable.
treacherous: characterized by disloyalty, hidden dangers, or a violation of trust.
equate: compare.
irrespective: regardless.

groups who were wronged in the past. Lungren proposed an amendment to the bill that would have eliminated all payments to the Japanese Americans.

Along with Representative Mineta, who delivered an emotional plea of his own in favor of the bill, Matsui spoke movingly of his reasons for supporting H.R. 442. He urged his fellow legislators to approve it in its entirety, including the part that awarded compensation to former Japanese American prisoners of the United States. His remarks during that debate are excerpted here from the Congressional Record, 100th Congress, 1st Session, U.S. Government Printing Office, 1988.

This is a very difficult issue for me to speak on today, mainly because it is, I guess, so personal and perhaps some of you may think that I may lack **objectivity.** That may very well be the case. But I will try to be objective.

I would like if I may for a moment, however, to indicate to all of you perhaps what it was like to be an American citizen in 1942 if you happened to be of Japanese ancestry.

My mother and father, who were in their twenties, were both born and raised in Sacramento, California, so they were American citizens by birth. They were trying to start their careers. They had a child.... They had a home like any other American. They had a car. My father had a little produce business with his brother.

For some reason, because of Pearl Harbor, in 1942 their lives and their futures were shattered. They were given seventy-two hours' notice that they had to leave their home, their neighborhood, abandon their business, and show up at the Memorial Auditorium, which is in the heart of Sacramento, and then be taken—like cattle—in trains to the Tule Lake Internment Camp.

My father was not able to talk about this subject for over forty years.... I really did not even understand what had happened until the 1980s.... [He] finally [told me], "You know what the problem is, why I can't discuss this issue, is because I was in one of those internment camps, a prisoner of war camp,

objectivity: the ability to base judgments on fact and not on one's own opinions, emotions, or interpretations.

and if I talk about it the first thing I have to say is look, I wasn't guilty, I was loyal to my country, because the **specter** of disloyalty attaches to anybody who was in those camps."

And that stigma exists today on every one of those ... Americans of Japanese ancestry who happened to have lived in one of those camps.

specter: ghost.

They were in that camp for three and a half years of their lives and, yes, they have gotten out and they have made great Americans of themselves, and I think if my mother were alive today she would be very proud of what the U.S. Congress hopefully is about to do. Because the decision we make today really is not a decision to give $20,000 to the 66,000 surviving Americans [of the original 120,000 imprisoned], the decision today is to uphold that beautiful, wonderful document, the Constitution of the United States.

You know, because this is the 200th celebration [today, September 17, 1987], we have been talking about those fifty-five individuals who put together [the Constitution], and I do not think there is any question that there was some Supreme Being that gave them the inspiration to put that document together.... It is only because of the American people that that document is a living document with meaning, not only 200 years ago, but for 200 years in the future as well.

The real issue here today is an issue of fundamental principle. How could I, as a ... child born in this country, be declared by my own government to be an enemy alien? How can my mother and father, who were born in this country, also be declared a potential enemy ... to their country? That is the underlying issue here. They did not go before a court of law, they did not know what charges were filed against them. They were just told, "You have three days to pack and be **incarcerated.**" That is the fundamental issue here.

Now I would like to just, if I may, discuss some of the principles that were raised by the proponents of the Lungren amendment just for a moment.

The gentleman from Minnesota said, "Why should today's generation pay for the tragedies of the past generation?" I do not look upon America in terms of generations.... We are not talking about a generation in the 1940s and a generation today. We are talking about fundamental principles because the Constitution does not change from generation to generation. It is a living document that exists forever, for eternity. So it is not a question of generations.

I know that some would say, "Well, we as Americans in time of war have responsibilities, and everybody suffers in

incarcerated: confined or imprisoned.

time of war." You know, that is true. Ron Packard from California gave an eloquent presentation of the fact that his father had been incarcerated during World War II by the Japanese government, a prisoner of war. Many families lost their husbands and their sons and many families were broken because of tragedies like divorce because of the separations. Everybody suffers during times of war, so why should not the Japanese Americans also share in that suffering? Let me say this: every one of us, if war were declared today, would volunteer to fight on behalf of our country and our democracy; that is a fundamental principle.... That is a fundamental responsibility of a democracy, a fundamental responsibility of our government, that if our security is jeopardized we have a responsibility to defend it.

We have a responsibility to die for our country, but I tell you one thing, that in a democracy—this democracy with our Constitution—a citizen does not have a responsibility ... to be incarcerated by our own government without charges, without trial, merely because of our race. That is what our constitutional fathers meant 200 years ago when they wrote the Bill of Rights....

I hope that each and every one of the members will find it in their hearts to look at this issue not as an individual tragedy for 60,000 Americans of Japanese ancestry but look at it in terms of the real meaning of this country. We are celebrating 200 years of a great democracy, and I think we can today uphold and renew that democracy with a vote in favor of this bill and a vote against the **pending** [Lungren] amendment.

Thanks in large measure to the pleas of Matsui and his colleague, Representative Mineta, H.R. 442 was approved in a landslide vote, including the part that awarded payments to survivors of the camps. The Senate went on to pass its version of the proposal—known as the Civil Liberties Act of 1988—in April 1988. President Ronald Reagan signed it into law that August.

pending: not yet decided; awaiting a vote.

Sources

Books

Bosworth, Allan R., *America's Concentration Camps,* Norton, 1967.

Congressional Record, 100th Congress, 1st Session, U.S. Government Printing Office, 1988.

Daniels, Roger, *The Politics of Prejudice: The Anti-Japanese Movement in California and the Struggle for Japanese Exclusion,* University of California Press, 1962.

Daniels, Roger, *Concentration Camps USA: Japanese Americans and World War II,* Holt, 1972.

Daniels, Roger, *Asian America: Chinese and Japanese in the United States Since 1850,* University of Washington Press, 1988.

Girdner, Audrie, and Anne Loftis, *The Great Betrayal: The Evacuation of the Japanese Americans During World War II,* Macmillan, 1969.

Grodzins, Morton M., *Americans Betrayed: Politics and the Japanese Evacuation,* University of Chicago Press, 1949.

Hosokawa, Bill, *Nisei: The Quiet Americans,* Morrow, 1969.

Hosokawa, Bill, *JACL: In Quest of Justice,* Morrow, 1982.

Japanese-American and Aleutian Wartime Relocation: Hearings Before the Subcommittee on Administrative Law and Governmental Relations of the Committee on the Judiciary, House of Representatives, 98th Congress, 2nd Session, U.S. Government Printing Office, 1985.

The Japanese American Incarceration: A Case for Redress (booklet), 3rd edition, edited by Clifford I. Uyeda, National Committee for Redress of the Japanese American Citizens League, 1980.

Personal Justice Denied: Report of the Commission on Wartime Relocation and Internment of Civilians, U.S. Government Printing Office, 1983.

tenBroek, Jacobus, Edward N. Barnhart, and Floyd W. Matson, *Prejudice, War and the Constitution,* University of California Press, 1954.

Periodicals

A. Magazine, "Power Brokers," fall 1993, pp. 25–34; "The Power of Two," fall 1993.

Christian Science Monitor, "Japanese Americans Detained in WWII Have Hope of Redress," September 16, 1987.

Los Angeles Times, "House Votes to Pay Japanese WWII Internees," September 18, 1981.

New York Times, "Seeking Redress for an Old Wrong," September 17, 1987; "House Votes Payments to Japanese War Internees," September 18, 1987.

San Francisco Examiner, "House OKs Reparations for Internees," September 18, 1987.

Time, "The Burden of Shame," September 28, 1987, p. 31.

Washington Post, "House Votes Apology, Reparations for Japanese Americans Held During War," September 18, 1987.

Spark M. Matsunaga

1916–1990

Japanese American member of the U.S. Senate

"WITHOUT BEING CHARGED OR INDICTED, WITHOUT TRIAL OR HEARING, WITHOUT BEING CONVICTED OF A SINGLE CRIME, [JAPANESE AMERICANS] WERE EN MASSE ORDERED INTO WHAT CAN ONLY BE DESCRIBED AS AMERICAN-STYLE CONCENTRATION CAMPS...."

As one who was very familiar with the devastating effects of war, Spark M. Matsunaga made peace the focus of his career in the United States Senate. For nearly twenty years, he tried to persuade his colleagues to establish a cabinet-level Department of Peace as well as a National Academy of Peace and Conflict Resolution. While Matsunaga knew that his dream faced a tough uphill climb, he pursued it until the end of his days. "This is a nation which is built upon men who have dared to do the impossible," he once declared. "I feel that we must show the world that peace can be a way of life...."

Along with his zeal for ending war, Matsunaga sought redress for a particular group of war victims: the 120,000 people of Japanese descent who were unjustly incarcerated in the United States during World War II. It was a hard-fought battle, but Matsunaga and those who fought with him prevailed.

War Reshapes Young Man's Future

Matsunaga was born in Hawaii to parents who had immigrated from Japan. He and his brothers and sisters grew up in extreme poverty. Yet their parents passed along the belief that hard work would bring them success.

As a result, Matsunaga held a variety of jobs while he was still in high school. He also worked his way through the University of Hawaii, from which he graduated with honors in 1941. Postponing his plans to go on to law school, he joined the U.S. Army and was made a second lieutenant. But on December 7 of that year, Japan bombed the American naval base at Hawaii's Pearl Harbor, bringing the United States into World War II.

In the weeks and months following the attack, Japanese Americans became targets of prejudice and fear, as some questioned their loyalty to America. The greatest blow occurred on February 19, 1942, when President Franklin Roosevelt issued Executive Order 9066. (Also see entries on **Daniel K. Inouye, Robert T. Matsui, Norman Y. Mineta,** and **Clifford I. Uyeda.**) It called for the evacuation of some 120,000 Japanese Americans (about two-thirds of whom were U.S. citizens) from the West Coast to large "relocation centers" in isolated areas of Arizona, Arkansas, inland California, Colorado, Idaho, Utah, and Wyoming. A number of smaller camps were also set up in other states.

Imprisoned with Other Japanese Americans

For the most part, Japanese Americans who were not living on the West Coast were not affected by Executive Order 9066. As a member of the military, however, Matsunaga was looked at with suspicion—even though he had given no cause for anyone to doubt his loyalty to America. He, too, was shipped off to an internment camp in Wisconsin.

Many young Japanese American men wanted the chance to fight for their country and prove their loyalty. Before long, a number of them (including prisoners such as Matsunaga) began asking the U.S. government to allow them to serve in the armed forces. Finally, in January 1943, the War Department announced that it would accept fifteen hundred Japanese American volunteers for a new unit, the 442nd

Regimental Combat Team. Matsunaga joined up and fought for the 100th Infantry Battalion in Italy, where he was wounded twice. The now-legendary 442nd went on to become the most decorated unit in U.S. military history. Matsunaga himself returned home as a captain with many medals and commendations.

Political Goal of Furthering Peace

After the war, Matsunaga headed to Harvard University in Massachusetts, where he earned his law degree in 1951. Returning to Hawaii, he worked as a prosecutor in Honolulu until 1954. He then entered politics as a member of Hawaii's Territorial House of Representatives. (He later became majority leader.) He was also active in the administrative ranks of the Democratic party, serving as an executive board member of the local organization and as a delegate to county and state conventions. When Hawaii became a state in 1959, the popular Matsunaga was elected to its new senate.

In 1962, Matsunaga made the leap to national office when he was elected to the U.S. House of Representatives. He went on to serve seven consecutive terms in that body before being elected to the U.S. Senate in 1976. Matsunaga worked tirelessly on behalf of peace, nuclear arms control, safeguarding the environment, and obtaining redress (compensation or payment) for Japanese Americans interned during World War II. Time and time again, he brought those issues to the attention of his colleagues and gained their support for proposed legislation.

From the moment Matsunaga arrived in Washington, he sought ways to carry out his dream of establishing a cabinet-level Department of Peace that would set up and maintain a National Academy of Peace and Conflict Resolution. Matsunaga thought of the academy as a place where young Americans could go to learn how to settle national and international disputes without resorting to violence. As he once explained to members of a special Congressional committee that was studying his idea, "Peace, like war, is an art which must be studied and learned before it can be waged well...."

In 1984, a part of Matsunaga's dream finally became reality. While Congress did not approve the creation of a

Matsunaga (left) poses in front of the Capitol with other members of Hawaii's Democratic Congressional delegation, Daniel Inouye (center), and Thomas Gill (right)

Department of Peace within the cabinet, it did vote in favor of establishing a peace academy. It awards graduate degrees to people who help resolve national and international disputes.

Leads Movement to Investigate Japanese American Internment

Perhaps the most significant achievement of Matsunaga's legislative career, however, involved the fight to obtain redress for Japanese Americans who were victims of the infamous Executive Order 9066 during World War II. Under the terms of this act, men, women, and children of all ages and backgrounds—who had not been accused of any crime— spent as long as three years imprisoned in tar-paper shacks behind barbed wire and guarded by armed military police.

Many had been forced to give up everything they owned. The incarceration was a tremendous blow to their dignity and sense of security. They could not understand why their loyalty was being questioned or why the government was so willing to ignore their constitutional rights.

On August 2, 1979, Matsunaga co-sponsored a bill known as S. 1647 that proposed creating a commission to investigate the wartime incarceration of Japanese Americans and determine what, if any, compensation was owed to them for the emotional and economic losses they had suffered. The bill was signed into law by President Jimmy Carter on July 31, 1980.

Nearly a year later, on July 14, 1981, the Commission on Wartime Relocation and Internment of Civilians (CWRIC) began gathering testimony from people who had been victimized by the relocation program. Hearings were held in Washington and in various cities around the country. In all, more than seven hundred people appeared before members of the CWRIC.

In 1983, the commission published a report of its findings entitled Personal Justice Denied. *In this document, CWRIC members condemned the relocation of Japanese Americans, insisting it was done not out of military necessity but as a result of "race prejudice, war hysteria and a failure of political leadership." The CWRIC later issued several recommendations for redress. One suggested that Congress and the president formally apologize to Japanese Americans and acknowledge the injustice done to them. Another recommended that the government pay $20,000 to each of the estimated sixty thousand survivors of the camps.*

Urges Colleagues to Support Redress

Finally, on April 19, 1988, a bill known as S. 1009 (originally introduced by Matsunaga and seventy-three co-sponsors) proposing that the CWRIC's recommendations be adopted made it to the Senate floor. At various times during the bill's long journey through the legislative process, Matsunaga had given impassioned speeches urging his fellow senators to pass the bill. Few legislators had a problem with the idea of apologizing to Japanese Americans. But some questioned the fairness of holding present-day taxpayers responsible for wrongs committed many years earlier. Since they were afraid that approving this payment would open the door to similar claims from African Americans and other groups, they wanted to eliminate from the bill the payment of cash compensation to former Japanese American prisoners.

Matsunaga took the floor to argue against dropping the part of the bill that authorized such payments. His persuasive defense of S. 1009 is excerpted here from the Congressional Record, *100th Congress, Second Session, U.S. Government Printing Office, 1988.*

...As of September 17 of last year [1987], we have been observing the bicentennial of the greatest human document ever written—the U.S. Constitution. With pride in our unique heritage, we Americans should reaffirm our commitment to the proposition that the United States is one nation with liberty and justice for all....

In the life of every individual, and every nation, there are certain events which have a lasting, lifelong impact and which change the shape of their future. For some Americans, the October 1987 stock market decline brought back frightening memories of the Crash of 1929 and the Great Depression which followed it. For others, the image or words of a slain president or civil rights leader remind them of a turning point in their lives.

For Americans of Japanese ancestry who are over the age of forty-five years, the single, most traumatic event, the one which shaped the rest of their lives, is the wholesale relocation and incarceration in American-style concentration camps of some 120,000 Americans of Japanese ancestry and their parents and grandparents, who were legal resident aliens barred by United States law from becoming naturalized American citizens.

All Americans of that generation no doubt recall with great clarity where they were and what they were doing on December 7, 1941, the day that Japan attacked the American naval base at Pearl Harbor. I myself was in active military service on the Hawaiian Island of Molokai as an Army officer in temporary command of an infantry company. In fact, I was one of

Wreckage of the U.S.S. Arizona after Japanese attack on Pearl Harbor, December 7, 1941

prevailed: became widespread; predominated.

rampant: widespread.

1,565 Americans of Japanese ancestry who had volunteered for and were in active military service before Pearl Harbor, and who, with other Americans, stood in defense of the Territory of Hawaii against the enemy.

We remember vividly the atmosphere which **prevailed** in this country immediately after the bombing of Pearl Harbor. Rumors of a Japanese attack on the West Coast of the United States were **rampant** and numerous false sightings of enemy war planes off the coast were reported. A great wave of fear and hysteria swept the United States, particularly along the West Coast, where a relatively small population of Japanese Americans had, even before the outbreak of war, been subjected to racial discrimination and often violent attacks.

Two months after the attack on Pearl Harbor, in February 1942, President Franklin D. Roosevelt issued Executive Order 9066. The Executive Order gave to the Secretary of War the authority to designate restricted military areas and to exclude any or all persons from such areas. Penalties for violation of the restrictions were subsequently established by Congress in Public Law 77–503, enacted in March 1942.

At about the same time, the military commander of the western district, Lieutenant General John DeWitt, issued public proclamations establishing restricted military zones in eight western states, instituting a curfew applicable to enemy aliens and persons of Japanese ancestry, and restricting the travel of Americans of Japanese ancestry and enemy aliens. The first "civilian exclusion order" was issued by General DeWitt on March 24, 1942, and marked the beginning of the relocation and internment of the Japanese American population on the West Coast.

Significantly, the military commander of the then-Territory of Hawaii, which was under **martial law**, did not believe that it was necessary to order the wholesale evacuation of all Americans or resident aliens of Japanese ancestry, although about 1,400 leaders of the Japanese American community in Hawaii were rounded up immediately after the attack and sent to detention camps on the mainland.

J. Edgar Hoover, then director of the Federal Bureau of Investigation [FBI], opposed the mass incarceration of Japanese Americans, pointing out that the FBI was capable of apprehending and arresting any spies or saboteurs. Japanese diplomats, consular officials and military attachés who were in this country at the outbreak of war between the United States and Japan were not incarcerated in detention camps. On Hoover's orders, they were confined to house arrest and treated courteously, because the FBI director hoped that American citizens in Japan would be treated in a similar manner. The Office of Naval Intelligence had also informed President Roosevelt that the

martial law: a state in which law and order is maintained through the use of military forces rather than the police, usually in response to an emergency situation.

wholesale incarceration of Japanese Americans was unnecessary, pointing to the lack of evidence of any acts of espionage or sabotage by Americans of Japanese ancestry or their parents, before, during or after the attack on Pearl Harbor.

Of the 120,000 individuals who were ordered on seventy-two hours' notice to pack, leave their homes, and report to assembly centers prior to being moved to camps in the interior United States, about eighty percent were native-born American citizens—many of them young children and teenagers. The remainder, including many elderly people, were legal alien residents of the United States who were prohibited by the Oriental Exclusion Act of 1924 from becoming naturalized American citizens regardless of how much they wanted to be, like my father and mother. All of them, citizens and alien residents alike, were entitled to the protection of the U.S. Constitution, but their constitutional rights were **summarily** denied. Without being charged or indicted, without trial or hearing, without being convicted of a single crime, they were **en masse** ordered into what can only be described as American-style concentration camps surrounded by barbed-wire fences with searchlights, watchtowers and armed guards—and there they remained, many for over three years.

In 1980, thirty-eight years after the beginning of the relocation and internment of Japanese Americans, Congress authorized a thorough study of the circumstances surrounding the event. A distinguished nine-member commission, appointed by the president of the United States, was **mandated** to examine the facts surrounding the issuance of Executive Order 9066 and the subsequent relocation and internment of Japanese Americans. In addition, the commission was authorized to study the circumstances surrounding the evacuation of the Aleutian and Pribilof Islands in Alaska and the relocation of Native American Aleuts....

In 1983, following twenty days of public hearings which included more than 750 witnesses, and extensive review of federal records, contemporary writings, personal accounts and historical analyses, the commission filed its report, entitled *Personal Justice Denied*.

The commission's comprehensive report was welcomed by Americans of Japanese ancestry who had lived through the

summarily: quickly; without any formal proceedings.

en masse: as a group.

mandated: ordered.

relation and internment. It revealed publicly for the first time what they had always known: the relocation and internment of Japanese Americans was not justified by military necessity or national security but was the result of racial prejudice, wartime hysteria and the failure of political leadership.

The commission found that the **precipitous** action had been taken under the leadership of men like General DeWitt, who believed, and stated to the U.S. House of Representatives Naval Affairs Subcommittee on April 13, 1943:

> A Jap's a Jap. They are a dangerous element, whether loyal or not. There is no way to determine their loyalty.... It makes no difference whether he is an American; theoretically, he is still a Japanese, and you can't change him.... You can't change him by giving him a piece of paper.

At the war's end, interned Japanese Americans live in crowded barracks while awaiting processing to return home, 1946

precipitous: hasty, sudden.

Moreover, the commission found that the exclusion of Japanese Americans from the west coast and their detention continued long after the initial panic following the attack on Pearl Harbor had **abated**....

While revelation of the truth at last by a congressionally-created commission is a great relief to Americans of Japanese ancestry who were victims of this grave wartime mistake, the public report alone is not enough to provide them with justice too long denied—any more than it would be for any other American falsely imprisoned for years on **trumped-up** charges. In our great society, the victims of such errors in justice are entitled to more **tangible** relief.

What kind of relief is appropriate? The commission recommended and S. 1009 provides, first, for an official acknowledgement of the injustice and an apology to the surviving internees. Second, the bill establishes a civil liberties education fund which would conduct educational research and fund projects designed to inform the public of the events surrounding the relocation and internment of Japanese Americans, to ensure that such a thing never happens again. S. 1009 also provides that court cases wherein Japanese Americans were convicted of violating curfew and travel restrictions imposed by the western military district be reviewed by the U.S. Department of Justice, and that presidential pardons be recommended where appropriate. Finally, S. 1009 provides for the payment of $20,000 to each of the approximately 60,000 former internees who are still alive.

This last provision is perhaps the most controversial in the bill ... and I would like to take a few minutes to address it....

Those who contend that token payments are an inappropriate way to redress this injustice overlook the basic fact that compensatory remedies are deeply rooted in American **jurisprudence.** It has long been considered proper for our courts to award monetary damages to individuals who have been unjustifiably injured [as a result of being] falsely arrested or imprisoned, on nonracially motivated grounds.

The amounts of damages in such cases vary considerably, ranging from several hundred dollars to well over $100,000. The vast majority of reported awards stem from detentions lasting no more than a few days in duration, as compared to

abated: eased, decreased.

trumped-up: made up; invented.

tangible: real; capable of being assigned a definite value.

jurisprudence: law or legal system.

three years in the case of Japanese Americans. In many jurisdictions, an award for false arrest or imprisonment can include an amount for mental suffering. Humiliation, shame, and fright are elements that are considered in determining mental suffering. In addition, many jurisdictions include **punitive damages** where the conduct of the wrongdoer was particularly **egregious** or outrageous....

When one considers the fact that most of the internees were detained for three years or more, the $20,000 lump-sum payments simply cannot be considered excessive. The funds authorized for these payments are **allocated** over a period of five years and will constitute but a tiny fraction of our trillion-dollar federal budget. In addition, as was pointed out several times during the House debate on this legislation, the $20,000 lump-sum payments are equivalent to less that $3,000 in 1945 dollars, a very small amount of compensation considering the degree of economic, social, and emotional injury incurred by the internees during their three-year confinement.

In addition, opponents of S. 1009 often express the concern that enactment of the bill will set a dangerous **precedent** and invite similar claims by other minority groups.

It should be noted that under the provisions of S. 1009, payments are to be made only to those living individuals who were victims of the federal government's wartime policy. No payments are to be made to heirs or descendants of the former internees. S. 1009 would, therefore, not open the door for claims by descendants of former slaves or the descendants of Native American victims of the federal government's nineteenth-century policies with respect to American Indians. When we look for cases of people alive today who were themselves directly injured by the federal government because of their race or ethnicity, the incarceration of Japanese Americans is **unprecedented.**

Finally, I am often asked about the case of American citizens who were held captive by Japan during World War II. The War Claims Act of 1948 compensated each civilian American citizen who was held by the Imperial Japanese Government in the amount of $60 per month. The act was later extended to cover civilians captured by North Korea during the Korean conflict. Later still, it was extended to cover American civilians captured

punitive damages: money awarded to an injured person that goes beyond normal compensation in order to punish the wrongdoer.

egregious: obviously bad.

allocated: spread out.

precedent: an act or decision that may later be used to justify another act or decision similar to it.

unprecedented: extraordinary; unlike anything that has happened before.

by North Vietnam during the war in Vietnam. Civilians captured in Vietnam were compensated in the amount of $150 for each month they were imprisoned. Like the Japanese Americans, these Americans suffered a loss of liberty; the difference is that Japanese Americans were deprived of their freedom through the actions of their own government—the United States of America, not the enemy.

Federal courts have also addressed constitutional violations and false imprisonment in individual or class-action settings. In [a case involving] the mass arrests of demonstrators at the 1972 May Day demonstration in Washington, D.C., damages for false imprisonment were awarded in amounts ranging from $120 for twelve hours or less to $1,800 for forty-eight to seventy-two hours of detention.

Individual payments have also been made to Americans held hostage as a consequence of terrorism. Of the fifty-two Americans held hostage in Iran for 444 days, all but one were U.S. government employees. Congress voted each of these fifty-one a special bonus of $50 per day for that period—a total of $22,200 for each former hostage.

So it is clear that Congress can act to provide appropriate compensation to individuals who were the victims of such a grave injustice. Such compensation is long overdue. Since the end of World War II, many who were directly or indirectly involved in the mass evacuation and detention of Japanese Americans and resident aliens of Japanese ancestry have acknowledged the wrong inflicted on the evacuees.

President Roosevelt, in approving the induction of Japanese Americans into the U S. Army, observed that "Americanism is a matter of the mind and heart—not race or ancestry." Henry L. Stimson, then Secretary of War, recognized that "to loyal citizens, this forced evacuation was a personal injustice." Francis Biddle, then the attorney general of the United States, expressed his belief that "the program was ill-advised, unnecessary, and unnecessarily cruel." Milton Eisenhower, the first director of the War Relocation Authority, described the evacuation and detention of Japanese Americans as "an inhuman mistake." The late chief justice of the U.S. Supreme Court, Earl Warren, who, as attorney general of the state of California, urged evacuation of Japanese Americans, stated, "I have since deeply regretted the removal order and my own testimony **advocating** it, because it was not in keeping with our American concept of freedom and the rights of citizens."

S. 1009 also has the strong support of a large number of contemporary individuals and organizations....

It is time that Congress, too, recognized the grave injustice inflicted by the federal government on American citizens of Japanese ancestry and move to make amends. Passage of S. 1009 would remove a longstanding blot on our national Constitution—a most appropriate way to commemorate its bicentennial. It would also remove a cloud which has hung over the heads of innocent Americans of Japanese ancestry since World War II.

advocating: recommending; urging.

When the Japanese American 442nd Regimental Combat Team, described by General Mark Clark as the "most fightingest and most highly decorated military unit in the history of the United States," marched up Pennsylvania Avenue to the White House, upon its return from the European Theater at the end of World War II, President Harry S Truman, in presenting the team with its seventh Presidential Unit Citation said, "You fought not only the enemy, but prejudice—and won."

...As a twice-wounded veteran of the 100th Infantry Battalion, which is the first battalion of the 442nd Regimental Combat Team, I plead with my colleagues to make that victory complete and meaningful by passage of S. 1009.

The debate over S. 1009 continued the next day, April 20. Matsunaga again rose to speak in support of the bill and against any attempts to eliminate the payments to former internees. Shortly before a vote was taken, Matsunaga made the following speech, also excerpted here from the Congressional Record, *100th Congress, Second Session, U.S. Government Printing Office, 1988. Newspaper accounts noted that he wept as he recalled the suffering of some prisoners.*

...I rise in opposition to the amendment offered by the senator from Nevada [Mr. Hecht].

The Hecht amendment would **delete** from the bill funds provided to compensate each of about 60,000 surviving former internees and would also delete funds provided for the establishment of a *civil liberties education fund.* Further, the Hecht amendment would delete title III of the bill, pertaining to compensation for Aleuts, in its entirety.

Those who contend that monetary compensation is an inappropriate way to redress this longstanding injustice overlook the fact that monetary compensatory remedies are an integral part of our system of jurisprudence.....

delete: eliminate.

During hearings of the Commission on Wartime Relocation and Internment of Civilians ... former internees, many telling their stories for the first time, told of infants, young mothers, and elderly persons who died for lack of adequate medical care and facilities; of families who were separated, with elderly parents or in-laws going to one camp while their married children were sent to another; of large families forced to live together in one small room; of the constant, nagging uncertainty about the future, both near and long term; of the strains which this placed on their families and on the close-knit Japanese American community as a whole; and, most dramatically, of internees who were shot and killed by camp guards because they inadvertently wandered too close to the camp barbed-wire fences.

In one such incident, an elderly man and his grandson were playing pitch-catch ball near the fence late one afternoon. Under the camp rules, one was never to be seen between the two barbed-wire fences after six P.M. Although it was after six o'clock, on this day it was a bright summer day and it was still broad daylight. The grandfather, having missed the ball, chased after it, and when he got in between the two fences the guard up on the watchtower yelled, "Get back," and the elderly gentleman said, "Oh, I am only going for the ball," and continued his chase; whereupon the guard up on the watchtower fired the machine gun, killing the elderly man instantly. His grandson and members of his family still bear the scars of that incident.

And I myself become overly emotional when I think about it even to this day.

It is also reported ... that an elderly American veteran of World War I committed suicide because he was so ashamed of being branded as "disloyal" to the United States. Indeed, the stigma of disloyalty has haunted Japanese Americans for the past forty-five years, and it is one of the principal reasons that they are seeking congressional action to remove that cloud over their heads....

The sponsors of the bill do not pretend that history can be erased, but the measure would provide for the first time an official acknowledgement of the grave injustice which was done, and it would provide token monetary compensation to those who suffered irreparable losses. Without such compensation the bill would be meaningless....

Perhaps of greater significance, as I stated yesterday, is that S. 1009 would remove forever a longstanding blot on that great Constitution of the United States, and its passage, as reported by the committee, will prove that our beloved country is great enough to acknowledge and correct its past mistakes.

99

Later that day—April 20, 1988—the Senate voted 69 to 27 in favor of S. 1009 (also known as the Civil Liberties Act of 1988), including the part awarding a $20,000 payment to former internees. President Ronald Reagan signed the bill into law in August of that year.

Sources

Books

Bosworth, Allan R., *America's Concentration Camps,* Norton, 1967.

Commission on Wartime Relocation and Internment of Civilians Act: Hearing Before the Committee on Governmental Affairs, United States Senate, 96th Congress, Second Session, U.S. Government Printing Office, 1980.

Congressional Record, 100th Congress, 1st Session [and] 2nd Session, U.S. Government Printing Office, 1988.

Daniels, Roger, *Asian America: Chinese and Japanese in the United States Since 1850,* University of Washington Press, 1988.

Daniels, Roger, *Concentration Camps USA: Japanese Americans and World War II,* Holt, 1972.

Daniels, Roger, *The Politics of Prejudice: The Anti-Japanese Movement in California and the Struggle for Japanese Exclusion,* University of California Press, 1962.

Girdner, Audrie, and Anne Loftis, *The Great Betrayal: The Evacuation of the Japanese Americans During World War II,* Macmillan, 1969.

Grodzins, Morton M., *Americans Betrayed: Politics and the Japanese Evacuation,* University of Chicago Press, 1949.

Hosokawa, Bill, *Nisei: The Quiet Americans,* Morrow, 1969.

National Academy of Peace and Conflict Resolution: Hearings Before the Subcommittee on International Operations of the Committee on International Relations, House of Representatives, 95th Congress, 2nd Session, U.S. Government Printing Office, 1978.

Personal Justice Denied: Report of the Commission on Wartime Relocation and Internment of Civilians, U.S. Government Printing Office, 1983.

tenBroek, Jacobus, Edward N. Barnhart, and Floyd W. Matson, *Prejudice, War and the Constitution,* University of California Press, 1954.

Uyeda, Clifford I., editor, *The Japanese American Incarceration: A Case for Redress* (booklet), 3rd edition, National Committee for Redress of the Japanese American Citizens League, 1980.

Norman Y. Mineta

1931–

Japanese American business executive and former member of the U.S. House of Representatives

"WHY SHOULD AN AMERICAN, WHO BY ACCIDENT OF BIRTH HAPPENS TO BE OF ASIAN ANCESTRY, HAVE TO FACE THE PROSPECT OF BEING BEATEN WITH A BASEBALL BAT, OR HAVE HIS CAR SPRAY-PAINTED WITH THE WORDS 'DIE NIP'?"

In Congress as well as in the business world, Norman Y. Mineta's specialty has involved public works and transportation issues. Yet he has also served as a voice of conscience on the subject of redress (compensation or payment) for Japanese Americans who were forced to leave their homes and relocate to concentration camps during World War II. It is a painful episode from America's past with which he is personally very familiar. As a ten-year-old boy, Mineta was one of those imprisoned for no other reason than his Japanese ancestry.

Childhood Internment

A native of San Jose, California, Mineta was one of five children born to Japanese immigrants. His father had arrived in the United States in 1902 at the age of fourteen. He worked as a farm laborer for a number of years before he opened his own insurance agency. The Mineta family's life was comfortable and fairly uneventful until December 7, 1941—the day the Japanese bombed Pearl Harbor, an action that brought the United States into World War II.

A little more than two months later, on February 19, 1942, President Franklin Roosevelt issued *Executive Order 9066*. (Also see entries on **Daniel K. Inouye, Robert T. Matsui, Spark M. Matsunaga,** and **Clifford I. Uyeda.**) This infamous proclamation authorized the evacuation of some 120,000 Japanese Americans (about two-thirds of whom were U.S. citizens) from the West Coast to relocation centers in remote areas of nearly two dozen states, including Arizona, Arkansas, inland California, Colorado, Idaho, Utah, and Wyoming. No similar action was taken against German Americans or Italian Americans, even though the United States was also at war against Germany and Italy.

The Minetas, like many others, were given just a couple of days to make arrangements for their evacuation. Government officials shut down the family insurance business and confiscated their bank savings. Norman's older sister had to quit her job and his older brother had to leave school. Norman had to give away his dog.

On May 29, 1942, the Minetas were loaded on to a train with what few personal possessions they could carry and sent to a camp established at the Santa Anita racetrack in suburban Los Angeles. Later that year, they were transferred to the Heart Mountain relocation camp in Wyoming, and found themselves surrounded by barbed wire, guard towers, and armed military police.

The family remained in the camp until late 1943. Mr. Mineta was then offered a job in Chicago, Illinois, teaching Japanese to U.S. Army personnel enrolled in a special program. After the war, the Minetas were allowed to return to California. Once they were settled again in San Jose, they tried to resume the lives they had known before Executive Order 9066 turned everything upside down.

Rebuilding the Family Business

Following his graduation from high school, Mineta attended the University of California at Berkeley, where he received his bachelor's degree in business in 1953. He then served in the U.S. Army as a military intelligence officer *before heading back to San Jose to help out his father, who had reopened his insurance agency.*

Mineta worked in the family business throughout the rest of the 1950s and into the 1960s while also becoming involved in community affairs and joining civic groups, including the Chamber of Commerce, the Rotary Club, and the Japanese American Citizens League (JACL). He moved into local politics in 1962, when he joined the city's Human Relations Commission and later served on the Housing Authority. In 1967, Mineta became San Jose's first minority councilman when he was appointed to fill a vacancy. Two years later, he was elected to the position in his own right.

In 1971, Mineta successfully ran for mayor of San Jose. The victory made him the first Japanese American to head the government of a major city. One of the major hurdles he faced was managing the tremendous growth then under way in the area. (San Jose is located in the heart of the booming Silicon Valley, home to many computer-related firms.)

National Office

After completing his mayoral term in 1974, Mineta aimed for a seat in the U.S. Congress. People were especially eager for change that year in the wake of various political scandals in the Republican administration of President Richard Nixon. A reform-minded Democrat, Mineta won in a district long dominated by Republicans.

In Washington, D.C., Mineta quickly rose in the ranks. He served as deputy whip for the House Democratic leadership and as a member of the Budget Committee, the Policy and Steering Committee, and the Post Office and Civil Service Committee. He also chaired several subcommittees of the Public Works and Transportation Committee and chaired the committee itself from 1992 until the Republicans gained control of the House after the 1994 elections.

In these various roles, Mineta earned praise for his ability to bring together people with very different opinions and make them agree on a single course of action. As a former colleague once described him, he is "always nice and always tactful, but can be tough as nails."

In addition, President Bill Clinton asked the California representative to serve in his cabinet as Secretary of Transportation, but Mineta felt he could be of more use to the administration by staying in Congress. There he continued to help shape the nation's policy on numerous construction and environmental projects involving highways, railroads, federal buildings, airports, clean water and wetlands regulation, and other related concerns.

Mineta as newly elected mayor of San Jose in front of City Hall, 1971

A Leading Role in the Redress Movement

Mineta particularly stands out as a spokesperson for Japanese Americans who were unjustly imprisoned during World War II by their own country. He believed the importance of the fight for redress went beyond obtaining monetary damages *from the government—it was a fight for the preservation of constitutional rights. As he once explained, those who lived through the concentration-camp experience emerged "without any rancor [hatred] or bitterness, but with a very strong conviction that this should never, ever happen again to anybody else."*

On September 28, 1979, Mineta became one of the co-sponsors of H.R. 5499. This House bill proposed creating a commission to investigate the wartime relocation of Japanese Americans and determine what, if any, compensation was owed to them for the losses they had suffered both emotionally and economically. A Senate version of the bill, S. 1647, passed in mid-1980. A year later, the new Commission on Wartime Relocation and Internment of Civilians (CWRIC) began holding hearings to gather testimony. Over seven hundred people shared their stories with commissioners.

In 1983, the CWRIC published a report of its findings entitled Personal Justice Denied. *In the report, members of the group condemned the relocation of Japanese Americans as a measure undertaken not for military reasons but out of "race prejudice, war hysteria and a failure of political leadership." They later issued several recommendations for redress. First of all, they suggested that Congress and the president formally apologize for the government's actions and acknowledge the injustice done to Japanese Americans as a result of Executive Order 9066. They also expressed their belief that each of the estimated sixty thousand survivors of the camps should be paid $20,000 in damages.*

Finally, on September 17, 1987, a bill proposing that the CWRIC's recommendations be adopted came to the floor of the House of Representatives for debate. The date was especially significant—it was the 200th anniversary of the signing of the Constitution.

To those who opposed H.R. 442, as it was known, awarding monetary damages was the sticking point. Republican Congressman Dan Lungren of California (who had been a

member of the CWRIC) questioned the fairness of holding present-day taxpayers responsible for wrongs committed decades earlier. He also raised the prospect that approving such payments would open the door to similar claims from African Americans and other groups. Lungren proposed an amendment to the bill that would have eliminated all payments.

An Emotional Plea on Senate Floor

In response to Lungren's proposal, Mineta stood before his colleagues—his voice often quavering with emotion, his hand occasionally brushing away a tear—and delivered an impassioned plea in favor of the bill. His remarks that day are excerpted here from the Congressional Record, 100th Congress, 1st Session, U.S. Government Printing Office, 1988.

Mineta speaks at rally outside the Capitol about protecting the environment, 1985

66

To me this is a very, very emotional day, in sharp contrast to May 29, 1942, when, as a ten-and-a-half-year-old boy wearing a Cub Scout uniform, I was herded onto a train under armed guard in San Jose, California, to leave for Santa Anita, a race track in southern California. And here, on the 17th of September, 1987, we are celebrating the 200th anniversary of the signing of that great document, the Constitution of our great land. It is only in this kind of a country, where a ten-and-a-half-year-old can go from being in a Cub Scout uniform to an armed-guard-guarded train to being a Member of the House of Representatives of the greatest country in the world....

I rise now to urge my colleagues' opposition to the amendment offered by our fine friend, the gentleman from California [Mr. Lungren]. Today we can truly celebrate the bicentennial of our great Constitution by passing this legislation without any weakening amendments. H.R. 442, including compensation, will reaffirm and strengthen this very, very vital document that we are celebrating today.

H.R. 442 may not deal with events either as distant or as proud as those in Philadelphia two hundred years ago, but the bill does address events just as central and just as fundamental to our rights and to our laws.

The gentleman's amendment would eliminate a key provision of this bill, the payment of monetary compensation to the present-day survivors of a shameful episode in our nation's long and proud history. Beginning in 1942, the federal government ordered and sent 120,000 Americans of Japanese ancestry to isolated camps scattered throughout the Western United States, and those who were interned and evacuated had but days, sometimes only hours, to dispose of their property and set their affairs in order, and then, carrying only what their arms could hold, these Americans were summarily shipped off to parts unknown for up to three years.

Because the government of the United States was responsible for the violation of the rights of 120,000 lives, that government, our government, has a legal and moral responsibility to compensate the internees for the **abrogation** of their civil and human rights.

abrogation: withdrawal; cancellation.

An internment camp in Manzanar, California, 1942

Now, some are saying that these payments are inappropriate, that liberty is priceless and we cannot put a price on freedom. That is an easy statement to make when you have your freedom, but it is absurd to argue that because constitutional rights are priceless, they really have no value at all. Would you sell your civil and constitutional rights for $20,000? Of course not. But when those rights are ripped away without **due process**, are you entitled to compensation? Absolutely....

One night in early 1942, when we did not know what events were to come, my father called our family together. I had one sister in San Francisco, but the rest of us, the four of us, were still in San Jose. He said he did not know what the war would bring to my mother and to him since they were resident

due process: formal legal proceedings carried out according to established rules and principles.

aliens, my dad having come in 1902 and my mother in 1912, but with the Oriental exclusion law of 1924 they were not able to become citizens because they were prohibited by that racial exclusion law from becoming U.S. citizens. However, he was confident that his beloved country would guarantee and protect the rights of his children, American citizens all. But his confidence, as it turned out, was misplaced.

I was born in this country, as were most of those who were interned, yet at that time even citizenship was not enough if your parents or grandparents had come from Japan. So on May 29, 1942, my father loaded his family upon that train under armed guard which was taking us from our home in San Jose to an unknown distant barracks. He was later to write to friends in San Jose, and he wrote in that letter about his experience and his feelings as our train pulled out of the station. I quote from the letter:

> I looked at Santa Clara's streets from the train over the subway. I thought this might be the last look at my loved home city. My heart almost broke, and suddenly hot tears just came pouring out, and the whole family cried out, could not stop, until we were out of our loved county.
>
> We lost our homes, we lost our businesses, we lost our farms, but worst of all, we lost our most basic human rights. Our own government had branded us with the **unwarranted stigma** of disloyalty which clings to us still to this day.

So the burden has fallen upon us to right the wrongs of forty-five years ago. Great nations demonstrate their greatness by admitting and redressing the wrongs that they commit, and it has been left to this Congress to act accordingly.

Injustice does not dim with time. We cannot wait it out. We cannot ignore it, and we cannot shrug our shoulders at our past. If we do not **refute** the shame of the indictment here and now, the specter of this tragedy will resurface just as surely as I am standing here before you, and the injustice will recur.

This bill is certainly about the specific injury suffered by a small group of Americans, but the bill's impact reaches much deeper into the very soul of our democracy. Those of us who support this bill want not just to close the books on the sad

unwarranted stigma: undeserved mark of shame or disgrace.

refute: prove false.

events of 1942, we want to make sure that such blatant constitutional violations never occur again.

I must confess that this is a moment of great emotion for me. Today we will resolve, if we can finally lift the unjust burden of shame which 120,000 Americans have carried for forty-five painful years.

It is a day that I will remember for the rest of my life. I hope the members will help me, too, to remember it as a day when justice was achieved, and so with all my heart, I urge the members to oppose this amendment and to support H.R. 442, the Civil Liberties Act of 1987, and in so doing, to reaffirm our Constitution on this very historic day....

*Mineta's moving appeal, along with that of another Japanese American in the House, **Robert T. Matsui**, helped secure passage of H.R. 442 in a landslide vote. The Senate went on to pass its version of the proposal (known as the Civil Liberties Act of 1988) in April 1988. President Ronald Reagan signed it into law that August.*

Several years later, on February 15, 1992, Mineta spoke to an audience gathered in San Francisco, California, to observe the fiftieth anniversary of Executive Order 9066. But he used the occasion to do more than reflect on that event. In short, he warned, the United States must continue to be on guard against discrimination. Mineta provided the editor with a copy of his speech, a part of which is reprinted here.

I am proud to join you here today. Very proud. And as I stand before you—my friends and neighbors here in San Francisco—I feel a great sadness, but I also feel an even greater hope.

I know my sadness is shared throughout this center, throughout this city, and throughout the Japanese American community here in the United States. Our sadness is not for ourselves, but for our parents and grandparents who did not live to see this day. These pioneers and survivors would have been proud of this moment, and proud of us. Proud of us all.

There would have been a time, not all that many years ago, when I would have wondered if anyone other than Americans of Japanese ancestry would—or could—feel the power of this anniversary, as we do. Some would say that no one could truly know the tragedy of our internment by the United States government as we know it. And this is true. But today, the difference is that people from all across the country—and indeed, from around the world—*want* to know....

The fact that our nation—the United States of America—has now apologized to us for our internment fifty years ago tells me how much this nation has changed, and that the changes have been for the better. With those changes have come understanding, reflection, and the recognition that basic human rights either apply to us all—or they belong to no one. *However,* there is no escaping another truth: that the **specter** of racism is lurking in us all.

In times of acute economic hardship or **jingoistic** pressures, this evil can surface all too easily. We've seen that when Vincent Chin was beaten to death in Detroit by unemployed auto workers. [See entry on **Helen Zia** for more information.] We've seen that during the war in the Middle East, when Arab Americans were the target of bigotry and suspicion. And we see it today as a result of Japan-bashing.

Why should an American, who by accident of birth happens to be of Asian ancestry, have to face the prospect of being beaten with a baseball bat, or have his car spray-painted with the words "Die Nip"? The answer is, there is no answer. No one should have to face such crimes of hate. So, too, was it in 1942.

It was here in California and the West Coast fifty years ago that this standard was put to the test. Our life as a community was forever transformed by an attack that struck at the heart of the U.S. Constitution. This was an attack not of our making. But three thousand miles away in Washington, D.C., the government of the United States—our government—decided that Americans of Japanese ancestry were a categorical threat to the United States.

specter: spirit, ghost.
jingoistic: extremely and aggressively patriotic.

No matter that these threats were unproven, or that we were either American citizens or permanent resident aliens. All were tarred with the same **indiscriminate** brush of racial hatred and fear.

We were all scared, those of us who were alive at the time. The entire world was at war. The United States had been brought into this war—the Second World War—after the Empire of Japan had attacked Pearl Harbor, Hawaii, on December 7, 1941. One of the first casualties of that attack was faith and trust within our American nation.

America quickly saw little value in distinguishing between the attackers that Sunday morning and loyal Japanese Americans who were every bit as much the target of that dawn air

Police "round up" Japanese Americans in California, March, 1942

indiscriminate: haphazard; not thought out with judgement.

Norman Y. Mineta | 151

raid in Hawaii. All too much effort was invested, instead, in **expedience**. And the search was on for **scapegoats**.

Headlines told this story. And by February of 1942, those headlines had reached a fevered pitch.

Wednesday, February 18. The *San Francisco Chronicle*. Headline: "Enemy Aliens: Demand for State **Martial Law** Sent to General DeWitt by Impatient Congressmen."

Thursday, February 19. Headline: "Enemy Aliens: Congressmen Demand All American-Born Japs Be Moved from Coastal Areas."

Friday, February 20. Headline: "Enemy Aliens: Second Generation Japs to be Evacuated from Coast, War Department Predicts. Civil Liberties May Go by the Boards."

And finally, on Saturday, February 21. Headline: "Drive Against Enemy Aliens: FDR [President Franklin Delano Roosevelt] Orders Army Rule for All Strategic Areas. Even Citizen Japs May be Cleared from Coast."

And the story in the *Chronicle* read, in part: "Bringing California only a step short of martial law, the president slashed through a web of legal entanglements, directed military commanders to mark whatever zones they need, and to oust immediately any unwanted aliens and citizens."

And the story continued: "His orders smashed directly at 60,000 American-born Japanese on the West Coast, all hitherto protected under a cloak of U.S. citizenship."

Think about that for a moment. "A cloak of U.S. citizenship." When you came down to it in 1942, that was all the **illusory** protection we had: a cloak. [See box on Japanese Immigration and U.S. Citizenship for more information.]

When the signs went up telling us, as Americans of Japanese ancestry, that we would have to leave our homes, the signs said, "ATTENTION: ALIENS AND NONALIENS." Our own government wouldn't even acknowledge us as citizens.

In a way, that was not surprising. Our parents and grandparents had not even that much, since they were forbidden by racial exclusion laws from becoming American citizens. So, with the stroke of a pen at the White House, even that illusory

expedience: carrying out something quickly and efficiently.

scapegoats: people who are unfairly blamed for something.

martial law: maintaining law and order through the use of military forces rather than the police, usually in response to an emergency situation.

illusory: apparent, misleading; coming from an illusion.

cloak—which my father thought would protect his children—was stripped away.

One by one, Japanese American communities along the West Coast disappeared: removed into stark, barren camps scattered throughout some of the most **inhospitable** regions of the United States. The myth that this forced relocation was being done for our protection was a lie exposed by the first sight of camp guard towers with their machine guns pointed in at us, instead of out.

Tens of thousands of us spent up to four long years in these camps. The vast majority of us cooperated with our government, determined to prove our loyalty in the long run by sacrificing peacefully in the short run our most basic rights as Americans. And we served this country well. Far above and beyond the call of duty.

The all-**nisei** 442nd Regimental Combat Team and its 100th Battalion were volunteers from the camps, enlistees fighting Nazi Germany and fascist Italy while their families remained behind barbed wire. These men became the most-decorated Army fighting force in all of American history. They gave of themselves, they gave of their blood, and they gave of their lives to protect America even though America did not see fit to protect their rights.

In the Pacific, a top-secret war was fought by Japanese Americans in the Military Intelligence Service—a story untold for decades. But it was they, these volunteers, who cracked code after code—saving countless American lives. And yet, after the war, the stigma of shame born of the internment lived on in all of us.

Internment drained and crippled many Japanese American families. Homes, farms, and businesses were lost. Lives were ruined. The hot brand of disloyalty hung over our heads like a thundercloud ready to burst at the mention of our **subjugation** as second-class citizens.

The result was that once the war had ended and the camps were closed, we tried to forget the internment.

Parents never spoke of it to their children. But here there was an inescapable **contradiction:** How can you prove your loyalty once and for all, as we had tried to do, if you allow personal

inhospitable: unlivable.

nisei: a Japanese word that describes the U.S.-born children of parents who had immigrated from Japan.

subjugation: the act of conquering or bringing under control.

contradiction: a situation in which one thing is inconsistent with another or opposite of the other.

U.S. Policy on Japanese Immigration

There were almost no Japanese immigrants to the United States until the mid-nineteenth century due to Japan's rigid laws against travel. In 1868, however, Hawaii began to import Japanese laborers to work on the sugar plantations. In 1869, a small group of Japanese established a colony in California. During the 1880s, the number of Japanese living in the United States increased from 148 to 85,716. By 1924, about 200,000 Japanese had located in Hawaii, and another 180,000 had moved to the mainland United States, primarily California.

Japanese who settled in California faced so much racial hostility that they were usually shut out of the skilled trades and many factory jobs. They often turned to self-employment, becoming farmers or shopkeepers. Others managed to earn a living as migrant farm laborers, railroad workers, and cannery employees. As the number of immigrants increased, so, too, did anti-Japanese sentiment. In 1907, tensions over Asian immigration led Japan and the United States to reach an agreement: Japan would no longer issue passports to Japanese workers to go to the United States. California and several other states banned Japanese immigrants from owning or leasing land on the grounds that they were not eligible to become U.S. citizens. (According to a 1790 law, only "white" people could be U.S. citizens.)

This racial intolerance, along with a growing tendency toward **isolationism** in the years following World War I (1914-18), eventually led to a series of tough immigration laws. In 1917, the U.S. government passed a law intended to slow down the rate of immigration, which had climbed to over a million people per year just before the war.

---

justice denied to stand silently in a specter of shame? The answer is, you can't.

And the lesson I learned was that wronged individuals must stand up and fight for their rights if our nation is to be true to its principles, without exception. That's what our successful effort to redress the internment was meant to do.

For me, that ten-year struggle in Congress won back for us our dignity. In the Civil Liberties Act of 1988, there is a passage that is more everlasting a testament than any I know to our national ethic. I am proud that this legislation was written in my office... It says, and I quote:

The Congress recognizes that, as described by the Commission on Wartime Relocation and Internment of Civilians, a grave injustice was done to both citizens and permanent

isolationism: a national policy of remaining detached or separated from international affairs.

Under its terms, those seeking to come to America had to prove that they could read and write (any language, not necessarily English) and that they met certain minimum standards as to their mental, physical, moral, and economic state. Large numbers of potential immigrants—especially Asians—were denied entry into the United States.

In 1921, the Dillingham Bill (also known as the Emergency Quota Act), established a quota system to restrict immigration even further. It allowed only three percent of the people of any nationality who had lived in the United States in 1910 to enter the country each year. The most severe blow came in 1924 with the Johnson-Reed Immigration Act. It limited the annual quota to two percent of the people of any nationality who had lived in the United States in 1890 and denied entry to all aliens who were ineligible for citizenship. Together, these restrictions totally excluded all Japanese while making it easier for people from northern and western Europe to enter the country.

Such discrimination continued throughout the mid-1940s, until after the end of World War II, when more and more people realized that America could not stand tall as a world leader if it tolerated prejudice and ignored human rights and freedom. In 1948, the Supreme Court struck down laws prohibiting Japanese from owning and leasing land as "outright racial discrimination" and therefore "unconstitutional." In 1952, the McCarran-Walter Act ended all racial restrictions having to do with becoming a U.S. citizen, finally making it possible for Japanese immigrants be naturalized. And in 1965, Congress eliminated quotas based on national origin.

resident aliens of Japanese ancestry by the evacuation, relocation, and internment of civilians during World War II.

As the Commission documents, these actions were carried out without adequate security reasons and without any acts of espionage or sabotage documented by the Commission, and were motivated largely by racial prejudice, wartime hysteria, and a failure of political leadership.

The excluded individuals of Japanese ancestry suffered enormous damages, both material and intangible, all of which resulted in significant human suffering for which appropriate compensation has not been made.

For these fundamental violations of the basic civil liberties and constitutional rights of these individuals of Japanese ancestry, the Congress apologizes on behalf of the Nation.

That last sentence means more to me than perhaps any other in law, for it represents everything that our government is designed to do when it works at its best. And today, fifty years after Executive Order 9066 was signed, the successful effort to redress that wrong stands as a reminder of what ultimate **accountability** can and should mean in the United States.

It should mean truth. It should mean justice. And it should mean universality of the rights guaranteed by the U.S. Constitution.

But today, we must remain vigilant to ensure that these truths hold true for our children and grandchildren. The most recent wave of Japan-bashing and America-bashing holds for us a special danger. Those who prefer not to learn from the mistakes of the past, those who prefer a jingoism of hate, those who prefer to seek scapegoats continue to pose a threat.

We have seen these latest headlines, and experienced these latest hate crimes. And the specter of tragedy remains all too real. But today, unlike fifty years ago, we have the political strength to bear witness—and to protect ourselves and our neighbors from more senseless tragedies.

The war in the Middle East last year [the Persian Gulf War of 1990–91] demonstrated how genuine a concern this is for every minority community. In 1942, Japanese Americans were threatened and interned. But in 1991, when Arab Americans were threatened, there were voices within government and without to bear witness. We helped stop history from repeating itself.

None of us can predict who might next fall target to hysteria, racism, and weak political leadership. But with our strength of conviction, and witness to history, I do believe that we can ensure that such a tragedy as our internment never befalls anyone ever again here in the United States.

99

In September 1995, Mineta announced he was quitting Congress as of October 10 (midway through his eleventh term) to join Lockheed Martin Corp., the nation's biggest weapons contractor. There he was named senior vice-president of transportation systems and services.

accountability: responsibility.

Sources

Books

Bosworth, Allan R., *America's Concentration Camps,* Norton, 1967.

Congressional Record, 100th Congress, 1st Session, U.S. Government Printing Office, 1988.

Daniels, Roger, *Asian America: Chinese and Japanese in the United States since 1850,* University of Washington Press, 1988.

Daniels, Roger, *Concentration Camps USA: Japanese Americans and World War II,* Holt, 1972.

Daniels, Roger, *The Politics of Prejudice: The Anti-Japanese Movement in California and the Struggle for Japanese Exclusion,* University of California Press, 1962.

Girdner, Audrie, and Anne Loftis, *The Great Betrayal: The Evacuation of the Japanese Americans During World War II,* Macmillan, 1969.

Grodzins, Morton M., *Americans Betrayed: Politics and the Japanese Evacuation,* University of Chicago Press, 1949.

Personal Justice Denied: Report of the Commission on Wartime Relocation and Internment of Civilians, U.S. Government Printing Office, 1983.

Takaki, Ronald, *A Different Mirror: A History of Multicultural America,* Little, Brown, 1993.

Uyeda, Clifford I., editor, *The Japanese American Incarceration: A Case for Redress* (booklet), 3rd edition, National Committee for Redress of the Japanese American Citizens League, 1980.

Periodicals

A. Magazine, "Power Brokers," fall 1993, pp. 25-34.

AsianWeek, "Remembering a Painful Era: Honoring the Strength of Japanese Americans," February 28, 1992, p. 16.

Business Journal, "Norman Mineta: World War II Injustice Drives His Political Life," May 2, 1994, p. 12.

Time, "The Burden of Shame," September 28, 1987, p. 31.

Patsy Takemoto Mink

1927–

Japanese American attorney and member of the U.S. House of Representatives

"THE GREATNESS OF OUR COUNTRY LIES IN OUR PEOPLE, DIVERSE AND OF ALL POSSIBLE IMMIGRANT BACKGROUNDS, WHO ARE BOUND TOGETHER BY THEIR COMMON LOVE OF FREEDOM AND LIBERTY. NO LAW IS NEEDED TO REQUIRE THIS LOYALTY; NO PUNISHMENT ... CAN OBLITERATE THIS LOYALTY."

Patsy Takemoto Mink is a third-generation Hawaiian who has battled discrimination both as a woman and as an Asian American to succeed in the world of politics. Although a member of the Democratic party, she has often taken positions that put her at odds with her fellow Democrats in order to remain true to her own beliefs.

Enters Law and Politics

Mink was born on the island of Maui, the second-largest of the islands that make up Hawaii. Her father was a civil engineer and both of her parents were of Japanese descent. From the time she was very young, Mink dreamed of becoming a doctor, and attending medical school was still her goal when she began studies at the University of Hawaii. Gradually, however, she came to realize that she was drawn more to the humanities than to science. After spending several semesters on the mainland at Pennsylvania's Wilson College and the University of Nebraska, Mink earned her bachelor's degree in zoology and chemistry in 1948. Eventually, she enrolled in law school at the University of Chicago in Illinois.

In 1953, Mink returned to Hawaii with her law degree. She then went into private practice in Honolulu. She also taught business law at the University of Hawaii and served as house attorney for the Hawaii House of Representatives.

In 1954, Mink became involved in Democratic politics at the local level. By 1956, she was heading the state's Young Democrats group. That year, she was elected to the Hawaii House of Representatives, and two years later, she won a seat in the Hawaii Senate. Mink's growing prominence as a liberal party activist led to her selection as a member of the platform committee at the 1960 Democratic National Convention. (A platform committee is responsible for coming up with the official statement of beliefs and principles supported by a political party or candidate.) In that role, she helped shape the party's position on civil rights. Several months later, she won a second term in the Hawaii Senate.

The First Asian American Woman in Congress

After Hawaii became a state in 1959, Mink was one of several people who ran in a special primary election to determine who would represent Hawaiians in the U.S. House of Representatives. Her first bid proved unsuccessful, but she won on her second try in 1964, thus becoming the first Asian American woman ever to serve in Congress.

Once in Washington, Mink focused on a number of areas that were important to her, including children, the elderly, education, health care, housing, equal rights for women and minorities, and the war against hunger and poverty. She supported normalizing relations with the People's Republic of China (the United States had never officially recognized Communist China since its creation in 1949) and even testified before the United Nations on the subject. She was also one of her party's most outspoken opponents to the military draft and U.S. involvement in the Vietnam war. She strongly defended the right of people to protest against it without fear of being labeled "un-American."

In June 1967, a controversy erupted in Congress over the burning of an American flag in New York's Central Park *during a demonstration against the Vietnam war. Eager to punish the protesters, a number of angry legislators proposed a bill making it a federal crime to show "contempt" for the flag by "publicly mutilating, defacing, **defiling** or trampling upon it."*

In the heated debate that followed the introduction of the bill, an equally angry Mink stood up to challenge the idea that patriotism is somehow connected to how one looks or behaves. Her impassioned defense of the right of all Americans to protest is excerpted here from the Congressional Record, *90th Congress, 1st Session, Volume 113, Part 12, U.S. Government Printing Office, 1967.*

I rise on a matter of personal privilege for myself and for my constituents in the state of Hawaii, to call to the attention of this House a **defamatory** and highly insulting letter which was placed in the [*Congressional Record*].... This was a letter submitted by one Aaron E. Koota, district attorney of Kings County, Brooklyn, New York. His letter referred to a recent court decision by a distinguished jurist in my state....

This case involved a student from the state of New York attending the University of Hawaii's East-West Center who had drawn a large caricature of the flag with dollar signs for stars and the stripes dripping as with blood. The student was arrested under state law which makes it a crime to show contempt for the flag of the United States. The judge after reviewing the case ruled that the drawing was symbolic of the defendant's feeling about certain policies of his country, but that he did not intend by his drawing to dishonor the flag which to him still symbolized everything that he loved and honored about America.

Mr. Koota in trying to dismiss the legal significance of this case said in his letter:

> *Although it is true that the act in the latter case was condoned by the court as symbolic speech, we must realize that the background of the state of Hawaii is not as steeped in the same spirit of Americanism as are the other states of the*

defiling: contaminating; dishonoring.

defamatory: harmful to the reputation of someone.

*Union. Hawaii has a foreign **ideology** as its background and that is probably explanatory of the Court's attitude.*

By this outrageous statement the loyalty, patriotism, and Americanism of my entire state has been **impugned**, as well as that of my esteemed friend the Honorable Masato Doi, the judge in this case whose learned opinion took tremendous courage and conviction to write.

This is precisely the outrage that will be **perpetrated** by this bill on all Americans who do not conform in ideas or beliefs or color of skin or shape of their eyes or nose.

A disagreement on what we believe to be the real meaning of our Constitution will lead to emotional, irrational accusations like Koota's that the reasons for disagreement is due to lack of love of our country or lack of Americanism.

According to Attorney Koota, I wonder how many generations must we be Americans to be steeped with this spirit of Americanism with which he believes he is possessed? Can it be said that only Hawaii has a foreign ideology as its background and not Brooklyn, New York, or any city in this country where its people are of immigrant stock?

We feel that same pride when our colors are presented, our skin like yours rises in goose pimples at the playing of the national anthem, our eyes like yours wept as many tears over the death of our late President [John F.] Kennedy, our blood has been shed in three wars for the defense of our country and is now being shed again in Vietnam.

I am willing to match the love and devotion to our country of the people of my state whose only difference is the color of their skins, with any group of people anywhere in America.

The greatness of our country lies in our people, diverse and of all possible immigrant backgrounds, who are bound together by their common love of freedom and liberty. No law is needed to require this loyalty; no punishment, not even confinement in wartime relocation camps with complete denial of due process, can obliterate this loyalty.

The love for our country cannot be destroyed; the nation cannot be injured by the mere burning or defiling of one flag. America stands for too much that is a tribute to freedom that

ideology: belief system.

impugned: attacked; opposed as something that is false or lacks integrity.

perpetrated: carried out; committed.

no few foolish acts of contempt can dishonor its greatness. Rather these childish tantrums now cast only ridicule upon the perpetrators of this insane and irrational behavior.

I cannot believe that these few extremists in our society endanger the honor of this country; if they truly do, then no mere $1,000 fine or year in jail would be punishment enough.

Ramsey Clark, the Attorney General of the United States, in commenting on this bill states:

> *Particular care should be exercised to avoid infringement of free speech. To make it a crime if one "defiles" or "casts contempt ... either by word or act" upon the national flag is to risk **invalidation.** This broad language may be too vague under standards of constitutional law to constitute the basis of a criminal action. Such language reaches toward conduct which may be protected by First Amendment guarantees, and the courts have found vagueness in this area.*

I stand four-square behind our attorney general and more particularly behind the honored jurist of my state whose Americanism has been questioned because he chose to place the Constitution above his own popularity and to ignore the passionate demands of people who seek to punish all offbeat conduct without regard for the true meaning of liberty and freedom.

America is not a country which needs to punish its **dissenters** to preserve its honor. America is not a country which needs to banish its atheists to preserve its religious faith. America is not a country which needs to demand conformity of its people, for its strength lies in all our diversities converging in one common belief, that of the importance of freedom as the essence of our country and the real honor and heritage of our nation, which no trampled flag can ever symbolically desecrate.

I did not intend to speak against or even vote against this bill, but when my Americanism has been challenged and that of the people of my state, by persons who see only disloyalty in dissent, then I must rise to voice my faith and my belief that America is too great to allow its **frenetic** fringes to curb the blessings of freedom and liberty, which are the cornerstones of our democracy.

When the flag desecration bill came up for a vote, Mink was one of only 16 legislators who voted against it. A total of 387 legislators voted for it. A revised version of the bill that

invalidation: being made invalid, meaningless, weak, or ineffective.

dissenters: people who disagree with the opinions of the majority.

frenetic: frantic, frenzied.

specifically added the word "burning" to the list of acts it banned passed in the Senate in 1968.

Mink has spoken out on intolerance—especially racial intolerance—on numerous other occasions as well. On November 6, 1971, she gave the keynote address at the Thirtieth Anniversary and Installation Banquet of the West Los Angeles Japanese American Citizens League (JACL). In her speech, Mink reflected on the anger and frustration that was then causing many young people to protest in ways their elders often found disturbing. Her words are excerpted here from Representative American Speeches: 1971–1972, *edited by Waldo W. Braden, Wilson, 1972.*

I am delighted to participate in this memorable occasion. It must be difficult to look back thirty years to 1941 and relive the pains and agonies that were inflicted upon you [during World War II, when Japanese Americans were branded as "enemy aliens" and imprisoned in concentration camps]; as citizens, unloved and unwanted in their own country of their birth. Loving this land as much as any other citizen, it is difficult to fathom the despair and fury which many must have felt, yet who fought back and within a few years had reestablished their lives and their futures. Most of us remember these years vividly. Our faith in justice was tested many times over. Our patriotism was proven by blood of our sons upon the battlefields.

Yet today, thirty years later, to many even in this room it is only a part of our history. Our children, thirty years old and younger, cannot follow with us these memories of the forties. They tire of our stories of the past. Their life is now, today ... tomorrow....

It is quite evident that I am standing before an affluent group whose surface appearance does not reveal the years of struggle and doubt that have ridden behind you.

Sociologists have generally described the Japanese Americans as an easily **acculturated** people who quickly **assimilated** the ways of their surroundings. This has always been in my view a friendly sort of jab at our cultural background, for what

acculturated: changed through exposure to another culture.

assimilated: became part of; blended into.

it has come to mean for me is a description of a **conformist**, which I hope I am not!

I still dream that I shall be able to be a real participant in the changing scenario of opportunity for all of America. In this respect, I share the deep frustration and anguish of our youth as I see so much around us that cries out for our attention and that we continue to neglect.

Many factors have contributed towards a deepening sense of frustration about our inability to solve our problems of poverty and racial prejudice. Undoubtedly the prolonged, unending involvement in Vietnam has contributed to this sense of hopelessness. At least for our youth who must bear the ultimate burden of this war, it seems unfair that they should be asked to serve their country in this way when there are so many more important ways in which their youth and energy can be directed to meet the urgent needs at home. They view our government as **impotent** to deal with these basic issues.

It is true that Congress has passed a great many civil rights laws. The fact that new, extra laws were found necessary to make it easier for some people to realize their constitutional guarantees is a sad enough commentary on the American society, but what is even worse is the fact that the majority of our people are still unready, personally, to extend these guarantees to all despite the Constitution and all the civil rights laws, and despite their protestations to the contrary.

Certainly, no one will admit his bigotry and prejudice—yet we always find ways to clothe such feelings in more presentable forms—and few will openly advocate suppression or oppression of other men, but nevertheless, it exists.

Although Congress has repealed the Emergency Detention Act [see box], the fight for freedom is not over. We now see a new witch hunt proclaimed in which all government employees will be examined for their memberships and organizations. It seems that we have not yet succeeded in **expunging** the notion that "dangerous" persons can be identified by class or group relationships and punished accordingly.

I believe that nobody can find safety in numbers—by huddling with the larger mass in hopes of being overlooked. Those who seek to suppress will always find ways to single out others.

conformist: someone who goes along with established customs.

impotent: powerless.

expunging: erasing, getting rid of.

The Emergency Detention Act

During the Korean War in the early 1950s, the U.S. was in a state of near-hysteria over the possibility that Communist spies had infiltrated the government and were planning to overthrow it. Congress responded to these fears by passing the Emergency Detention Act. It allowed for the imprisonment of Americans merely suspected (but not convicted) of espionage or sabotage whenever the president declared a national security emergency. These prisoners were to be held in camps similar to those established for Japanese Americans during World War II. (For more information on the World War II-era camps, see entries on **Robert T. Matsui, Spark M. Matsunaga, Norman Y. Mineta,** and **Clifford I. Uyeda.**)

The Emergency Detention Act was never used against anyone, and by 1957 the federal government had abandoned the prison camps once set aside for detaining potential troublemakers. During the social unrest of the 1960s, however, some people feared that the law might end up being used against black militants and student radicals. So, led by Representative Spark M. Matsunaga of Hawaii, some members of Congress launched a successful movement to repeal the Emergency Detention Act.

Matsunaga's bill, passed in 1971, removed the Justice Department's authority to round up and detain suspected spies and saboteurs. To make sure there would be no repeats of what had happened to Japanese Americans during World War II, it also eliminated the president's power to create prison camps just by issuing an executive order. Congressional approval was required before any action could be taken against possible enemies inside the country.

Instead, we must change the basic attitude that all must conform or be classed as renegades and radicals. Our nation was founded on the idealistic belief in individualism and pioneering spirit, and it would be tragic for our own generation to **forswear** that ideal for the false security of instant assimilation.

It seems to me that our society is large enough to accept a wide diversity of types and opinions, and that no group should be forced to try to conform to the image of the population as a whole. I sometimes wonder if our goal as Japanese Americans is to be so like the white Anglo-Saxon Protestant population as to be indistinguishable from it. If so, we will obviously never succeed!

There has been and continues to be prejudice in this country against Asians. The basis of this is the belief that the Oriental is "**inscrutable.**"

forswear: abandon.

inscrutable: mysterious, difficult to understand.

Having such base feelings, it is simple to stir up public outrage against the recognition of the People's Republic of China in the United Nations, for instance, even though reasoned judgment dictates otherwise, unless of course a yellow [Chinese] communist is really worse than a red [Russian or Soviet] one!

The World War II detention overnight reduced the entire population of one national origin to an enemy, stripped of property, rights of citizenship, human dignity, and due process of law, without so much as even a stifled voice of conscience among our leading scholars or civil libertarians. More recently, the Vietnam war has reinforced the view of Orientals as something less than fully human. All Vietnamese stooping in the rice fields are pictured as the enemy, subhuman without emotions and for whom life is less valuable than for us.

During the trial of Lieutenant [William] Calley [see box on page 168], we were told about "MGR," the "Mere Gook Rule" which was the underlying basis for Calley's mindless assertion that the slaughter of defenseless women and children, our prisoners of war, was "no big thing." The "Mere Gook Rule" holds that life is less important, less valuable to an Oriental.

Laws that protect other human beings do not apply to "gooks." One reporter noted before the verdict became known that the essence of the Calley case was to determine the validity of this rule. He described it as the "unspoken issue" at the trial.

The issue was not as unspoken as most would prefer to believe. The indictment drawn up by the Army against Lieutenant Calley stated in six separate charges that he did at My Lai murder four "Oriental human beings"... murder not less than thirty "Oriental human beings"... murder three "Oriental human beings"... murder an unknown number of "Oriental human beings" not less than seventy ... and so on numbering 102. Thus, the Army did not charge him with the murder of human beings as presumably would have been the case had Caucasians been involved, but instead charged the apparently lesser offense of killing mere "Oriental human beings."

The Army's definition of the crime is hardly surprising inasmuch as the Army itself could have been **construed** as on trial along with Calley for directing a genocide against the Vietnamese. Indeed, the lieutenant pleaded he was only doing

construed: understood to be.

The My Lai Massacre

On March 16, 1968, during the Vietnam war, a savage and shameful episode in American military history took place in the South Vietnamese village of My Lai. It was there that some members of Company C of the U.S. Army's American Division brutally murdered around five hundred women, children, and elderly men on orders from their platoon leader, Lieutenant William Calley. First the Army and then the U.S. government covered up the massacre. But when the story finally hit the newspapers twenty months later, some of the horror and brutality of U.S. participation in the Vietnam War was brought home to the American public.

The incident grew out of an attempt by U.S. troops to flush out some Viet Cong from a group of villages in the general area of My Lai. (The Viet Cong were Communist rebels and guerrilla fighters operating within U.S.-backed South Vietnam. They carried on the war against the United States with help from the regular troops of Communist North Vietnam.) Company C was assigned to sweep through the village of My Lai and burn houses, kill livestock, poison the drinking water, and destroy crops and food supplies. Several men later claimed that they had also been ordered by company commander Captain Ernest Medina to kill any people they found there, a charge Medina denied.

Beginning just before eight in the morning and over the next two to three hours,

Calley's platoon swept through My Lai and nearby rice fields, killing, mutilating, and raping the people they found there. They used machine guns and rifles to mow down groups of villagers, often pausing to "finish off" the wounded before moving on. The majority of those who died were women and children, along with some elderly men. No one ever fired upon the Americans during the operation; in fact, the soldiers confiscated a total of only three guns that day.

The truth about what happened at My Lai was covered up for a year despite attempts by some soldiers to bring it to the attention of their superiors. In March 1969, Vietnam veteran Ronald Ridenhour informed top Army officials about stories he had heard about the massacre from several different soldiers who had taken part in it or witnessed it. The Army investigated the incident and its findings led to murder charges against Lieutenant Calley in September 1969. But it was not until November that the public learned in more detail about what had gone on at My Lai. That month, the *New York Times* ran interviews with men from Company C, the *CBS Evening News* broadcast additional interviews, and *Life* magazine published photographs of the victims.

U.S. and world reaction to the news varied considerably. Most people were horrified by the massacre itself but had very different opinions on its overall significance and

what he thought the Army wanted. It seems clear to me that the Army recognized the "Mere Gook Rule" officially by distinguishing between the murder of human beings and "Oriental

Calley's guilt. Some, for example, accepted that "things like that happen during war." They felt it was unfair to hold Calley and his men responsible for the tragedy, especially since they were only doing what they had been trained to do—namely, kill the enemy (or people they thought might be the enemy). Others were convinced that the soldiers deserved to be executed for the cold-blooded murders of innocent civilians. Many believed the United States and its Vietnam policy were to blame for the deaths at My Lai.

Of the twenty-five men Army investigators identified for court-martial (a trial by the Army) in connection with the My Lai massacre, twelve men were initially recommended to be charged with the war crime of murdering civilians. Of the twelve, only Calley and two other officers of Company C (including Captain Medina) and one enlisted man were court-martialed.

During the trials, Calley was identified from the start as the one who had specifically ordered his men to shoot women and children, and Calley alone was found guilty of war crimes and sentenced to life in prison in 1971. But the Army soon reduced his term, first to twenty years and then to ten years. As a result, Calley became eligible for parole in the fall of 1974 and was released that November.

In their final report, Army investigators listed several factors they believed had contributed to the massacre. They noted poor

Lieutenant William Calley (right) leaving preliminary court-martial hearing for the murder of 102 South Vietnamese civilians at My Lai, August, 1970

training and an overall climate of permissiveness and lack of leadership. In addition, they cited the atmosphere of anxiety that existed throughout Company C, which had suffered quite a few casualties from mines and booby traps, although they had not confronted the enemy face-to-face. But "most disturbing" of all, noted the investigators, was that some soldiers regarded the Vietnamese as "subhuman, on the level of dogs.... Some of the men never referred to Vietnamese as anything but 'gooks,' 'dinks,' or 'slopes.'" The Army concluded that this attitude of extreme prejudice was in part responsible for the vicious treatment the residents of My Lai received at the hands of U.S. soldiers.

human beings." When Calley was convicted, the resulting thunder of criticism verified that many in the public also went along with the concept of differing scales of humanity.

Somehow, we must put into perspective Dean Rusk's dread of the "yellow peril" expressed as justification for a massive antiballistic missile system on the one hand, and on the other, a quest for improved relations with Peking. [Dean Rusk was the U.S. Secretary of State during the 1960s. He was a firm believer in the idea that communism could only be stopped by strong military action.] This latter event could have a great meaning in our own lives as Japanese Americans. We could help this country begin to deal with Asians as people....

Instead of seeking refuge, we should seek to identify as Asians, and begin to serve America as the means by which she can come to understand the problems of the East. Our talents have not been used in American diplomacy, I suspect, largely because we are still not trusted enough.

We must teach our country that life is no less valuable, and human dignity no less precious, in Asia than elsewhere. Our detractors point to the large-scale killings that have occurred in China, Vietnam, Pakistan, and elsewhere in Asia, but we hear remarkably few references to the mass slaughter of six million Jews in Nazi gas chambers in World War II—that was done by Aryans, not Asians, and the total far exceeds the loss of life in the Orient that has been used to justify the debasement of "mere gooks."

I am not trying to compare one group against another, but merely to point out that a lack of appreciation for the value of human life can occur wherever totalitarian government exists. This makes it more than vital for us to oppose such influences within our own country wherever they may occur. The war in Vietnam has lasted for seven years. If Americans believed there was the same worth in the life of an Asian, this war would have ended long ago. If Americans were willing to **concede** that the Asian mind was no different than his, a peace would have been forged in Paris long ago. I am convinced that racism is at the heart of this immoral policy.

I know that many of you are puzzled and even dismayed by actions of some of your sons and daughters who have insisted on a more aggressive role in combating the war and other evils that exist in our society. I plead with you for understanding of this Third World movement in which not only young Japanese Americans but many minority groups are so deeply involved.

concede: admit.

U.S. Marines fire into rubble of a South Vietnamese village believed to be Viet Cong headquarters, 1965

We are confronted with what seem to be many different revolutions taking place all over the world ... the black revolution, the revolution of emerging nations, the youth revolution here and in other countries as well—and something that was even more unheard of, the [Roman Catholic] priests challenging the Vatican on the most basic issues of celibacy and birth control. It is no accident that these things are all happening at the same time, for they all stem from the same great idea that has somehow been rekindled in the world, and that is the idea that the individual is important.

All of the systems of the world today have this in common: for they are mainly concerned with industrialization, efficiency, and gross national product; the value of man is forgotten.

The children of some of you here tonight are involved in the great protests of today—are they chronic **malcontents** and **subversives**? I think not—I think they are probably fairly well-educated, thoughtful people who see certain conditions they don't like and are trying to do something about it. I'm not sure they know exactly what they want to do. I do know they are clearly dissatisfied with the way their world has been run in the past.

So, the problem is not what to do about dissent among our young people—the problem is what to do about the causes of this dissent. The question is not "how to suppress the dissent" but how to make it meaningful ... how to make it productive of a better society which truly places high value on individual human beings as human beings and not merely as so many cogs in the great, cold and impersonal machinery of an industrialized society.

I, for one, believe that the grievances of our youth are real and that they are important. Merely because the majority of students are not involved ... merely because the dissidents are few ... should not minimize the need for serious efforts to **effectuate** change....

Our sons and daughters seek to establish a link with the past. They want to discover who they are, why they are here, and where their destinies are to take them. So many of our children are growing up in complete isolation in a society that places a premium on conformity, in middle-class homes where parents still want to play down their differences, and prefer to **homogenize** with society. Some of these children are rebelling and are seeking ways to preserve their uniqueness and their special heritage. I see pride and strength in this.

One of the most promising avenues for this renewed search for one's heritage is in our school systems—the logical place for instructing children in the knowledge they need. Programs of ethnic heritage studies are needed in our schools....

It seems to me that we as Asians have a large stake in encouraging and promoting such a program. We cannot and must not presume knowledge about Asia merely because we are Asians. This requires concentrated study and dedicated determination. Of course, we do not need to become scholars **cloistered** in the ivory tower of some campus. We need to become

malcontents: people who hold a grudge against the world or are always dissatisfied; complainers.

subversives: people who are secretly dedicated to overthrowing or weakening the government.

effectuate: bring about, achieve.

homogenize: blend different elements into a unified whole.

cloistered: secluded; hidden away.

Patsy Takemoto Mink

aware of the enormous history of Asia and through our daily lives, regardless of what our profession, translate it to all the people with whom we deal. We have not fully met our responsibility to educate the public about Asia and its people.

I hope that all Japanese American organizations and others with strong beliefs in the magnificent history and culture of the Orient will now help lead the way to a more enlightened

America. We have an immense story to tell, for as I have said, the public at large too often assumes that all civilization is Western and no worth is given to the human values of the East. As long as this belief persists, we will have future Vietnams. The way to counteract it is to build public knowledge, through school courses, travel, and dedicated emphasis on increased communications, so that our people will know and appreciate all that is Asian....

We are so few and they who do not care to understand us are so numerous.

It is fine for all citizens to pursue the good life and worldly goods on which our society places such emphasis, but there is increasing recognition that all will be ashes in our mouths unless our place as individuals is preserved. This is what the young are seeking—and I am among those who would rejoice in their goals.

They need the guidance and support of their parents to succeed, but in any event with or without us, they are trying. It **behooves** us to do all we can to accept their aspirations, if not all of their actions, in the hope that this new generation will be able to find a special role for themselves in America, to help build her character, to define her morality, to give her a depth in soul, and to make her realize the beauty of our diverse society with many races and cultures of which we are one small minority.

"

In 1972, Mink mounted a campaign for the presidency of the United States. However, she was unable to attract enough delegate support to be taken seriously as a candidate. Four years later, she decided not to run for a seventh term in the House and instead tried for a seat in the U.S. Senate. She lost in the Democratic primary to Spark M. Matsunaga .

Mink nevertheless remained active in government and politics in other positions. In 1977 and 1978, for example, she served in the administration of President Jimmy Carter as assistant secretary of state for oceans and international

behooves: is necessary or proper for us.

environmental and scientific affairs. She then spent three years as president of Americans for Democratic Action.

Returning home to Hawaii, Mink was elected to the Honolulu City Council. She remained a member of that body until 1987, spending two years (1983 to 1985) as chair. In 1986, while she was still on the council, Mink ran an unsuccessful campaign for governor of Hawaii. She followed that in 1988 with a failed bid to become mayor of Honolulu. In the meantime she kept busy with her law practice and also lectured at the University of Hawaii.

Mink returned to the U.S. House of Representatives in 1990 after winning a special election held to fill the vacancy created when Representative Daniel K. Akaka (see entry) resigned to take the late Spark M. Matsunaga's place in the U.S. Senate. There she once again served as an advocate for civil rights and equal opportunity, as well as universal health care and family and medical leave programs.

Sources

Books

Braden, Waldo W., editor, *Representative American Speeches: 1971–1972,* Wilson, 1972.

Congressional Record, 90th Congress, 1st Session, Volume 113, Part 12, U.S. Government Printing Office, 1967, pp. 16491-16492.

Notable Asian Americans, Gale, 1995.

Peers, W. R., *The My Lai Inquiry,* Norton, 1979.

Periodicals

Commonweal, "The Battle Hymn of Lt. Calley ... and the Republic," April 30, 1971, pp. 183-187.

National Catholic Reporter, "My Lai Massacre Was an American Tragedy: Lessons Unlearned as Warrior Culture Lives," February 24, 1995.

New Republic, "Mental Gymnastics on My Lai," February 21, 1970, pp. 14-16; "Forgetting My Lai," January 15, 1972, p. 8.

New York Times, "Agency Asks End of Detention Act," March 19, 1971, p. 32; "Detention Camps Opposed by House," September 15, 1971.

Irene Natividad

1948–

Filipina American activist, feminist, and educator

"The one constant in my life is that ... I could get people together to fight a cause," declared Irene Natividad in an International Examiner *article. Taking action on behalf of women and minorities (especially Asian Americans) is a path she has followed for over twenty-five years. During that period she has headed several major organizations, including the National Women's Political Caucus, the National Commission on Working Women, and the Philippine American Foundation. The common goal that links these activities is Natividad's commitment to making sure that people who are often overlooked or ignored gain power and influence through political action. "The price of citizenship is political involvement," she explained. "To be silent is to not be counted, and we can't afford not to be counted."*

An International, Multilingual Childhood

Natividad is a native of Manila, the capital and largest city of the Philippines. As the oldest of four children born to a chemical engineer whose job took him around the world, she spent her childhood in a number of different countries, including Japan, Iran, Greece, and India, and is fluent in a half-dozen languages. To this day Natividad credits her family's frequent moves with making it easier for her to work with people from other cultures. It also made her especially sensitive to the limited opportunities women have in some countries, where they are not allowed to hold jobs outside the home.

Natividad completed her high school education in Greece. From there she went on to attend New York's Long Island University. After graduating in 1971 at the top of her class, she enrolled in Columbia University. There she earned two master's degrees, one in American literature in 1973 and one in philosophy in 1976. She has since completed the course work toward her doctoral degree, but increasing demands on her time have made it impossible for her to finish her dissertation.

During the early 1970s Natividad taught at Lehman College of the City University of New York and at Columbia University. The late 1970s and early 1980s saw her move out of the classroom and into college administration. She served first at Long Island University as director of continuing education and then in the same role at New Jersey's William Paterson College.

Takes a Stand on Political and Social Issues

Natividad's first brush with activism came while she was working as a waitress. Using her natural talent for organizing, she rallied her fellow waiters and waitresses to demand higher wages. Although she lost her job as a result, Natividad was not discouraged. Instead, she became active politically. In 1968 she distributed campaign leaflets for Democratic presidential candidate Eugene McCarthy.

Later, as her interest in women's issues grew, Natividad became involved in a number of organizations devoted to women's concerns. In 1980 she founded and headed a group known as Asian American Professional Women. She was also a founding director of both the National Network of Asian-Pacific American Women and the Child Care Action Campaign.

Natividad became active on the national political scene at the beginning of the 1980s. After serving two years as chair of the New York State Asian Pacific Caucus early in the *decade, she went on to serve as deputy vice chair of the Asian Pacific Caucus of the Democratic National Committee. (A caucus is a group of people united in a common cause.) Later, during Walter Mondale's 1984 presidential campaign, she was chosen by Democratic party officials to act as a link between the Asian American community and Mondale's choice for vice president, Geraldine Ferraro.*

Even though Mondale and Ferraro lost the election to Republicans Ronald Reagan and George Bush, Natividad refused to consider the outcome a total defeat. As she explained to a reporter for the Honolulu Star-Bulletin, *because Ferraro had been the first woman ever nominated by a major U.S. political party to run as vice president, she "broke the* **credibility gap** *for all women candidates.... I don't consider '84 a loss. I consider it a win."*

Heads the National Women's Political Caucus

In 1985 Natividad made history herself when she became the first minority woman to head a mainstream political organization—the National Women's Political Caucus. It was established in 1971 by a small group of prominent feminists, including congresswomen Shirley Chisholm, Patsy Takemoto Mink (see entry), and Bella Abzug. Based in Washington, D.C., the National Women's Political Caucus is a bipartisan, or two-party, group that concentrates its efforts on electing more women to public office.

During her four-year term as head of the organization, Natividad took steps to make sure there was a steady flow of potential women candidates for national office. She focused her efforts on helping interested women gain political experience at the local level first. To that end, the caucus conducted training sessions throughout the country for women candidates and their staffs (including the first-ever program for minority women) on how to run a successful campaign. Members of the caucus also collected and analyzed data to help them understand the influential factors in congressional races involving women. In addition, the caucus monitored political appointments of women at the state and national level and promoted women candidates to fill such posts.

credibility gap: a lack of trust, in this case among voters.

In 1991 Natividad was invited to deliver a keynote address at a special gathering held in Washington, D.C., at the National Museum of American History, which is part of the Smithsonian Institution. In her speech she reflected on the many achievements of women in American political life over the past few decades. Natividad provided a transcript of her remarks.

Irene Natividad and supporters react to her election as president of the National Women's Political Caucus, 1985

When the **scribes** of history sit down to write a chapter on the past three decades, they ought to call it "The Wonder Years."... From the first shaky steps out of our kitchens in the late fifties, to the fortifying sessions of **consciousness-raising groups** formed in our own parlors during the sixties, and the

scribes: learned authors.

consciousness-raising groups: gatherings of people who want to increase their awareness of and concern about a social and/or political issue.

Irene Natividad | **179**

growing pains of entering the work world in the seventies and eighties, women in the nineties have indeed come of age. Unquestionably, we are now enjoying the largest measure of personal and political freedom in this country's history. There are those among you in this audience who will agree that the path to progress has been a bumpy one, but no one doubts that indeed we have moved forward.

As we have come of age, from the very basic and revolutionary struggles of our early **foremothers** ... through ... our more recent fights for equality, we have all learned that the personal is indeed the political. You might say we have gone public over the years, and the world has not been the same. The result today is that we are in the fortunate position of having power, serious power, within our reach—power to win our rights, to fulfill our dreams, and to assume full partnership in the public business of this nation....

We have come to accept that certain **notoriety** that comes with being the first woman to enter the rooms of power, be they economic, political or social. Men have entered those rooms in the past, assuming their rightful place as if they had been expected. Well, we are not yet expected in large numbers, for the time being, but as more women enter the room the spotlight will dim and not focus exclusively on the newest member of the club. Instead, the focus will shift to our numbers. Women are now the majority of students in colleges and graduate schools all across this nation. Large numbers of women are studying in medical schools, law schools, and business schools. Women are projected to be the majority of workers in the next century, and the majority of new small businesses are now started by women.

But the most important numerical fact, which underscores our power to shape the forces of twenty-first century America, is that women are the majority of voters in every state of the United States. That means that no one can get elected without our votes, not to the House, not to the Senate, not to the presidency, let alone to school boards. The **gender gap**—or the women's vote, as I prefer to call it—provided the margin of victory for [Texas governor] Ann Richards in the last election, for Governor Doug Wilder in Virginia, and for Mayor David Dinkins in New York City in the 1989 elections.

foremothers: women who preceded us historically.

notoriety: fame.

gender gap: the difference in voting patterns between men and women.

Speakers at a 1971 meeting of the National Women's Political Caucus: (left to right) Betty Smith, Dorothy Haener, Fannie Lou Hamer, and Gloria Steinem

Equally important, the threat of the women's vote propelled the issue of child care into the 1988 presidential campaign. And we saw candidates for the first time tripping over themselves at child care centers. It's not that they had discovered children lately. It's just that the **mediagenic** politics of the last decade dictates that you go to a child care center because it **resonates** among women voters.

Lastly, the large female electorate has encouraged officeholders interested in re-election to make record numbers of women's appointments at both the state and the federal levels....

The successes of the past three decades that I've been recounting to you were the result of efforts from the early **suffrage** movement to the modern women's movement. These extraordinary gains challenge us to reach yet another **plateau**

mediagenic: being attractive to the media.

resonates: relates harmoniously.

suffrage: right to vote.

plateau: stable, high level.

The Equal Rights Amendment (ERA)

Although it most recently generated headlines in the 1980s, the Equal Rights Amendment (ERA) was actually first introduced in Congress in the early 1920s. It proposed adding to the U.S. Constitution a declaration that "equality of rights under the law shall not be denied or abridged by the United States or by any State on account of sex." Under the terms of the ERA, no law could be enacted that would give one sex different rights than the other.

The original amendment was the work of Alice Paul (1885–1977), a lifelong champion of women's rights. In 1918 she helped gain passage of the Nineteenth Amendment, which extended to American women the rights of all citizens, including the right to vote. She was also the founder of the National Woman's Party (NWP), a political organization devoted to establishing equal rights for women.

Paul and her fellow activists believed that women needed to have full equality under the law before they could ever achieve full equality in other areas of life. So they focused their efforts on drafting constitutional amendments that would address the equality issue at both the state and federal level.

Some women and men—even those who generally supported women's rights—feared that passage of an equal rights amendment might reverse some of the workers' protection laws they had fought so hard to achieve—laws like the one that limited a female factory laborer's workday to ten hours. While Paul acknowledged that improving working conditions for women was an important goal, she warned that in many cases the laws protecting women actually succeeded in shutting them out of certain kinds of jobs. For her, nothing less than full equality would do.

To that end, the NWP managed to persuade Congress to bring the Equal Rights Amendment up for a vote in 1923. But it failed to capture the two-thirds majority it needed to move on to the states for approval. Year after year, each time it was reintroduced, the ERA went down to defeat.

Then, during the 1960s, the political climate began to change. The success of the African American-based civil rights movement inspired other groups, including women, to mount their own struggle for equality and justice. The newly formed National Organization for Women (NOW) made approval of the ERA its major goal.

in history—to top our gains, so to speak. But I didn't come here tonight merely to sing the praises of women's achievements of these past thirty years. I came to provide, if I can, a frank assessment.

The organized women's movement is far from being a small band of feminists doing consciousness-raising, or "hell-raising," as some would have said a few decades ago. Over the

Over the next few years the amendment gained support among leading Democratic and Republican politicians, including President Richard Nixon. Finally, in 1972, both houses of Congress passed the ERA by wide margins. It then faced its next major hurdle—winning the approval of three-fourths of the states before the 1979 deadline ordered by Congress.

Despite the enthusiastic backing it received in Congress, the ERA met with strong resistance at the state level. Religious and political conservatives joined forces to oppose it. They relied on many of the same arguments that had been used against it back in the 1920s: an equal rights amendment, they insisted, would have a negative impact on social institutions such as marriage and the family; it would eliminate the economic protections women enjoyed as a result of their dependence on men, such as alimony payments in the event of divorce; it would also force women to take on roles usually filled by men, including combat duty in the military.

In addition, opponents tried to appeal to members of the anti-abortion movement by declaring that the ERA would make it impossible to pass any restrictions on abortion.

They also charged it was immoral and destructive because it would legalize homosexual marriage and allow homosexuals to adopt children.

By 1974, the ERA had managed to win the approval of thirty-three of the required thirty-eight states. Yet it ran into trouble when only three more states had signed on by the 1979 deadline. Congress responded by granting ERA backers until June of 1982 to drum up the necessary votes, but the extra time did not help. The ERA fell short of its goal. And when it was reintroduced in Congress in July 1982, it could not even attract enough support to make it out of the House of Representatives.

Since 1982 the ERA has been reintroduced at every opening session of Congress. Each time it has quickly faded from view. Meanwhile, more than a dozen states have changed their own constitutions to ban discrimination based on sex. And in 1996 Supreme Court decisions in cases challenging the legality of one-sex schools such as the Citadel and the Virginia Military Institute (VMI) have raised new hopes about a possible revival of the ERA.

years the movement has acquired sophisticated, **grass-roots organizing** [and] **coalition-building**, political skills that have helped to win many a victory. The quest for equality in employment, education, in all areas of public life, has been embraced by this nation. The pioneers of women's freedom of the late sixties have been transformed into the largest mainstream movement of the late eighties.

grass-roots organizing: persuading people to get involved in an activity at the local level (away from established centers of power).

coalition-building: creating an alliance of different people or groups who come together to take action.

Yet the test that confronts this movement is one of durability. It is, in effect, a dare—a dare to continue to thrive when powerful vehicles, such as the presidency and the courts, are no longer available to support basic rights won earlier in the struggle for social reform along gender lines. All successful movements must face the fact that with successes come failures.... To sustain themselves, movements must not only grow, they must change.... It [is] difficult to chart a future course as **definitive** as that pursued during the seventies, when equal rights, **embodied** in the fight for the Equal Rights Amendment [ERA; see box], made the mission so clear and seemingly so simple.

The contradictions to women's successes have proved most frustrating. The public **consensus** we had for women's equality has had little effect on the wage gap. Today [on the average] women still earn only two-thirds of what men earn, no matter what area or level of employment. As [African American civil rights leader] Jesse Jackson said so well, the loaf of bread does not cost the woman any less, so why pay her less? It seems so clear, but no one is listening. The consensus for women's equality has not produced a **coherent** and caring system of child care for families and for the women that society has encouraged to work. The equal rights majority has not been able to gain recognition and protection for the rights of women in the nation's most basic legal document, the Constitution of the United States. Reproductive choice [a woman's right to an abortion during the first three months of pregnancy] has been won and now is threatened state by state.

These mixed results confuse and confound. So while women are **buoyed** by their successes, they are simultaneously **bedeviled** by the inability to sustain the fast pace they had set for themselves in the sixties and seventies. The result is frustration.

Frustration is inevitable for a country in which we still must reargue the basics of reproductive choice, **affirmative action,** and civil rights as a whole. Frustration is justified when a group that is fifty-three percent of the population numbers as its representatives only two percent of the Senate, only six percent of the House, only sixteen percent of the state legislatures, and only nine percent of the federal district court judges. Frustration is justified when there seems to be an **inverse** relationship between the number of women in public life and the degree of

definitive: clear.

embodied: represented.

consensus: agreement, understanding.

coherent: logical, orderly.

confound: baffle, puzzle.

buoyed: supported, nourished.

bedeviled: troubled, confused.

affirmative action: programs that promote educational, employment, and economic opportunities to women and minorities in an effort to make up for past discrimination.

inverse: opposite or contrary to what might be expected.

power that they exercise. The higher you go, the less accessible it seems. Frustration is justified when a majority of the poor are still women and children and women workers are still clustered, for the most part, in low-paying clerical, sales, and service jobs. Frustration is justified when the largest industrialized nation in the world is unable to pass a family and medical leave bill at a time when two-earner families are the norm in this country. [The Family Leave Bill was passed during President Bill Clinton's first term in office.]

These frustrations make the organized women's movements' efforts seem **Sisyphean** at times. For every step up the hill, we roll back a few times. But women are **resilient** and persistent, and so are our organizations. Women's groups didn't fold up their tents and go home when the ERA failed.... Instead, they

Alice Paul, women's rights champion in the 1910s and 1920s, broadcasts for the National Women's Party, 1922

Sisyphean: like the labors of Sisyphus, a king in Greek mythology who was condemned to roll a rock up a hill in Hades (the underworld) only to have it roll back down again as he neared the top.

resilient: able to recover easily from misfortune or adjust quickly to change.

learned to **coalesce**, not just among themselves, but with civil rights groups, labor groups, and, in some instances, even business groups to fight for issues demanding their attention.... In addition, women have become experts in using the media to reach the majority of Americans, so that more than any one piece of legislation, the women's movement's best achievement of late is the creation of a growing **constituency** for a family support system in a society where women's **disproportionate** responsibilities for work at home and work at work often make time more valuable than money....

The women's vote remains the most powerful tool for social change in the coming decades. Not always voting as a **bloc**, except recently on the issue of choice, women have increasingly come to view their vote as the expression of their hopes and dreams for a better world. The candidate who makes direct appeals to this vote wins.... Women are also much more likely to cross party lines to vote their interests....

Infrequent women voters were asked in 1988 what the issues were that propelled them to vote. The results were not surprising. "Not earning as much as a man" was the number-one answer.... Crime, or personal vulnerability as a whole, was the second most important issue. Employment. Environment. And the **prism** through which women saw all of these issues—children.

It is important to note that there is a strong **correlation** between the increasing number of women in the workplace and the increasing number of women voters. The more women become charged with their economic destiny, the more likely they are to vote. [Former congresswoman] Shirley Chisholm phrased it well when she said that women vote according to their pocketbooks. The truly liberating issue for women is economic security.

The task that remains, however, is how to **mobilize** that vote. Like most Americans, women are still voting only half their strength—a fact which I find personally frustrating. I have told women all across this country that if they do not vote, then they have not earned the right to complain about crime, about education, about discrimination, about the environment. I remind them that in other countries—in Latin America, for instance—people get shot for exercising their

coalesce: cooperate, join together.

constituency: group of supporters.

disproportionate: out of balance, lopsided.

bloc: a group united for a common purpose.

prism: something that changes or colors the look of whatever is viewed through it.

correlation: relationship.

mobilize: bring together in an effective way in order to take action.

right to vote. But in this country, we take that right for granted. On election day, many of us go shopping, which is all right as long as we shop as well for a candidate who represents our interests....

There is no substitute, however, for promoting social reform through our own leaders, our own representatives.... [Our impact] would be even more dramatic if there were 290 of [us] in Congress out of 435 instead of 29 out of 435. Clearly, **token** numbers of us on the inside cannot speak for the millions of us who are out here. And it remains the most challenging task of the women's movement to make those numbers grow bigger. It is not an easy task. It is an effort that's a little bit like carving a woman's face on Mount Rushmore [a mountain in South Dakota in which the faces of four former U.S. presidents—George Washington, Thomas Jefferson, Abraham Lincoln, and Theodore Roosevelt—have been carved]. It will take years to chip away at stubborn rock before a woman's face begins to emerge. But trust me, emerge it will.

A 1987 survey of voters' attitudes towards women candidates, commissioned by the National Women's Political Caucus, revealed that the future of women candidates is positive. From school board to Congress to the presidency, the poll showed that the **bias** against women candidates is **eroding**. In part, this is due to the public's becoming more accustomed to the **notion** of women holding office....

Given the changing **demographics** of the United States, which project a next century when minorities will be the majority, the [women candidates] of the future will come from various ethnic groups. The next plateau for the women's movement, which so far has been largely white and middle class, is how to embrace **pluralism** in its maturity. How to arrive at consensus in the future—given the possibility of emerging political tensions between the ethnic groups that will **come into ascendance**—will pose a difficult challenge for many of us.

Where the women's movement will be in the new political **mosaic** of the coming decades will be interesting to see, as Hispanics conflict with Asian or African Americans, or vice versa, in carving out new districts. How do you coalesce the interests of the young with the interests of the old? Will it be child care

token: only symbolic; not impressive in force.

bias: prejudice.

eroding: being broken down.

notion: idea.

demographics: the statistical characteristics of the human population.

pluralism: the social, racial, ethnic, and religious differences within a larger society.

come into ascendance: gain influence or rise to power.

mosaic: picture or pattern made up of many small pieces.

versus Medicare at a time when twenty-five percent of the American population will be older Americans, the majority of whom will vote, when children can't?

Clearly the task before us is enormous. But we women are more than up to it.... We are smart, we are patient, we are **persevering**. There are more of us and we live longer [than men]. The hurdles that we face are real. But we cannot move forward if we spend our time **bemoaning** our fate and the **foibles** and **arrogance** of the other gender [men].

Nancy Astor, the first woman to sit in the British House of Commons, said it best when she said, "Mercifully, women have no political past. We have all the mistakes of one-sex legislation with its **appalling** failures to guide us. We should know what to avoid. It is no use blaming the men. We made them and now it's up to us, the makers of men, to be a little more responsible."

Thank you very much.

99

Since stepping down as head of the National Women's Political Caucus, Natividad has remained busy with a number of other activities on both the national and international level. In 1991 she became chair of the National Commission on Working Women, which is devoted to improving the economic status of working women in the United States. Natividad has also organized and led political workshops outside the country. For instance, she directs the Global Forum of Women, a biennial (occurring every two years) gathering of women from around the world who meet to discuss and develop leadership strategies. And in 1995 Natividad was involved in planning a meeting on political leadership that ran in conjunction with the United Nations Fourth World Conference on Women.

Natividad maintains affiliations with many Asian American organizations as well, among them the Philippine American Foundation, for which she serves as executive director. Its efforts to reduce poverty in her native Philippines include working with local area activists to encourage rural development.

persevering: persistent.

bemoaning: expressing displeasure and regret about something.

foibles: failings, shortcomings.

arrogance: showing feelings of superiority.

appalling: shocking, outrageous.

In addition, Natividad heads her own consulting firm, Natividad & Associates. It provides services to groups that are trying to reach specific segments of the voting population. Her skills in this area were put to the test during the 1992 presidential election campaign, when she served as co-chair of the Women of Color Committee for Clinton/Gore.

Sources

Books

Asian American Almanac, Irene Natividad, editor, Gale, 1995.

Notable Asian Americans, Gale, 1995.

Periodicals

AsianWeek, "Women Shape the Course of Their Future During Conference," October 23, 1992, p. 12.

Honolulu Star-Bulletin, "Leading the Fight to Give Women Political Might," July 9, 1985.

International Examiner, "Activist Natividad Wants APIs to Make Themselves Heard," November 3, 1993, p. 1.

USA Today, "Asian-American Leads National Group," July 1, 1985; "Women's Caucus Loses Cornerstone," August 2, 1989, p. 2A.

Syngman Rhee

1875–1965

Korean political activist and founding president of South Korea

Syngman Rhee, the first president of the newly liberated South Korea in 1948, spent much of his life in the United States and was a respected leader among Korean Americans. He received his college education here and, while going to school, he found inspiration for his political beliefs in American-style democracy. Later, he spent most of the three decades he was in exile from his native land on American soil. When Korea was freed from Japanese rule after World War II, the United States supported his leadership in South Korea and he strongly influenced U.S. policy toward Korea.

International Influences Form the Young Activist

Rhee was born in Hwanghae Province, located in present-day North Korea. He was a descendant of the family that had ruled Korea since 1392. For many centuries, his country had enjoyed close cultural ties with China. Rhee's father therefore saw to it that his son received a classical Chinese education to prepare him for a high-level career in government service. Rhee was an excellent student who took first place one year in the annual national examinations held in the capital city of Seoul. Learning English was not part of the Chinese curriculum, however. Since Rhee felt that English language studies would be important to his future, he remained in Seoul after completing his Chinese education and enrolled in a school run by Methodist missionaries.

In the mission school Rhee was introduced to the idea of democracy. He embraced it wholeheartedly, and in 1894—to the dismay of his father—he joined a group of young reform-minded student activists known as the Independence Club. The organization called for changes in the ancient Korean monarchy (a government in which the head of state is usually a king and/or queen, and ruling power is passed along from generation to generation). The Independence Club also insisted on an end to the growing Japanese influence in the government. Since the 1870s, Japan's goal had been to weaken Korea's longstanding ties to China, Japan's major rival in the region. China in turn tried to lessen the impact of Japan's actions by encouraging Korea to develop a closer relationship with the United States. Those efforts helped pave the way for young people like Rhee to become familiar with western-style politics and society.

As a member of the Independence Club, Rhee founded and edited a newspaper devoted to the activists' cause. It was Korea's first daily newspaper as well as the first published solely by a Korean. In 1895, he became head of the reform movement after the leader of the Independence Club was forced to flee the country.

Imprisoned for Reform Activities

Two years later, Rhee was arrested and jailed after leading a massive student demonstration in Seoul. He then suffered through seven months of torture in prison, during which time he converted to Christianity. Later, he was sentenced to a life term and moved to another prison. There he organized classes for his fellow prisoners in religion, economics, and English and also conducted religious services. In addition, he translated several books from English into Korean and from Korean into English and wrote a book of his own entitled The Spirit of Independence.

In 1904, Rhee gained his freedom when the Korean king unexpectedly declared a general amnesty (pardon) for all political prisoners. He then headed to the United States and spent the next six years pursuing his education. Rhee earned a bachelor's degree from George Washington University, a master's degree from Harvard University, and a doctorate from Princeton University. While he was at Princeton he came to admire the school's president, Woodrow Wilson— just a few years before Wilson became president of the United States. Wilson's philosophy of international justice strongly influenced Rhee in the years to come.

Rhee headed home to Korea around 1911. He then worked as an official for the YMCA, established and led the Korean Christian Student Movement, and served as a teacher for the Methodist Mission Board. His return came shortly after the Japanese had essentially taken over Korea, which they renamed Choson. They assumed control of all major government functions, including foreign relations, the armed services, police, money and banking, and communications.

From 1910 until 1918, the Japanese tightened their grip on the country. They got rid of their opponents, took charge of the land system, and carried out strict changes in the government. They even outlawed the Korean language and banned the use of Korean names. In 1919, millions of Koreans insisting on an end to Japanese domination—including Rhee—took to the streets in a series of nonviolent demonstrations for independence known as the March First Movement. The uprising was quickly and brutally crushed, however, and Rhee was again forced to flee for his own safety.

Establishes Korean Government-in-Exile

From a base he established in Hawaii, Rhee spent the next twenty-two years as president of the Korean Provisional Government in Exile. He also established the Korean Methodist Church and the Korean Christian Institute there. He had been the unanimous choice to lead the provisional government among fellow activists who had settled in Hawaii as well as in China and the mainland United States. Before long, Rhee emerged as the voice and inspiration of the entire Korean independence movement.

Inside Korea, the rebels used passive-resistance techniques (the nonviolent refusal to cooperate with authorities) and guerrilla warfare (a type of war in which small, independent groups of people carry out acts of harassment and sabotage) to disrupt daily life and put pressure on the Japanese. Meanwhile, outside Korea, Rhee worked tirelessly to achieve international recognition for his government. Although he concentrated his efforts on the United States in particular, he wanted very much to present his case before all the democratic governments of the west. His pleas fell largely on deaf ears. Throughout the 1920s and 1930s, Japan successfully persuaded world leaders that Korea was not worth their attention.

Rhee was regularly re-elected president of the government-in-exile until 1941, at which time the post went to another

Japanese police massacre Koreans who rose in revolt in the March First Movement, 1919

independence leader. Rhee continued to wage his campaign on behalf of his country throughout World War II as head of the Korean Commission. The commission was an agency he had set up in Washington, D.C., to serve as a sort of diplomatic arm of the provisional Korean government.

Ultimately, Korea's bid for freedom had to wait until the end of World War II. In August 1945, Japan admitted defeat and gave up the territories formerly under its control, including Korea. The victors—the United States and the Soviet Union—then occupied Korea together while negotiating its fate. U.S. troops were in charge of the peninsula south of the 38th parallel, and Soviet troops held the territory north of that point. All Koreans wanted unification of their land, but as the Cold War between the United States and the Soviet Union mounted, unification conferences broke down.

Launches Battle for Independence on Korean Soil

Two months after the Japanese surrender, Rhee returned to his homeland amid widespread popular support and began the second phase of the battle for independence. Over the next three years, he argued that the only acceptable solution for Korea was to hold immediate elections to allow the Korean people to decide their own future. He opposed all agreements that left Korea divided, even on a temporary basis. (Rhee, an anti-communist, feared that allowing the Soviets to remain in the north would eventually cause the entire region to fall under communist control.) Rhee watched in frustration as the two emerging superpowers continued to bicker over his country. Often, his disappointment at their lack of progress was so great he went over the heads of U.S. government officials to take his case directly to the American people to win their support.

Finally, on May 10, 1948, elections were held throughout the U.S. zone under the supervision of the United Nations. U.S. officials had hoped a moderate candidate would emerge who could work not only with Rhee and his fellow right-wing anti-communists but also with the growing number of leftist activists. But when no such candidate appeared on the scene, the U.S. threw its support behind Rhee and helped restrain the left-wing movement. Despite several rivals who challenged his leadership, Rhee ended up winning the right

to represent Seoul in the National Assembly. His colleagues in the assembly then voted him president of the newly-formed Republic of Korea.

On August 15, 1948, a ceremony was held marking the formal transfer of power from the U.S. Military Government of South Korea to the new regime of Syngman Rhee. (In the north, a separate government was formed one month later, with the support of the Soviet Union, under the leadership of Kim Il Sung, a communist who had led anti-Japanese guerrilla forces in China.) On the occasion of the formation of an independent South Korea, Rhee briefly reflected on the past before discussing the challenges of the future—including the need for unity not only within South Korea itself but also between the northern and southern sections of the country.

Rhee working in exile for Korean independence from the Japanese in his New York office, 1942

An excerpt from the remarks he delivered is reprinted here from Vital Speeches of the Day, *September 15, 1948.*

The ceremonies of this day mark the third anniversary of the liberation of our nation from the Japanese Empire. As we receive, in the name of the whole Korean people, our **sovereign** government once more into our own hands, our national independence is solemnly and fatefully restored. This day is the **culmination** of four decades of hopes, dreams, struggles, and sacrifices. To stand in this hour in my own country as a free citizen under our own government is the greatest moment of my life. I speak to you on this occasion as your duly elected president, but speak in greatest humbleness as the servant of all our people.

But, my fellow citizens, the final destination toward which we are bound lies yet ahead, at the end of a road that may be both long and rough. We have answered the doubters who questioned our ability to govern our own destinies—even though we had already so governed them for more than forty-two hundreds of years—with an overwhelming and spontaneous demonstration of democratic self-determination in the election of May 10. We have answered the doubters with patience and with deeds, rather than with cries of anger or distress. We must continue in this same spirit to meet the critical problems that overshadow our rejoicing today. This is no time to relax and take our ease. Rather than to brood upon the past, or to rejoice in the present, we must plan and work for the future.

Ours is now the task to forge in labor, in love, and in loyal devotion the foundations upon which our Republic can rise securely and in peace. From you who have given so much and endured so much there must come yet greater sacrifices and an even stronger determination. Wearied and distraught though we may be from the struggles of the past, we can face the future with renewed strength, in the proud realization that we labor not only for ourselves but also for the peace and security of all mankind.

sovereign: free from control by others.

culmination: realization, final achievement.

As we turn our thoughts ahead, there are certain strong foundations upon which we must build anew the structure of our national life....

We should place our full trust and faith in democracy. It is my greatest regret that among our people are some who believe that only a dictatorship can guide us through the troubles that beset our way. Still others, shuddering at the destructive tactics of communism, and fearing that the people have not within themselves the strength and wisdom to meet the needs of the time, have reluctantly come to believe that a dictatorship may be necessary for the immediate future at least. But we must not permit temporary doubts or uneasiness to prevent our laying the basis of fundamental principles that will stand the test of time.

History has proved that dictatorships cannot establish peace and prosperity. The democratic way will be slow and hard, but we must hold to the faith that only righteousness can defeat evil. If we would make a mountain, we know from experience that we must carry every load of earth. Democracy is the faith of our friends in every part of the world. Dictatorship is the method of government against which our friends have fought. Democracy is the only form of government under which the liberties of the people will be secure....

We must protect civil rights and fundamental freedom. The essence of democracy is the protection of the fundamental freedom of individuals. Both citizens and government must be alert to protect freedom of speech, of assembly, of religion, and of thought, by all proper means. Any who try to buy food at the price of freedom will end by losing both. We have endured a generation of **tyranny** in which not only our words and our deeds but our very thoughts were subject to the harsh restraints of an alien police. But this is not the native habit of our historic experience. In the strength of our local government, in the justice of our courts, in the responsibility of the police to the people, in the principle that he who would lead must serve, and most of all, in the unshakable **integrity** of our own hearts there lies the fundamental guarantee we seek and demand.

Liberalism must be understood, respected, and protected. Liberals, certain intellectuals, and progressive-minded youth are often critical of the necessary processes of establishing an

tyranny: oppressive power exercised by a government.

integrity: honesty; firm belief in following high standards.

South Korea since 1950

The division of Korea into two separate nations after World War II led to brutal consequences. In 1950, two years after the nations were formed, the Korean War erupted when North Korean troops attacked in South Korea. North Korean leader Kim Il Sung apparently believed that the political conflicts among South Koreans would pave the way for his forces to invade the South, overthrow the Rhee government, and reunite Korea. International forces, however, quickly became involved, and Cold War politics turned the civil war into a global struggle between Communist and non-Communist forces. United States troops, entering the war with allies under the sanction of the United Nations, fought aggressively under the command of General Douglas MacArthur. When the allied troops pushed too far north, China entered the war in support of the North Koreans. After one year of fierce fighting, the Soviet Union proposed cease-fire negotiations. The talks lasted for two more years before a truce was signed by major powers in July 1953. By this time, 415,004 South Koreans and 36,700 U.S. and other allied troops were dead. The physical, social, political, and economic destruction to Korea was immeasurable.

An uneasy peace has existed on the Korean peninsula after the outright hostilities ended in 1953. North and South Korea never signed a treaty officially ending the war, and in many ways have remained bitter enemies.

Both nations have struggled with authoritarian rule. In the South, Syngman Rhee's regime was followed briefly by that of John M. Chang, a reform-minded president. He was ousted in May 1961 after only a year in office by members of the South Korean military, who feared that growing political and economic instability as well as unrest among college students might result in reunification with the North.

Park Chung Hee, leader of the group that had overthrown Chang, governed South Korea throughout the rest of the 1960s and into the 1970s. Park's ambitious economic reforms, which included attracting extensive Japanese investments, helped South Korea industrialize and become a major exporter of manufactured goods. But Park's strong-arm political and social policies often touched off violent protest demonstrations, especially among college students. Dissidents were kept under close watch by government spies who harassed and intimidated them. In 1972, Park transformed South Korea into a true dictatorship, issuing a new constitution that virtually guaranteed his rule. The South Korean economy continued to grow and prosper, but so, too, did political tensions under this repressive regime.

In 1979, Park was assassinated by the head of the Korean Central Intelligence

organized state. Many patriots, judging too quickly of their words and deeds, have condemned such critics as dangerous and destructive. Actually, freedom of thought is the basic

Agency (KCIA). As soon as the opportunity presented itself, General Chun Doo Hwan took charge of the military, crushed the opposition movement, and prevented any attempts to reform the constitution. South Korea simmered for seven more years under a brutal dictator who used violent force to repress his opposition.

After a series of massive, violent protest demonstrations in 1987, Chun was forced to support democratic reforms, including a presidential election. That December, South Koreans chose Roh Tae Woo, a member of Chun's Democratic Liberal political party, as their new president. The following year (1988), a new constitution took effect, and national elections were held in which opposition parties won a majority in the country's legislature. Roh resigned as president in 1992 amid charges that his party had bought votes in the 1991 elections.

In late 1992, South Koreans elected their first civilian president in over thirty years, Kim Young Sam. A former anti-government protester who spent two years under house arrest during the regime of President Park Chung Hee, Kim Young Sam is a supporter of gradual economic and political reform.

In 1996, South Korea very publicly condemned its turbulent past. At the end of what South Koreans consider their "trial of the century," former presidents Chun Doo Hwan and Roh Tae Woo were found guilty of treason for seizing power after the assas-

Korean refugees flee south to escape North Korean forces, Korean War, 1951

sination of President Park and crushing the opposition with brutal and deadly force. Chun was sentenced to death, and Roh was sentenced to more than twenty-two years in prison. Military officers and business executives involved in the killing and corruption also received prison sentences.

In the mid-1990s South Korea, once impoverished and decimated by war, was the world's eleventh-largest economy. Activism was alive and well in the nation, however. In January 1997 South Korean unions captured international attention with a nationwide strike protesting a labor law that threatened job security. The South Korean government was forced to negotiate.

foundation of a democratic state. Such people must be protected in their right to disagree. If we seek to overwhelm them, it must be with embarrassment from the fullness of our respect

North Korea after the Korean War

North Korea also experienced authoritarian rule following the war. North Korea was at the mercy of one man—Kim Il Sung, who ran his country with an iron fist from 1948 until he died in 1994. At first a close ally of the Soviet Union and then of China, Kim Il Sung eventually fashioned his own style of dictatorship that distanced him and his country from the rest of the world. It blended elements of a Soviet-style communist police state with strong Korean nationalism. Under this system, Kim Il Sung was raised to god-like status in his country. This created an air of mystery about North Korea that was difficult for outsiders to penetrate.

Under Kim Il Sung's leadership, North Korea's economic recovery lagged far behind that of its neighbor to the south. Late in the 1960s, the North showed a renewed sense of hostility toward the South and its chief ally, the United States. First, a North Korean assassination squad very nearly succeeded in killing South Korea's President Park Chung Hee. A series of guerrilla raids into the South followed. In 1968, North Koreans seized the *Pueblo,* a U.S. intelligence ship, and held its crew prisoner for a year. Then, in 1969, the North shot down a U.S. reconnaissance plane.

North Korea's economic problems, isolation, and unpredictable behavior continued into the 1990s. Industrial output has been shrinking since at least 1989, and energy supplies seem to be quite low. Foreign trade is in a slump because North Korea has so few trading partners left after the fall of the Soviet Union and its satellite nations in eastern Europe. Farm production fell, and the possibility of famine loomed.

North Koreans flee south, 1950

In 1993, the world learned that North Korea had a secret nuclear weapons program that violated the terms of an international treaty agreement it had signed. Negotiations aimed at ending that particular crisis were just getting under way at the time of Kim Il Sung's death from a heart attack in mid-1994. Several months of uncertainty and confusion followed before his son, Kim Jong Il, emerged as the leader of North Korea.

The border between North and South Korea was the most heavily fortified border in the world in the mid-1990s. Growing numbers of South Koreans were calling for reunification in light of reports that their family members in North Korea were living under desperate conditions. Yet signals from the North continued to be unpredictable and at times provocative, and negotiation about reunification seemed remote.

and tolerance for their views. In the eternal struggle between right and wrong, we must stand firm in the faith that truth eventually will prevail....

Generosity and cooperation should be the **keystones** of our new government. The greatest need of our new national life, to establish its stability at home and its dignity abroad, is that it be a government of, by, and for all the people. Our country needs the active support of every citizen, whatever his former beliefs may have been. We must start our new government in the hope that our people from every political group will stand together behind the ideals and the program set forth in our Constitution. Like all true democracies everywhere in the world, we must close ranks after an election is held and unite not in **partisanship** but in patriotism....

We must strive to unite our divided nation. We await with hope and determination the missing third of our representatives from the north. The 38th parallel division is no part of our choice and is wholly foreign to our destiny. Nothing must be neglected to keep wide open the door to reunion of the whole nation. The Everwhite Mountains are as surely our boundary to the north as are the Straits of Korea to the south. No temporary international situation can obscure what has been established through the centuries as historic fact.

We must not allow ourselves to be hurried into any conviction that we have a duty to conquer and reclaim the north. Instead, we must be content to proceed slowly and carefully, in accord with the program already laid down by the United Nations. This program can never be complete until the provinces of the north are enabled to hold an election internationally approved and to unite with us fully in the formation of a truly national government. No matter what the obstacles to this program may be, it is our duty and our strong determination to give to the people in the north every opportunity to join with us in common and equal brotherhood. A peacefully united nation is the only kind of nation we have known or wish to know. We shall never rest until this goal has been achieved....

Our foreign policy is devoted to world peace. In all our dealings with foreign nations, our solemn endeavor is to

keystones: foundations.

partisanship: strong and often blindly followed beliefs in a particular cause, side, or person.

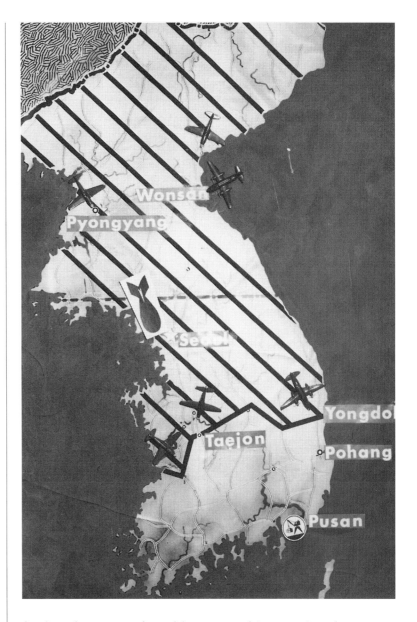

further the cause of world peace and international cooperation. It is in this spirit that we gratefully accept the aid **tendered** us by the United States. We have known a time when foreign aid was deeply distrusted, as meaning in effect foreign control. It is true that our request for such aid must always reflect the most careful consideration of potential effects. However, the old conception has given way to a new concept of

tendered: offered, presented.

202   Syngman Rhee

the relationship of all nations, both great and small, recognizing the independence of all nations and the inseparability of the problems of peace and war. The freedom of small nations has come to be of concern to the great powers both individually and through the United Nations. Experience has shown and we believe the future will continue to show that it is to the interest of the entire free world that the largest possible portion should remain free. Therefore, aid is not given to **entrench** selfish **imperialism** but in the hope of maintaining world peace.

Today the American Military Government in South Korea is ending, and the Republic of Korea is beginning. This day marks a fresh renewal of the friendship commenced between Koreans and Americans two generations ago. We owe our liberty to the destruction of the enemy by the armed forces of our friends. During the occupation of our country by American troops, the United States has proved its devotion to the principles of humanity and justice on which that great nation was founded. We wish to express the thanks of every Korean to the individuals who have participated in the Military Government....

Our relations with the United States of America are especially cordial. We are proud also of the close ties maintained with our neighboring government of China for **millenniums.** We shall never forget the participation of the United Kingdom in the ... pledge guaranteeing our independence. We are especially happy for the fine speech by Dr. Luna, of the Philippine Republic, Chairman of the United Nations Temporary Commission on Korea. Our deep gratitude is extended to all the nations that sent delegates to assist in the free and democratic elections from which this government is derived. Considering the particular problems that still confront us, we express our earnest wish to live at peace with the Union of Socialist Soviet Republics.

We realize that without the good will and assistance of free nations, the many problems before us might be **insuperable.** But we know we have their good will and feel we can count on their assistance. Above all, we need and we count upon the loyalty, the devotion to duty, and the determination of

entrench: reinforce.

imperialism: a nation's practice of extending its power by gaining indirect control over another nation's political and/or economic affairs.

millenniums: thousands of years.

insuperable: impossible to overcome.

People go about their business in the ruins of the great fire of Pusan, South Korea, after the truce of 1953

all Korean citizens. With hopeful hearts and minds alert we take into our own hands today a sovereign republican government that will long endure.

99

The hopeful tone of Rhee's address soon gave way to the harsh realities of the situation as he struggled to set up a working democracy. Within South Korea, he faced endless conflicts with his political opponents. Outside the country, tensions were increasing between the Soviet Union and the United States over the Soviets' continuing domination of

North Korea (which by that time was officially known as the Democratic People's Republic of Korea [DPRK]).

Korean War Brings Chaos

On June 25, 1950, following months of border skirmishes, North Korean troops—with the support of their Soviet ally—invaded South Korea. The United Nations quickly condemned the invasion, and within a week, U.S. ground forces arrived on the scene to prevent North Korea from moving farther south. They were later joined by troops from other countries who were also members of the United Nations. Before long, the communist government of China entered the dispute on the side of North Korea. The so-called Korean War ended in a standoff in July 1953, with armed troops (including U.S. forces) on both sides of the old border at the 38th parallel.

Meanwhile, South Korea had fallen into a state of complete social and economic turmoil. Rhee nonetheless remained very popular and easily won re-election to the presidency in both the 1952 and 1956 elections. But as time went by he became more fiercely anti-communist than ever and adopted an extremely tough stance against his political opponents, some of whom he threw in jail. During this period, the aging leader also fell under the influence of a number of corrupt friends and advisors. They cut him off from others and did not tell him how bad things really were in South Korea throughout the 1950s.

In 1960, Rhee was once again elected president amid widespread charges that the vote had been rigged to make sure he would win. Soon afterward, violent student demonstrations erupted in Seoul and spread throughout the country. Within just a couple of months, the government collapsed. And as he had done so many years before, Rhee left his homeland and took refuge in Hawaii. There he lived out the rest of his life in exile.

Rhee died in 1965 of complications from a stroke. His body was then returned to South Korea for a state funeral. As one official noted at the time, giving the fallen leader an honorable farewell was an acknowledgment of his "great contribution to national independence."

Sources

Books

Notable Asian Americans, Gale, 1995.

Periodicals

Chicago Tribune, "North Korea's Kim Il Sung Dies at 82," July 9, 1994; "The Kim Mystery," July 17, 1994; "Above the DMZ, an Enigma Lurks," May 27, 1996; "South Korea Ex-Chiefs Ruled Guilty," August 26, 1996; "South Korean Verdicts End an Era," August 27, 1996; "Reunification Remains Distant 'If' for Koreas," September 13, 1996.

Newsweek, "Reds on the Rocks," September 30, 1996.

New York Times, "Syngman Rhee Dies an Exile from Land He Fought to Free," July 20, 1965.

Vital Speeches of the Day, "The Goal We Seek: We Must Establish Our Own Government Ourselves," October 15, 1947, pp. 27-28; "Re-establishment of Korean Nation: We Must Plan and Work for the Future," September 15, 1948, pp. 709-710; "Where Do We Stand Today: United Resistance of Free Countries of Asia," March 15, 1950, pp. 346-348; "Korea Cannot Live Divided and Half-Occupied: Our Cause of Freedom Is the World's Cause of Freedom," September 1, 1952, pp. 703-704; "Death Is Scarcely Closer to Seoul Than to Washington: Destruction of the U.S. the Prime Objective of Kremlin," August 15, 1954, pp. 643-644; "America, Trust Yourselves a Little More: Have Faith in Your Own Ideals," April 1, 1955, pp. 1138-1140.

Clifford I. Uyeda

c. 1920–

Japanese American physician and activist

Although his name may be unfamiliar to most people, Clifford I. Uyeda played a key role in two important events in recent Japanese American history. Both involved moments during the 1970s and 1980s when he and other members of his community went public with their painful memories of the World War II era (1939-45). For many Japanese Americans, those memories were best forgotten. But to Uyeda, they were wrongs that deserved to be righted—not just for the benefit of Japanese Americans, but to emphasize how easy it can be to lose one's freedom in times of national stress.

A Medical Career Precedes Full-time Activism

Uyeda is a native of Olympia, Washington, but grew up in the nearby city of Tacoma. After graduating from his local high school, he earned a bachelor's degree from the University of Wisconsin. He then went on to the Tulane University School of Medicine, where he earned his medical degree. Heading to Boston, Massachusetts, Uyeda received

"WE MUST TAKE RESPONSIBILITY FOR WHAT WE DO AS A NATION. WE READILY TAKE CREDIT FOR WHAT OUR PAST GENERATIONS HAVE ACCOMPLISHED IN THE NAME OF HUMANITY. CAN WE SO EASILY EXCLUDE OURSELVES THEN FROM OUR PAST NATIONAL MISTAKES?"

additional specialized training in pediatrics at Harvard Medical School and Massachusetts General Hospital.

Uyeda's medical career began in Massachusetts, where he worked as a clinical and research fellow with the Harvard Pediatric Study and as a teaching fellow in pediatrics at Harvard Medical School. He then moved to California. There he served as staff pediatrician with the Kaiser-Permanente Medical Group in San Francisco from 1953 until his retirement in 1975.

For Uyeda, however, "retirement" was when he at last had more time to devote to the causes that interested him most. A longtime member of the Japanese American Citizens League (JACL), he became chair of the JACL's National Committee for Iva Toguri, a Japanese American woman better known as "Tokyo Rose."

Toguri was born in Los Angeles and educated at the University of California. She happened to be in Japan visiting a critically ill aunt when war broke out between the United States and Japan in December 1941. Unable to return home, she was pressured by the Japanese to broadcast propaganda aimed at American troops stationed in the Pacific region. She was actually just one of about a dozen women announcers whom soldiers nicknamed "Tokyo Rose."

Although she gave in to Japanese demands that she make the radio broadcasts, Toguri would not agree to give up her U.S. citizenship. Her refusal later made it possible for U.S. authorities to charge her with treason when she re-entered the country after the war ended. At her trial in 1949, Toguri was found innocent of any open acts of treason, but she was convicted of trying to undermine American morale. She was sentenced to ten years in prison and released on parole after serving a little more than six years.

The Movement to Obtain Pardon for Tokyo Rose

During and after Toguri's trial, the Japanese American community tried very hard to distance itself from her and her "crimes." In the early 1970s, however, Uyeda learned from someone who had closely studied the trial that Toguri's prosecution and conviction were based on evidence the government

Iva Toguri, also known as "Tokyo Rose," awaits trial for treason in a cell in Yokohama, Japan, 1945

knew was false. Officials had apparently threatened defense witnesses and bribed others to lie during their testimony.

Once he heard this, Uyeda was determined to correct the injustice. Overcoming opposition within the JACL—mostly from older members who did not want to get involved— he led the group's nationwide efforts to obtain a pardon for Toguri. Uyeda attracted support from politicians, the media, and the public at large for his cause. Success finally came in January 1977 when Gerald Ford pardoned Toguri in one of his last official acts as president.

But Uyeda faced a much tougher battle over the next issue that he took on—redress (compensation or payment) for Japanese Americans unjustly imprisoned during World War II just because they were of the same ancestry as one of America's enemies. *(See box for more information; also see entries on* **Daniel K. Inouye, Robert T. Matsui, Spark M. Matsunaga,** *and* **Norman Y. Mineta.***) Controversy raged both inside and outside the Japanese American community over whether it was right to approach the U.S. government about redress. As a result, few were inclined to step forward and call for action.*

Leader in Redress Movement

After President Gerald Ford officially apologized in 1976 for the U.S. government's treatment of Japanese Americans during the war, the JACL led the way in the campaign for justice. In 1977, Uyeda became chair of the group's National Committee for Redress. It immediately began compiling information needed "to clarify the issue of reparations [compensation], then [to] submit concrete alternative plans to the Japanese Americans for their review and comments," he explained at the time. To help Japanese Americans come to some sort of understanding and agreement on the issue, Uyeda contributed numerous articles on redress to the JACL's newspaper, Pacific Citizen, *throughout the rest of 1977 and into 1978. Five JACL districts also conducted a survey on redress among members to judge reactions to the idea.*

In 1978, Uyeda assumed the post of national president of the JACL. He then shared the recommendations of his National Committee for Redress with the rest of the organization. Among them was a controversial demand for $25,000 to be paid to each person (or their heirs) relocated to a camp as a result of Executive Order 9066. Also included was a call for the establishment of a $100 million-dollar trust fund to benefit Japanese Americans "to remind our nation of the continued need for vigilance [alertness to danger] and to render less likely the recurrence of similar injustice."

Uyeda's proposal was unanimously adopted by the JACL's national council, but proved to be a harder sell elsewhere. As Roger Daniels notes in his book Asian America: Chinese and Japanese in the United States Since 1850, *"Conservative forces within the organization, the community, and the nation were shocked that a 'model minority' should make such strident demands."*

Executive Order 9066

On February 19, 1942, just nine weeks after the bombing of Pearl Harbor pushed the United States into World War II, President Franklin Roosevelt issued Executive Order 9066. This infamous order called for the evacuation of some 120,000 Japanese Americans from the West Coast to large internment camps (called "relocation centers") in isolated areas of Arizona, Arkansas, inland California, Colorado, Idaho, Utah, Wyoming, and several other states.

The backlash of anti-Japanese sentiment after the attack on Pearl Harbor led to wild rumors that Japanese Americans were involved in espionage with Japan and had plotted the bombing. The executive order was apparently issued on the assumption that U.S.-born Japanese would bear allegiance to Japan and engage in acts of wartime sabotage. At the same time, the government claimed to be acting to "protect" Japanese Americans. However, no similar action was taken against German Americans or Italian Americans, even though the United States was also at war against Germany and Italy.

The people sent to internment camps included men, women, and children of all ages and backgrounds; about two-thirds of them were U.S. citizens. None of them had been accused of any crime, yet they spent as long as three years imprisoned in tar-paper shacks behind barbed wire fences guarded by armed military police. Many lost their homes, their businesses, their land, and everything else they owned, not to mention their civil rights, their dignity, and their sense of security in their own country.

It was not until February 19, 1976, that the U.S. government officially canceled Executive Order 9066. On the thirty-fourth anniversary of the original order, President Gerald Ford issued a special proclamation. In it, he apologized for the relocation and acknowledged that "Japanese Americans were and are loyal Americans."

*Senator **S. I. Hayakawa** (see entry) of California was among those Japanese Americans who were sharply critical of the redress campaign. A Canadian citizen living in Chicago, Illinois, during the war and therefore unaffected by relocation, Hayakawa even suggested that imprisoning Japanese Americans might have actually helped them in the long run because it pushed them out of their own little communities "to discover the rest of America." Hayakawa later reversed his position and supported redress.*

While virtually no other Japanese American agreed with Hayakawa's view of their ordeal, many did object to redress on other grounds. Some looked at it as a form of welfare and refused to have anything to do with it. Others maintained that no amount of money could possibly make up for what they had suffered and lost. Still others just did not want to bring up the past.

During the two years he headed the JACL, Uyeda often spoke to members of local chapters across the country to explain the reasons behind the fight for redress. One such occasion was on January 20, 1979, when he addressed the Twin Cities group at a dinner held in Minneapolis, Minnesota. Uyeda furnished the editor a copy of his remarks, which are excerpted here.

I appreciate this opportunity to appear before you tonight. I believe you will want me to speak out on the subject of redress which Japanese Americans seek for the injustices suffered as an official act of our own United States government. It happened in our lifetime. It is not an ancient wrong of the dim past.

There was no evidence or record of sabotage or espionage. There was no charge or indictment made against us. The [Supreme] Court, however, upheld the **proposition** that all persons of Japanese ancestry were enemies, that the war was not directed against Japan but at the Japanese race.

Losses sustained by the evacuees were far reaching. Property losses alone were estimated by the Federal Reserve Bank of San Francisco to be in excess of $400 million in 1942.

For those who point to the Evacuation Claims Act of 1948 [that granted some Japanese Americans compensation for their losses during the war], remind them that the amount returned was less than a single year's interest on the original sum. [That] $400 million would, in thirty-seven years, accumulate in interest alone billions of dollars.

For those who point to $25,000 per individual as too large a redress, ask them if they would be willing to be uprooted from their homes and without a charge be incarcerated in a desert camp for years with complete uncertainty about their future for a mere $25,000.

proposition: suggestion.

To some..., seeking redress is unacceptable, they say, because it is placing a price tag on our freedom and our rights.

Loss of freedom or injustice can never be equated **monetarily**. A meaningful redress, however, is a tangible expression of our own government's acknowledgment of the injustice and wrong committed against her own people.

Many fear backlash. It is fear of what their non-Japanese friends would say or think. There is also fear of reawakening in them their own feelings which had been so long suppressed.

Such fears may be well founded, but they are inappropriate in a responsible citizen. If we continue to ignore the past because it was unpleasant, and never even ask for a just **restitution** because it is not popular, then the experience **emasculates** the entire Japanese Americans as a group. To continue this **submissive** stance is **tantamount** to saying: "We prefer to be second class. Let someone else take the risk and the responsibility of a first-class citizenship."

If there are those amongst us who have achieved decent income, there are also others who have not. Let us not forget them....

Many elderly Japanese Americans have very low median income on which to subsist, many are below poverty level, and many live alone. Much of this was due to their having been expelled from the West Coast at the height of their productive years. They not only could not save for old age, they had lost everything they worked for.

It is the height of insensitivity to ignore our own people who must live in poverty because some of us are not in want.

We hear that because there will be recipients who are not at poverty level, redress is not justified. Since when has wealth or poverty of an individual had anything to do with one's right to be free from false imprisonment, his right to constitutional safeguards, and his right to redress the wrong committed against him?

We are talking about the fundamental rights guaranteed all Americans by our own Constitution. Are the guarantees of the Bill of Rights absolute, or are we free to suspend them at anytime according to the whims of those in power or the mood of

monetarily: in terms of money.

restitution: compensation.

emasculates: weakens.

submissive: willing to give in to the authority of another, or to be subjected to conditions created by others.

tantamount: the same as.

Japanese American internees prepare the ground for planting at Owens Valley Alien Reception Center in Manzanar, California, 1942

intimidated: frightened or threatened.

hysteria which may prevail? We must take responsibility for what we do as a nation. We readily take credit for what our past generations have accomplished in the name of humanity. Can we so easily exclude ourselves then from our past national mistakes? Japanese Americans were deprived of liberty and property without criminal charges, and without a trial of any kind.

We must not be **intimidated** by irrational statements from the public, or even by some amongst us. What are some of the major backlashes being heard in America?

1) That those other Americans drafted to fight in the war were also uprooted from their homes, lived in camps, suffered deprivations, pain and even death on the battlefields.

Clifford I. Uyeda

Japanese American soldiers—there were 33,000 of them during World War II—also went through the same sacrifices common to all citizens during wartime, and we seek no redress for such deprivations and sufferings.

Yes, there was a war going on. But to be regarded and treated as an enemy by one's own government without a shred of evidence, stripped of all constitutional and human rights, and then be told that your suffering is no different from those of any other American—any other American subjected to similar treatment by one's own government would have been equally outraged.

2) That if Japanese Americans seek redress, all Americans who suffered under enemy actions should be compensated. What about Americans who died at Pearl Harbor [Hawaii, during the surprise attack of Japanese bombers on December 7, 1941], and what about the sufferings of the POWs [prisoners of war], they say.

The plain answer is that Japanese Americans had nothing to do with Pearl Harbor. We were also the victims on that tragic day. The POWs were under the control of the Japanese military government, not Japanese Americans.

These are the very reasons why we must speak about the evacuation and the need for redress. The very fact that so many Americans associate Japanese Americans with Pearl Harbor and the sufferings of the POWs clearly indicates that America still does not see us as Americans but as former enemies.

This was the myth the 442nd boys went out to destroy. [During World War II, the U.S. Army's 442nd Regimental Combat Team included around fifteen hundred Japanese Americans who had volunteered for combat to prove their loyalty to the United States. It became the most decorated unit in U.S. military history.] They did a superb job, and paid for it in blood all out of proportion to a regiment of equal size. There is, however, much more to be done. This is the work of the redress campaign.

Thirty-five years ago it could be done only with sacrifices and more sacrifices on our own part, hoping against hope that these sacrifices would be recognized as a proof of our Americanism. When confronted with hostility from without, we punished ourselves to excel. We wanted the public to say, "Look, they're Americans after all." We were clearly a second-class citizen.

Today, as first-class citizens, we need no longer take just a submissive stance. We are ready to accept the responsibility and the risk of first-class citizens. We must claim our rights as Americans and claim the justice guaranteed us by our Constitution.

It is about time that Japanese Americans cut aside the second-class mentality with which we were forced to live.

On November 10, 1978, the West German Chancellor Helmut Schmidt and President Walter Scheel attended a memorial service to remember "Kristallnacht," the night 30,000 Jews were arrested and sent to concentration camps. It marked the beginning of the official anti-Semitism in Hitler's Germany exactly forty years ago.

Said Chancellor Schmidt: "Today's Germans are mostly innocent—yet we have to carry the political inheritance of the guilty and draw the consequences."

Germany can remember and make restitutions, but the United States cannot?

It took three hundred years before American blacks could demand to be treated with equality. It took thirty-five years for Japanese Americans to recover from the state of shock they were put into by the incarceration experience. And the American public is just beginning to understand that Japanese Americans were victims of gross injustice.

Japanese Americans in 1945 were just out of concentration camps. They had lost everything. Mere survival was the major concern.

Today there is increasing concerns for human rights, both here and abroad.

Japanese Americans are, finally, overcoming their reluctance to express their feelings. They realize that if they don't speak out for themselves, no one else will.

For those who are afraid of the backlash, cringing at every criticism thrown our way, let me state that there are also

friends out there whose sense of justice is keen and undaunted. They are also watching us.

We have received many heartwarming letters. Let me share a few with you. These are all from Caucasian Americans:

> Mamaroneck, New York, October 24, 1978: *I was one of the U.S. infantry privates ordered to serve eviction notices to Japanese Americans in Guadalupe, California. I have not forgotten the pain I suffered in helping to implement this unsavory and totally un-American order. I wish you to believe that the guilt has rested heavily with me.... I wish you would let me know in what manner I could be of help in your effort to obtain a redress from our government.* J.C.W.

Wrecked barracks at Pearl Harbor on December 16, 1941. "The very fact that so many Americans associate Japanese Americans with Pearl Harbor ... clearly indicates that America still does not see us as Americans but as former enemies," Uyeda stated.

Clifford I. Uyeda | **217**

Honolulu, Hawaii, August 13, 1978: *I'm so glad the time is finally right for you to take on this challenge. The redress is long overdue, and America will learn a great lesson by meeting its obligations to the Japanese Americans involved. By rethinking this whole matter, and finally doing the right thing, the black mark on our history will at least have some sunlight shine on it.* C.M.G.

Seattle, Washington, July 24, 1978: *Only by a drastic measure can we bring the lesson home to make the Constitution mean what it says.... Even in Germany they found that an apology was not enough and that the victims had to be redressed. We should not do anything less.* G.O.

Wheat Ridge, Colorado, October 27, 1978: *I am a German American, but I was never blamed for what the Germans did to six million Jews during World War II.... I hope your efforts prove successful.... You have opened some eyes, and reminded thousands of one of the most embarrassing incidents in American history.* D.P.L.

And finally,

Walnut Creek, California, October 20, 1978: *I was captured on Bataan by the Japanese Army in April 1942 and remained a prisoner of war for forty-two-and-a-half months. When the war was over and I returned to Chicago and was told that we sent our own American citizens of Japanese ancestry to American concentration camps, I could not believe that happened or could happen in America. Let me start off by saying $25,000 is too low a figure for compensation. It bothers me that there are those in your ranks that are still concerned about what their fellow white Americans will think.... Do not listen to the timid in your organization. Let the Hayakawas go their separate way. Let me assure you, there are thousands of white Americans who will stand behind you in this endeavor to right the great wrong. If I can be of some help to you or your organization, please be free to call on me.... I will pray for your organization's success.* E.A.F.

These are only few of the many letters of support we are receiving from fellow Americans. They're also expecting Japanese Americans to act like first-class citizens. Given the opportunity and the perfect case, let us not disappoint these concerned Americans. And most important of all, let us not disappoint ourselves....

99

Despite Uyeda's efforts, there was continued resistance inside and outside the JACL to the idea of pushing for redress. So the group downplayed its original recommendations and instead supported bills introduced in the U.S. Senate (S. 1647) and House of Representatives (H.R. 5499) in 1979. Both bills proposed creating a commission to investigate the wartime relocation and imprisonment of Japanese Americans and determine what, if any, compensation seemed appropriate.

The Senate version of the bill passed in mid-1980, and one year later, the new Commission on Wartime Relocation and Internment of Civilians (CWRIC) began hearings in Washington, D.C. Commissioners also gathered additional testimony during visits to Los Angeles and San Francisco, California; Seattle, Washington; Anchorage, Alaska; Chicago, Illinois; New York City; and Boston, Massachusetts. Over the course of several months, more than seven hundred people from all walks of life shared their often emotional recollections with members of the CWRIC.

Testifies Before Government Commission

One of those who testified before the CWRIC was Uyeda himself. He explained to members of the commission that while he was busy working his way through medical school in Wisconsin, some of his family members were rounded up and held in California prison camps at Tule Lake and Granada. He went on to give the reasons why he felt redress was necessary, concluding his testimony with the following observation: "The United States cannot insist on human rights abroad and then refuse to acknowledge and correct the wrong committed against her own people."

In 1983, members of the Commission on Wartime Relocation and Internment of Civilians published a report of their findings entitled Personal Justice Denied. *In it, they* condemned *Executive Order 9066* as an action U.S. officials took not for military reasons but out of "race prejudice, war hysteria and a failure of political leadership."

The commissioners later made several recommendations for redress. They urged Congress and the president to issue a formal apology for the injustice done to Japanese Americans as a result of *Executive Order 9066.* In addition, they suggested paying $20,000 to each of the estimated sixty thousand survivors of the camps.

For the next five years, the debate continued over the issue of whether it was fair to hold present-day taxpayers responsible for wrongs committed decades earlier. There were also widespread fears that approving such payments would open the door to similar claims from African Americans and other minorities. Finally, in April 1988, the Senate passed a bill (known as the Civil Liberties Act of 1988) enacting all of the Commission's recommendations, and President Ronald Reagan signed it into law that August.

In addition to his activities on behalf of the redress campaign, Uyeda has embraced other causes and interests as well. For example, he has long been involved in supporting the ban on commercial whaling. He served from 1974 until 1978 as chairman of the JACL's Whale Issue Committee, a group whose goal is to educate the public—especially the people of Japan and Japanese Americans—"on the plight of the whales as symbolic of our need to save our oceans." From 1982 until 1986, he was also chair of a special JACL committee that had been set up to keep the Japanese American community informed about efforts to force the Navajo Indians off their ancestral land in the American Southwest. And from 1988 until 1994, he served as president of the National Japanese American Historical Society in San Francisco. Part of his job involved editing its journal, Nikkei Heritage.

Sources

Books

Bosworth, Allan R., *America's Concentration Camps,* Norton, 1967.

Daniels, Roger, *Asian America: Chinese and Japanese in the United States Since 1850,* University of Washington Press, 1988.

Girdner, Audrie, and Anne Loftis, *The Great Betrayal: The Evacuation of the Japanese Americans During World War II,* Macmillan, 1969.

Hosokawa, Bill, *JACL: In Quest of Justice,* Morrow, 1982.

Personal Justice Denied: Report of the Commission on Wartime Relocation and Internment of Civilians, U.S. Government Printing Office, 1983.

Uyeda, Clifford I., *A Final Report and Review: The Japanese American Citizens League National Committee for Iva Toguri,* Asian American Studies Program of the University of Washington, 1980.

Uyeda, Clifford I., editor, *The Japanese American Incarceration: A Case for Redress* (booklet), 3rd edition, National Committee for Redress of the Japanese American Citizens League, 1980.

Periodicals

Pacific Citizen, "Reparations Committee," October 28, 1977, p. 6; "JACL Faces Stiff Redress Campaign," August 4, 1978; "Redress Campaign: A Brief Review," September 16, 1988, p. 5.

Helen Zia

1952–

Chinese American writer, media consultant, and activist

"I am not exactly sure when it happened, but somewhere during my childhood I decided I wasn't American." Thus observed Helen Zia in Essence *magazine, recalling her sense of feeling like an "outsider" among her friends because she "didn't match the national color scheme." In a society that recognized only white and black during the 1950s and 1960s, Asian Americans were very much the "forgotten minority"; their concerns seemed to matter little to the rest of the country. Zia has devoted her life to fighting against that trend. But she is not an activist working solely for Asian American concerns. She has taken up the cause of* all *people whose rights to justice and equality have been ignored.*

Spam with Rice

Zia was born in Newark, New Jersey, of parents who had immigrated to the United States from China. She grew up amid the traditions of two very different cultures. "I liked hot dogs, Kool-Aid, apple pie and the two-tone Chevy wagon my dad drove," she explained. "But I ate my Spam with rice and could use chopsticks as well as an abacus."

Because of their "foreignness" in the eyes of others, Zia and her family experienced a great deal of racial prejudice. By the time she was eight, she concluded: "America didn't want me, and in that case I didn't want to be a part of it." During her teenage years she identified closely with the black civil rights movement and its leaders. But she was also becoming aware of other battles waiting to be fought.

After receiving her bachelor's degree from Princeton University in 1973, Zia worked briefly for the U.S. Department of State as a public affairs specialist. She then enrolled for a short time in the Tufts University School of Medicine in Massachusetts. Her next stop was Detroit, Michigan, where she took graduate courses in industrial relations at Wayne State University and was a factory worker for Chrysler Corporation from 1977 until 1979. During this same period Zia began her career in journalism. She contributed articles to both local and national publications. And it was in Detroit, too, that she became involved in a landmark civil rights case involving the racially motivated beating death of a young Chinese American man named Vincent Chin (see box on page 224).

As the courts deliberated in the Chin case, Zia cofounded American Citizens for Justice, an organization set up to seek justice for Vincent Chin and to oppose anti-Asian prejudice. Members of the group circulated petitions and helped raise funds for legal expenses to challenge the court's decision. Zia served as the campaign's national spokesperson and was twice elected president of the organization.

Full-Time Writer, Lecturer, and Media Consultant

Zia moved into the field of journalism on a full-time basis in 1983 when she joined the staff of Metropolitan Detroit magazine as an associate editor. She left that post in 1985 to become executive editor of Meetings and Conventions magazine, part of the Murdoch Magazines/NewsAmerica group located in Secaucus, New Jersey. Zia remained with the company for the next four years, serving as editorial director of Travel Weekly from 1986 to 1987 and then as

The Death of Vincent Chin

In June of 1982 a twenty-seven-year-old draftsman named Vincent Chin went with three friends to a bar to celebrate his upcoming marriage. Also in the bar that evening was an unemployed white autoworker named Ronald Ebens. He blamed his joblessness on the success of Japanese auto companies in the United States. Thinking Chin was Japanese, Ebens made some racial slurs that led to a fight. As a result, Ebens, Chin, and everyone else who took part were forced to leave the bar.

Later that night Ebens and his stepson, Michael Nitz, who had also been involved in the bar fight, spotted Chin at a nearby fast-food restaurant. The two men waited for Chin to come out of the restaurant. Then, while Nitz held Chin, Ebens beat him with a baseball bat. Chin died several days later of his injuries.

Ebens and Nitz were arrested and charged with second-degree murder. (Most states recognize at least two degrees of murder. For a person to be charged with first-degree murder, there must be evidence that he or she deliberately developed a plan in advance to kill someone. For a charge of second-degree murder, there must be evidence that the killing was intentional, but not planned in advance.) Eventually, however, they bargained their way into pleading guilty to the lesser

Vincent Chin

charge of manslaughter—an unlawful but unintentional killing. As punishment for what they had done to Vincent Chin, Ebens and Nitz were each fined about $3,000 and put on probation for three years. Asian Americans everywhere reacted with outrage to this outcome.

Nationwide protests eventually forced federal authorities to investigate Chin's death. As a result, Ebens was charged with depriving Chin of his civil rights. Although he was tried and found guilty, he challenged the guilty verdict—and won. A civil suit against him proved more successful, however, and Chin's estate was awarded $1.5 million.

editor in chief of Meetings and Conventions *magazine from 1987 to 1989.*

In 1989 Zia moved to New York City to become executive editor of Ms. *magazine, a position she held until 1992. She*

Lillie Chin, mother of Vincent Chin, breaks down during the sentencing of her son's killers, Detroit, 1983

then headed to San Francisco, California, where she was vice president and editor in chief of WorldView Systems (an electronic publishing company) through 1994. She now works primarily as a freelance writer, lecturer, and media consultant. Zia is also a contributing editor to Ms. *magazine and is at work on her own books of fiction and nonfiction. In 1995 she served as coeditor of the reference book* Notable Asian Americans, *published by Gale Research.*

In addition to her efforts on behalf of Asian Americans, Zia is also active in the feminist and gay/lesbian movements. A number of other social justice causes have captured her attention as well. All of these interests figure prominently in her speeches. (She gives up to two dozen or so over the course of a typical year.)

On August 27, 1992, for example, Zia was in Washington, D.C., where she delivered the keynote address at the annual convention of the Asian American Journalists Association (AAJA). The subject of her talk was media coverage of Asian Americans—particularly by other Asian Americans. Zia provided the following transcript of her remarks.

Welcome to AAJA's annual national convention. I've been given the task of saying something meaningful (and hopefully rousing) on our role as Asian American journalists today. You know—something about whether we are Asian Americans who happen to be journalists, or journalists who happen to be Asian Americans. I have only a short time to address this complete question, and this will be a challenge. It's been an amazing year in the news for Asian Americans; news events that involve and directly impact the Asian American community have figured prominently in the national headlines.

We've been on the front pages as crime victims. Who can forget the sweet, youthful face of Konerak Sinthasimphone, the Laotian boy who was raped, murdered, and cannibalized by serial killer Jeffrey Dahmer [in Milwaukee, Wisconsin]? Police said they thought the fourteen-year-old was an adult.

And what about [the] front-page/front-cover/top-of-the-news image of the smiling, charming, victorious face of Olympic gold medal figure skater Kristi Yamaguchi, the fourth-generation Japanese American who defeated Midori Ito of Japan?

Then there was the media event of this half century—that is, of course, the fiftieth anniversary of the bombing of Pearl Harbor. Virtually every media outlet in the country played some special Pearl Harbor angle.

This was followed by very **cursory** coverage—if there was any coverage at all—of the fiftieth anniversary of the racist **incarceration** of 120,313 Japanese Americans into U.S. concentration camps....

Two major reports on Asian Americans [have been] released nationally, one by the U.S. Civil Rights Commission on the rise of anti-Asian prejudice, and one by AAJA—our media

cursory: superficial.
incarceration: imprisonment.

resource handbook on covering the Asian American community. Both reports were ridiculed by some national media (such as *U.S. News and World Report, New Republic*, and *Reader's Digest*) because they dared to discuss issues of sensitivity to Asian Americans.

But the most dramatic news involving Asian Americans this year took place during the LA rebellion—which, to Asian Americans, represents the selective targeting of an entire Asian nationality and **implicates** all other look-alike Asians. [Zia is referring here to the racial disturbances that took place in Los Angeles, California, during the spring of 1992. The rioting followed the trial at which four white police officers were found innocent of using excessive force to subdue black motorist Rodney King. His brutal beating at the hands of those officers had been captured on videotape and broadcast around the world. Anger over that verdict was only partly to blame for the riot, however. Some blacks were also very upset with the Korean American community in Los Angeles. They felt that Korean American storeowners in particular treated them rudely and with suspicion. As a result many of the stores that rioters destroyed were owned by Korean Americans, some of whom had armed themselves to shoot would-be looters, or robbers.] The riot coverage *also* represents the overall failure of our business to go beyond the surface in reporting on the Asian community. Not only was there inadequate reporting, but considerable mischaracterization and disinformation about Korean Americans **disseminated** in the name of news.

Those are just some of the Asian American news highlights since our last convention. Pretty big visibility for a community that's used to being invisible in the national news—and I think this change reflects the **dynamic** period of history that we're in. We are on the verge of the next **millennium**, tagged the century of Asia and the Pacific Rim.

As Asian Americans, we find ourselves at the **crossroads** of two major trends. First, there is the decline of U.S. economic might while the nations of Asia are on the **ascendancy**. This trend involves major shifts in global power relationships. Does anyone here doubt that there will be fundamental **repercussions** of all kinds for Asian Americans?

implicates: involves.

disseminated: spread, distributed.

dynamic: changing, forceful.

millennium: a period of one thousand years; here a reference to the coming of the year 2000.

crossroads: the intersecting point.

ascendancy: rise.

repercussions: consequences, effects.

Secondly, Asian America is changing. Our numbers have doubled every ten years for each of the last four census reports, making us the fastest-growing minority in the U.S. It wasn't so long ago that being Asian American meant being either Chinese or Japanese. But now we are so **diverse** that even many Asian Pacific Americans know little about their fellow Asian brothers and sisters.

And we, as Asian American journalists, have a very big role to play during this historic period, precisely because we are at the crossroads and in a position to give shape to who this Asian American community is to a nation that really doesn't have a clue.

I, like most of you, remember what it was like never to see people who looked like me in the world beyond my immediate circle. When I was growing up in the 1950s, Asians were nowhere to be found in the media, except occasionally in the movies. There, at the Saturday matinee, my brothers and I would sit with all the other kids in town watching old World War II movies—you know, where the evil [Japanese] zero pilots would be heading for their unsuspecting prey, only to be **thwarted** by the all-American heroes, who were, of course, always white. These movies would have their defining moment, that **crescendo** of emotion when the entire theater would rise up, screaming, "Kill them! Kill them! Kill them!" ("Them" being the Japanese.) When the movie was over and the lights came on, I wanted to be invisible so that my neighbors wouldn't direct their red-*white*-and blue fervor toward me.

When I was a little older, I was inspired by the civil rights movements of the 1960s. In my high school, the social unrest often took the form of bomb scares and other disruptions. One afternoon, as my classmates and I stood in the schoolyard talking about racism while waiting for the bomb squad, one of my black girlfriends turned to me and said somberly, "Helen, you've got to decide whether you're black or white."

These incidents took place many years ago. I wish I could say things have changed a lot since, but I can't. In spite of the news coverage this year and the relative visibility of Asian Americans, a closer look at the coverage shows that we're still **rendered** invisible.

diverse: varied, different.

thwarted: frustrated, stopped, or defeated.

crescendo: peak.

rendered: treated, made to be, or represented as being a certain way.

Helen Zia

Take the front-page coverage of Konerak Sinthasimphone. How much—or perhaps I should ask, how little—consideration was given to the fact that he was Laotian? What was the response of the Laotian community, which is a sizable and impoverished minority group in the Midwest? Does anybody know? Did any reporters bother to try to find out? Was there any mention made of the anti-Asian racism that was exhibited by the Milwaukee police, in addition to their **homophobic** and anti-black attitude?

What about the very interesting social/political implications of Kristi Yamaguchi's ancestry at this particular point in history, especially following all the Pearl Harbor hype? Not too many news organizations wanted to touch that one—or maybe it never occurred to them how. *Newsweek*'s long essay by Frank Deford described her **physique** down to the two "cute" little moles on her face, but not a bit of analysis about how her Japanese heritage might be playing in **Peoria**.

Speaking of Pearl Harbor, what news value is there really to have so many polls, in just about every media market, asking how much more do Americans hate the Japanese today than they did yesterday? (Of course, these "Americans" are presumed to be non-Asian.) And don't you agree that this is a strange question? Would we ever see such widespread polling on how much more we hate the Germans today than yesterday, or the Russians, or the Cubans? Somehow it is assumed to be accepted behavior to hate Japanese people—and this is **biased**, non-objective journalism coming from our news directors at some of our most **esteemed** news organizations. The *New York Times* runs this poll every few years, and both the *Wall Street Journal* and the *Los Angeles Times* asked, "Was America right in dropping the atom bomb on [the Japanese cities of] Hiroshima and Nagasaki [during World War II]?" (The surprise answer—a high proportion of respondents said yes.) Or their question, "Was America right to **intern** 120,313 Japanese Americans?" (Surprise again—a significant proportion said yes.) I mean, we might imagine a poll that asked, "Do you think Germany was right to try to exterminate the Jews?" and we might even get a considerable response that said yes. But what journalistic purpose would this question serve? And what assumptions are being made in even asking the question?

homophobic: marked by an irrational fear of homosexuals or homosexuality.

physique: the form of a person's body.

Peoria: a city in Illinois, often used as an example of the American heartland.

biased: prejudiced; based on personal views, experiences, or emotions rather than on facts and observations.

esteemed: highly regarded; valued.

intern: imprison.

Many of you may be involved in the coverage of Soon-Yi Previn, adopted daughter of [actress] Mia Farrow, who was raised as a daughter of [Farrow and her partner, director-actor] Woody Allen. [Previn and Allen became attached romantically, prompting a bitter battle between Allen and Farrow.] Some of our colleagues (or even some of us) call it a "love triangle." But would we be more likely to call it "incest" if she looked more like she could be his biological daughter instead of an Asian female, with all those sexual **connotations?** [Zia is referring here to the stereotype that portrays Asian women as exotically appealing to white men and easily dominated by them.] What does this so-called affair mean for an entire generation of adopted Korean children? Soon-Yi's Asian face is all over the news, but her Asianness is ignored and invisible.

This kind of invisibility was never so apparent than in the national coverage of Los Angeles, the story in which the nation's news media discovered Korean Americans, but then could only **fixate** on the image of Korean men with guns. A demonstration involving thousands of Korean Americans calling for justice for Rodney King was barely covered. [The ABC television news program] "Nightline" let only one Korean spokesperson, Angela Oh, appear for an abbreviated broadcast after days of prolonged interviews with African American gang members who made grossly incorrect statements about Korean people that largely went unchallenged, and only then after community protests. As John Lee and Dean Takahashi wrote in the AAJA newsletter, a *Los Angeles Times* post-riot survey reported only the responses of whites, blacks, and Latinos—and "other." As explanation, they said that Asians are not statistically significant enough to count, even though they comprise eleven percent of LA's population—and even when Asians were so strongly impacted by the rebellion.

At some points, the **insurrection** seemed to be portrayed as a black-Korean issue (forget about police brutality and economic injustice). There was virtually no news analysis on the potential impact on other Asian Americans, or the fact that several hundred stores owned by Cambodians, Chinese, Japanese, and South Asians were also looted and burned.

This stuff is simply poor journalism. It wouldn't get out of Reporting 101—you know, the section on how to ask the right

connotations: undertones.
fixate: focus, concentrate.
insurrection: uprising, riot.

questions. But when it comes to Asian Americans, some people just don't seem to know what questions to ask to get beyond the superficial stereotypes.

I know I'm making this sound a lot like "us versus them," even though as journalists, many of us are the "them." But the fact is that many of us—perhaps *most* of us—are still outsiders in our own newsrooms.... We're just not in the newsrooms in sufficient numbers yet or in enough positions of authority to be taken seriously. How many Asian American journalists were sent to cover LA? Shockingly few. I've heard several accounts of experienced Asian American journalists who requested to go and cover the riots and were turned down, even if the organization had no other Asian reporters. Yet if she or he pushed too hard or criticized too loudly, the consequences could be harsh, including the ultimate insult—being labeled as "not objective."

Now I'd like to deal with this **objectivity** issue for a moment. Somewhere, somehow, we ourselves have started to buy into this backlash mythology that to be a professional journalist means we can have no point of view—and if that were possible, that it would be a virtue. This is a fiction and an **hypocrisy** that only serves to keep us doubting ourselves.

Last year at the Seattle convention, I sat in a workshop and listened to a young woman in her first journalism job as an education reporter questioning her own ability to cover issues like bilingual education simply because she is Asian and *that* might be a conflict in and of itself. Obviously *every* story has **implicit** assumptions that steer the reader or viewer to some kind of impression. The issue is who determines those assumptions? Who decides what questions to ask, or not to ask?

For example, so much media **hype** is made on the point of Japanese investment. Yet in the news media itself several of the largest companies are owned by British, German, Australian, Canadian, and French interests. Imagine how differently the news coverage would play if the late [British investor and businessman] Robert Maxwell had been Japanese. Can you imagine the headlines? "Maxwell-san Says 'Sayonara' After Kamikaze Strike on Tribune Company." "Maxwell's Sons Make Sneak Attack on U.S. Workers' Pensions." But Maxwell was British, not Japanese, and instead we see very staid, very respectful coverage. Is this not an **inherent** bias?

Personally, I think the whole issue of objectivity is a **smokescreen** to make us and others think that *we* are somehow **deficient** for not fitting the mold that the traditional white male standard created in its own image. We of all groups should never forget that we work in an industry that was singularly responsible for the systematic **vilification** and exclusion of Asian immigrants. Some **venerable** newspapers played

objectivity: the ability to analyze facts on their own merit without allowing personal feelings or prejudices to distort them.

hypocrisy: pretending to have high moral standards but not living by them; pretending to be something one is not.

implicit: understood, implied.

hype: publicity.

staid: serious, proper.

inherent: inborn, natural.

smokescreen: something designed to confuse or mislead.

deficient: lacking in a necessary quality; not up to acceptable standards.

vilification: the act of saying things that are intentionally mean or false in order to hurt someone.

venerable: distinguished, respected.

a key role in the incarceration of Japanese Americans. Radio helped spearhead the "red scares" of the McCarthy era that led to the persecution of many Chinese Americans. [During the early 1950s U.S. Senator Joseph R. McCarthy became well known for accusing high-ranking government officials and others of being communist or otherwise "disloyal" to the United States—despite the fact that he had little or no proof that they had actually done anything wrong. Communism is a system of government in which the state controls the means of production and the distribution of goods. It clashes with the American ideal of capitalism, which is based on private ownership and a free market system.] More recently, the Kerner Commission in 1968 outlined how the news media and its lack of diversity contributed to the civil disorders of the 1960s—and sadly, progress has been at a **glacial** pace.

So when we get accused of not being objective, we need to be able to stand our ground and point out the double standard that is being applied to us at the expense of good journalism.

I should also note that I do not believe these editors and news directors and colleagues of ours are necessarily being deliberately racist. I think they're just doing what they've been taught, acting out some of their own biases. Don't you know that some of them were sitting near me—or near you—shouting, "Kill them! Kill them! Kill them!" Or perhaps they were explaining to another kid in another schoolyard how you have to decide whether you're black or white.

It's a vicious cycle—news gets shaped by people who are not even aware of their own prejudices. Journalists produce news that often reinforces their own beliefs, thereby steering public opinion in a way that **perpetuates** the same crap. And so on and so on. That's what we saw in LA—*some* black people using their prejudices toward Asians in general and Koreans in particular to **justify** their actions; and *some* Korean people using their prejudices toward blacks to justify their actions. And where did each group learn these prejudices? Mostly through news and entertainment media.

Indeed, this is our historic role at this historic time with the **confluence** of these trends. *We* can interrupt this crazy feedback loop of misinformation about our communities and cultural heritage. We are in a very powerful position to outline

glacial: very slow, like the movement of an enormous body of ice.

perpetuates: upholds, maintains.

justify: to prove or show that something is right.

confluence: coming together

Helen Zia   233

the public perception of who Asian Americans are—not only within our newsrooms but to build bridges with other communities through the various minority journalists organizations.

This is not an easy task. Look around in this room. What you see are pioneers in this effort. Every one of us is a pioneer. As you go through this convention picking up skills for professional development and networking for career advancement, remember that our **collective** development includes being role models for each other as part of this historic position we hold.

There will be times when an issue of fairness stands out so **blatantly** that you will be moved to act, and you will find strength in knowing that you don't have to act alone because there is an entire organization that stands with you. There's nothing radical about this—it's simply about trying to create the newsroom environment in which the Asian American journalists can reach their fullest potential without having to explain why they speak English so well, or having to deal with colleagues who try to second-guess if the color of their skin or the shape of their eyes had anything to do with a job, a promotion, or a story assignment.

As you look around this room and think how comfortable it is not to have a worry about such things, imagine being able to feel this way at a meeting of the Society of Professional Journalists, the American Society of Magazine Editors, the American Society of Newspaper Editors, and so on, or even your own newsroom. One day it will be that way for all of us, because of our pioneering efforts in AAJA. So enjoy the convention, be good role models to each other, and remember that history is on our side.

99

collective: shared by all members of a group.
blatantly: obviously.

Sources

Books

Daniels, Roger, *Asian America: Chinese and Japanese in the United States Since 1850,* University of Washington Press, 1988.

Periodicals

Essence, "Not Black, Not White," May 1993.

Additional information for this entry was taken from the video documentary "Who Killed Vincent Chin?".

A video of Zia's speech to the Asian American Journalists Association (AAJA) on August 27, 1992, is available through the C-SPAN cable channel.

Index

Entries on featured speakers are indicated by boldface; illustrations are marked (ill.)